RISC Architectures

RISC Architectures

J.C. Heudin

Technical Head Manager,
Sodima S.A. Paris,
France

and

C. Panetto

Professor of Electrical Engineering,
Paris,
France

CHAPMAN & HALL

London · Glasgow · New York · Tokyo · Melbourne · Madras

Published by Chapman & Hall, 2–6 Boundary Row, London SE1 8HN

Chapman & Hall, 2–6 Boundary Row, London SE1 8HN, UK

Blackie Academic & Professional, Wester Cleddens Road, Bishopbriggs, Glasgow G64 2NZ, UK

Van Nostrand Reinhold Inc., 115 5th Avenue, New York NY10003, USA

Chapman & Hall Japan, Thomson Publishing Japan, Hirakawacho Nemoto Building, 6F, 1-7-11 Hirakawa-cho, Chiyoda-ku, Tokyo 102, Japan

Chapman & Hall Australia, Thomas Nelson Australia, 102 Dodds Street, South Melbourne, Victoria 3205, Australia

Chapman & Hall India, R. Seshadri, 32 Second Main Road, CIT East, Madras 600 035, India

First edition 1992

© 1992 English edition Chapman & Hall

Original French language edition – Les Architectures RISC – © 1990 Bordas, Paris. Published by Dunod Editeur, Updated material © 1992 Bordas, Paris

Printed in Great Britain by T.J. Press (Padstow) Ltd, Padstow, Cornwall

ISBN 0 412 45340 1   ISBN 0 442 31605 4 USA

A catalogue record for this book is available from the British Library

Library of Congress Cataloging-in-Publiation data available

Contents

Contents

2 Principles of the RISC design methodology

Contents

Acknowledgements

Major support for the work on KIM20 reported in this book was provided by the DRET Research Department of the French Defense. This research could not have progressed as well as it has without the contribution of many contributors from the ETCA/CREA laboratory. Professor B. Zavidovique, and the staff from the IEF laboratory of the University of Orsay (PARIS XI – CNRS), as well as Professor F. Devos were also significant contributors.

Contributions were also made by R. Malka, H. Vilamosa, L. Bol, J.P. Courrier and E. Peltier of SODIMA S.A. We must also thank all the companies listed in this book for their courtesy and the information given to us, especially SUN Microsystems, MIPS Computer Systems, Motorola, Intel, Intergraph, VLSI Technology, Inmos and IBM.

KIM™ is a trademark of SODIMA S.A. (Phone (33.1) 69 07 32 18). All other trademarks are the proprietary of their respective owners.

Introduction

In 1980, the term RISC was coined as part of David Patterson's course in microprocessor design at the University of California at Berkeley. Since this date, we have seen a growing number of papers claiming the "Reduced Instruction Set Computer" revolution. It is true that most manufacturers of mainframe computers and workstation vendors have progressivey adopted RISC micro-processors. The goal of RISC is to provide superior overall system results. Actual computer implementations demonstrate that this goal has been achieved.

The traditional approach to meet the demand for greater performance was done in the past by increasing the complexity of architectures. In contrast, the RISC design philosophy states that a simpler architecture will be more efficient if the compiler and the processor make a matched set. Investigations of RISC versus CISC architectures (Complex Instruction Set Computer) indicate that RISC machines are faster than traditional ones for executing typical large programs. Unfortunately, the term "Reduced Instruction Set Computer" is somewhat misleading and most people think that the goal of RISC-based design is to reduce the number of executable instructions. What is the real meaning of these four letters ? Answering this question is the main objective of this book. Written for both novices and computer scientists, this book describes practical and theoretical aspects of the RISC design approach. Readers who want to go further and to study RISC architecture in detail, will find a complete indexed bibliography to the literature of RISC systems at the end of the book.

This book is basically composed of four chapters : the first, second and third ones discuss the history and technical foundations of the RISC architecture, the last chapter gives a more practical approach through the study of the KIM20 microprocessor.

From pioneers in Universities to major microprocessor vendors, the first chapter relates the early history of this new wave of computer systems. Then, it gives an overview of the research in RISC concepts that will influence all computer architectures for years to come.

The second chapter lays out the main characteristics of a RISC architecture and describes the underlying design methodology. The latter is compared to a more traditional approach to show what is really new within RISC system design.

The third chapter gives an architectural overview of some commercial RISC microprocessors. It concludes by a set of comparison tables, including technical features, performance evaluations, application areas and more.

The last chapter gives a detailed description of the KIM20 microprocessor. The latter was designed using a pure RISC methodology specifically for efficient symbolic processing. The study of the KIM20 architecture provides a more practical approach of RISC. It clearly shows the required relationship between hardware and software for designing high-performance microprocessors.

This book is not an exhaustive course on all techniques required for designing a new RISC microprocessor or for simply using an existing one. Rather, it gives a synthesis of principles and foundations that make RISC a unique and elegant approach for high-performance microprocessor design.

1

The RISC architecture history

1.1 CONSTRAINTS IN MICROPROCESSOR DESIGN

1.1.1 THE INCREASES IN COMPLEXITY

A general trend in microprocessor design is to increase functionalities of an earlier architecture, for example by adapting new concepts used in the design of mainframe computers. Since VLSI (Very-Large Scale Integration) has allowed more and more transistors on a single chip, this tendency has become more pronounced. Typical examples can be easily found within major microprocessor vendors. Thus, Motorola Inc. has produced the famous 6800, then the 6809, the 68000, 68010, 68020, 68030, 68040, etc. Its main rival, Intel Inc., has also adopted a similar design strategy : from the 8080, 8085, 8086, 80186, 80286, 80386 to the 80486.

Some vendors have resorted to more complex instructions to bring instruction sets up to the level of the desired high-level language, while others have incorporated peripheral circuitry or coprocessors as part of the processor architecture. Most of them have based their strategy on an instruction set compatibility with earlier products. That is to say that the new microprocessor's instruction set is identical to the one of its predecessor, but also possesses some additional instructions and features. As an example, the MC68030 object code is compatible with the MC68020 and earlier MC68000 microprocessors. In addition to the MC68020 features, the MC68030 has an internal data cache, an on-chip memory management unit, and an enhanced implementation of the 68020 instruction set [1].

Therefore, three main features for designing a new microprocessor architecture have previously been :

1. To provide a set of complex instructions in order to reduce the gap between the machine object code and high-level languages/operating systems.

2. To enable programs to be easily transported from one earlier member of the microprocessor family to another one in an upward compatible fashion.

3. To improve performance, in terms of the speed and efficiency of program execution.

1.1.2 RELATIONSHIP WITH HIGH-LEVEL LANGUAGES

The first point emphasizes the relation between compilers, operating systems and the design of the hardware architecture. Since the goal of most CISC microprocessors is to be general-purpose, taking into account a wide spectrum of applications and languages, the resulting architecture include a large set of functionalities, multiple addressing modes, a redundant and heterogeneous set of instructions. As an example, the MC68030 microprocessor instruction set from Motorola includes nearly 100 instructions. Most of them can operate on four basic data types (byte integers (8 bits), word integers (16 bits), long word integers (32 bits) and Quad word integers (64 bits)) and support 18 addressing modes.

Like other general-purpose CISC architecture, the MC68030 supports an impressive number of languages, but it is not dedicated to the efficient execution of one particular language, such as C, Pascal or Fortran.

1.1.3 UPWARD COMPATIBILITY OF INSTRUCTION SETS

The second point enables software to be transported from one earlier member of the microprocessor family to a newer architecture in an upward compatible fashion. That is, the user programming model remains unchanged from a previous implementation. However, the new architecture includes additional instructions, addressing modes or on-chip extensions. Both improved performance and increased functionality can be used by new compilers, but all the machine code produced for earlier members of the family can execute on the new architecture without any modification. The main goal of this approach is to guarantee that previous software developments can be directly reused and therefore not lost. This point is not a crucial requirement since most software developers use standardized high-level language compilers. Thus, porting a program to a new target microprocessor is not a particularly difficult or time-consuming task. However, upward compatible instruction sets are useful for engineers implementing compiler back-ends and low-level operating system features.

1.1.4 MICROPROCESSOR PERFORMANCE

The third point is to deliver high levels of performance for a wide range of applications. Performance is a notion directly related to the time spent executing a given task. Most microprocessors are designed using a clock running at a constant rate. Therefore, designers refer to a clock by its period or by its frequency. For example, a processor with a 100 ns clock period runs at 10 Mhz. Then, the CPU time spent for executing a program is the following [2] :

CPU time =
number of clock cycles for the program * clock cycle time (T)

In addition to the number of clock cycles, we can also count the number of instructions executed for that program :

I = number of instructions executed for the program

Then, we can calculate easily the average number of clock cycles required per instruction (CPI) :

CPI = number of clock cycles for the program
                              I

or
number of clock cycles for the program = CPI * I

If we replace the "number of clock cycles" in the first formula by CPI * I, we obtain a new definition for the CPU time :

5

$$CPU \ time = I * CPI * T$$

Expanding this formula into units of measure allows us to verify its homogeneity :

$$CPU \ time = \frac{Instructions}{Program} * \frac{Clock \ cycles}{Instruction} * \frac{Seconds}{Clock \ cycle}$$

$$CPU \ time = \frac{Seconds}{Program}$$

We can also invert CPU time in order to obtain the Performance in terms of the instruction rate :

$$P = \frac{1}{CPU \ time} = \frac{1}{I * CPI * T} \quad or \quad P = \frac{F}{I * CPI}$$

where F represents the inverse of T, that is the clock frequency.

$$P = \frac{F}{I * CPI}$$

P is the performance in MIPS
I is the instruction count
CPI is the average number of clock cycles per instruction
F is the clock rate

Examples :

Motorola 68030	I=1.0	CPI= 5.2	F= 16.67	P= 3.21
Intel 80386	I= 1.1	CPI= 4.4	F= 16.67	P= 3.44
SPARC	I=1.2	CPI= 1.3	F= 16.67	P= 10.69

(If I is in millions of instructions, then P is in MIPS)

Fig.1.1 Performance of a processor.

So, finally, we obtain the performance P of a processor proportional to the clock frequency F, and inversely proportional to the Instruction count I and the average clock cycle per instruction CPI, Therefore, if I indicates millions of instructions, then P is in Millions of Instruction Per Second (MIPS). This formula demonstrates that the performance of a processor is dependent upon three characteristics :

1. The number of instructions required to execute the program : I.

2. The average number of clock cycles required per instruction : CPI.

3. The clock frequency or rate : F.

Each of these three characteristics is related to one particular technology domain. The instruction count (I) is related to the adequacy of the instruction set to execute the code produced by the compiler. In other words, a small instruction count indicates a small gap between the machine code and the high-level language. A big instruction count shows that the processor is not well-suited for the language or indicates a bad compiler implementation.

The average number of clock cycles per instructions (CPI) is related to the basic architectural model of the microprocessor. Most RISC processors require between 1 and 2 clock cycles per instruction, while most CISC processors consume up to 10 clock cycles per instruction.

The clock rate (F) is directly related to the hardware technology used for the implementation of the processor. The period (1/F) can vary from a few nanoseconds for Gallium Arsenide (GaAs) or Emitter-Coupled Logic (ECL) based computers, to more than 10 times that for microprocessors using a more conventional technology, such as Complementary Metal Oxide Semiconductor (CMOS).

However, be careful that the basic technologies involved in each characteristic are strongly-coupled : the clock rate depends also upon the architecture, and so on.

Some performance measurements refer also to "VAX MIPS", where the performance of a processor is compared to the time needed by a VAX-780 to execute a given benchmark. By convention, the VAX has a performance of 1 MIPS and the performance metric is a ratio based on this definition. For example, a processor of 3.5 MIPS is 3.5 times faster than the VAX-780 in executing the benchmark.

However, remember that performance evaluation is a difficult task since results are always affected by the conditions of the experiment :

benchmark programs
programming language
compiler technology
computer architecture
implementation technology.

Since all these points affect the absolute performance, the ideal experiment would vary only the microprocessor. This condition is rarely possible in practice.

1.1.5 HORIZONTAL AND VERTICAL COMPLEXITY

During the last decades, these requirements (i.e. reducing the gap between high-level languages and machine code, upward compatibility, performance) have resulted in an increase of processor complexity. This complexity is both horizontal and vertical. Horizontal complexity refers to the microprocessor data-path. The first microprocessors had 4-bit and 8-bit data-paths. Then, microprocessor data-paths grew to 16- and 32-bit, mainly on the foundations of the first microprocessors, using larger microcode ROMs (Read Only Memories) and more elaborate micro-state machines. Vertical complexity is mainly due to the use of microcode. The latter evolved on mainframes as a method for eliminating complex combinatorial logic and because engineers could develop the software and hardware at the same time : minor changes in the architecture could be compensated by rewriting the microcode.

The increasing power of these microcode machines allowed architects to create increasingly elaborate instruction sets with a large number of addressing modes. This class of microprocessor was called CISC (Complex Instruction Set Computer) as opposed to RISC (Reduced Instruction Set Computer).

1.1.6 CISC PROCESSORS

Computer architects agree on the need to support high-level languages. CISC designers have all claimed that their architectures were designed with high-level languages in mind. The goal of these designs was first to provide a high-level and complex instruction set in order to reduce the number of executed instructions (I in the formula of section 1.1.4). This idea was reinforced since external memory-access times were so much slower than CPU execution times. Then, microcode was seen as a way of matching CPU and memory speed, providing an ideal solution for implementing elaborate instruction sets. When a CISC processor executes a machine-code operation, it is in fact executing a microprogram subroutine.

Each machine code instruction is interpreted as a sequence of micro-instructions stored in the microcode memory. As an example, an "add" instruction that adds the content of register A to that of register B, with the result stored in register C, might have micro-instructions to load from and store to registers, an internal register-to-register addition, and various tests for updating the status word of the processor and checking overflows.

Such an architecture is based on a multilevel execution model (Figure 1.2). The first level is the high-level language which produces machine code through the use of a compiler. The machine code is then interpreted by the processor control unit as a sequence of micro-instructions (microcode). Finally, at the lower-level, each micro-instruction is transformed into an executive word that directly controls and commands the elementary hardware units of the processor.

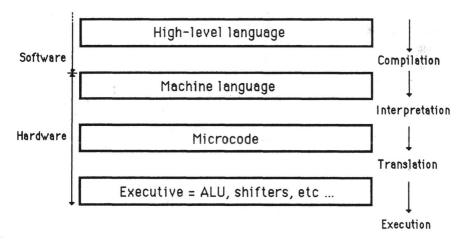

Fig.1.2 Execution scheme of a CISC processor.

Based on this general model, designers incorporate many high-level language constructs to assist compiler writers, such as simple stacking primitives for procedure calls and returns.

This approach is called "vertical microprogramming" because its major goal is to reduce the semantic gap between the high-level language and the instruction set.

A second important improvement to the CISC model was to reduce the number of micro-instructions required for one machine instruction. That is, reducing the gap between the hardware executive level and the instruction set by increasing the size of the command word. This approach is called "horizontal micro-programming".

CISC architecture attempts to gain a significant performance improvement by making internal microcode execute much faster than external instructions and by implementing high-semantic-content instructions, where such instructions reduce the number of external instructions that the processor must fetch. Most CISC advocates argue that elaborate instruction sets are ideal for compiled code, but their assertions turn out to be untrue.

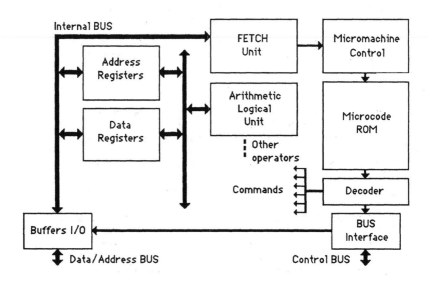

Fig.1.3 General structure of CISC processor.

1.2 THE TECHNOLOGY EVOLUTION

1.2.1 THE EVOLUTION OF THE TECHNOLOGICAL FRAMEWORK

The general trend in computer architecture was to increase the complexity of microprocessors commensurate with the increasing potential of silicon implementation technologies. CISC designers have largely taken advantage of this technology evolution to implement complex instruction sets. However, this progression was rather more historical than induced by scientific analyses. In particular, we can notice that the main idea was first to put in microcode a large set of high-level instructions and then to solve performance problems by adding more functions in hardware or executing more than one task at the same time. The latter is called pipelining. Pipelining usually requires some form of low-level parallel processing, such as paired logic units for address manipulation and instruction execution. Once again, these techniques result in an increase in the number of transistors required.

But, during the same period, the economical and technological framework changed.

1. Memory-access time has decreased significantly in recent years, thanks to semi-conductor advances. Thus, the difference in access-time to internal and external memories has been reduced.

2. The use of caches effectively provides a low access-time to large external memories.

3. Advances in CAE/CAD for electronics and VLSI deeply influence microprocessor design.

4. The large amount of available application software enables significant analyses of compiler behaviour.

1.2.2 THE EVOLUTION OF MEMORY

Since the access-time of external memory has decreased significantly, microcode is no longer useful. It makes little sense to keep making microprocessors more complex by fetching microcode subroutines instead of directly fetching simple instructions. Compilers that translate high-level language directly into simple instructions would be more efficient and overall execution would be faster. Since a single CISC instruction often involves many micro-instructions, a compiler translating directly into simple instructions could eliminate many intermediate instructions and thus, produce more efficient code. Moreover, CISC performance has not advanced as quickly as memory access-time, because each generation of microprocessors has become more complex than the preceding one. Thus, it takes longer to execute instructions, because each instruction specifies a large microprogram and therefore requires more cycles per instruction (CPI) and longer cycles (T).

1.2.3 CACHE MEMORIES

In recent years, there has been a growing interest in cache circuits for microprocessors. This technique allows the designer to reduce the memory traffic by temporarily holding those portions of the contents of main memory which are currently in use in a small, high-speed, memory buffer. Information located in cache memory may be accessed in much less time than that located in main memory. Thus, a microprocessor with a cache needs to spend far less time waiting for instructions and data to be fetched and/or stored.

The goal in using a cache is not just to achieve optimal processor performance. Rather, it is usually a more global objective, typically involving optimizing system performance within cost, size and power limits. Since a large and low-cost central memory associated with a cache minimizes the time to access information, this technique also reduces the overall advantage of using complex microcoded instructions.

1.2.4 CAE/CAD ADVANCES

Microprocessor design is directly affected by numerous technological advances in the fields of ASIC (Application Specific Integrated Circuit) and VLSI Computer Aided Design. This includes state-of-art software tools such as high-performance graphical editors, simulators, silicon data-path compilers and state machine compilers, automated placement, complex routing tools and more.

This new generation of CAE/CAD software associated with easy to use VLSI technologies such as gate-arrays and standard cells enables a wider range of companies to design their own architecture. This opens new opportunities for small firms to win a place in the electronic component marketplace, historically dominated by big companies. CAE/CAD tools have also introduced structured top-down design methodologies that directly influence the definition and implementation of microprocessor architectures.

1.2.5   HIGH-LEVEL LANGUAGE COMPILERS

However, the main point is certainly the advances in compiler technology. In recent years, researchers have looked at many millions of lines of compiled code and made a surprising discovery. Although elaborate instructions are helpful to human assembly-language programmers, compilers largely ignore them. Compiler writers simply do not take advantage of the enhanced CISC instruction set, because the complex CISC instructions do not perform a task precisely as needed. High-level language compilers are unable to use the complete instruction set, selecting in each case the optimal instruction, execution and addressing mode. Rather than using a complex instruction set, compiler writers usually elect to use the simpler instructions that produce no side effects and are easier to control. Such approaches can benefit from all the standard optimization techniques that compiler writers have been using for some time, because such tools are well-suited for simple instruction sets, where the instruction timings are predictable and regular.

Another point is that most compiler writers want their products to be portable onto a wide spectrum of hardware platforms. A simple way to ensure this goal is to define some kind of virtual machine based on a few frequently-used instructions. A compiler is generally divided into two parts : the front-end that handles the language syntax is essentially the same for all target hardware, and the back-end that generates the target-specific machine code by translating the virtual machine code into the given processor instruction set. This approach leads to portable compilers, but forces the code-generator to use only a small set of simple instructions that can be found in every microprocessor instruction set.

As an example of studies done on instruction sets, Dennis A. Fairclough of Brigham Young University published in 1982 a paper claiming a scientific approach to a unique instruction set design [3].

First, the author defines precisely the working vocabulary in instruction set design :

Instruction set
A computer instruction set is the set of all instructions that can be executed.

Instruction format
The instruction format is the binary configuration that the instruction-bit field, the address-mode-bit field, the address-modifier-bit field and all other instruction-bit fields are formatted into. The instruction format is in a form that the control unit may easily decode.

Instruction field
The instruction field is that portion of the instruction format that defines the unique bit configurations for the instruction (operation code).

Operation code
The operation code (also called OP-code) is an object that instructs the microprocessor control unit which operation to perform.

Address type
The address type refers to a general addressing method used to obtain the final effective address for a memory unit. The address type is made up of the address mode and the address modifier.

Address mode
The address mode is the algorithm by which the address of a memory unit is calculated. The address units include bit fields, registers and main memory.

Address modifier
The address modifier provides the modification to a memory address just prior to actually addressing memory. Indexing is an example of an address modifier.

Source address
The source address is the modified effective address from which data is read.

Destination address

The destination address is the modified effective address to which data is written.

D.A. Fairclough also divides instructions into eight categories :

1. Data Movement Instruction Group such as load, store and move.
2. Program Modification Instruction Group such as branch, jump, call and return.
3. Arithmetic Instruction Group such as add, subtract, multiply and divide.
4. Compare Instruction Group such as arithmetic and logical compare.
5. Logical Instruction Group such as and, or, xor and not.
6. Shift Instruction Group such as shift and rotate.
7. Bit Instruction Group such as bit set, bit clear, bit test.
8. Input/Output and Miscellaneous Instruction Group.

In research by the author, studies were made of programs used on four microprocessors : the Texas Intruments TMS9900, the MOS Technology MOS6502, the Motorola MC6800 and MC68000. A significant number and variety of programs were analysed including applications programs, assemblers, interpreters, compilers, monitors, kernels, operating system libraries and more.

INSTRUCTION GROUPS PER OCCURRENCE IN PROGRAMS	CORRESPONDING MC68000 INSTRUCTION SET PARTITION	INSTRUCTION GROUP (see text)	RELATIVE OCCURRENCE FOR MC68000
= 0.0%	30.3%	1	43.52%
<= 0.1%	3.9%	2	25.13%
<= 0.5%	21.1%	3	12.09%
<= 1.0%	11.8%	4	9.15%
<= 2.0%	10.5%	5	5.03%
<= 3.0%	13.2%	6	2.65%
<= 4.0%	0.0%	7	2.36%
<= 5.0%	6.6%	8	0.07%
> 5.0%	2.6%		
	TOTAL 100%		TOTAL 100%

Fig.1.4 Analysis of MC68000 instruction set occurrences.

The analysis show that 8.7% to 30.3% of all the microprocessor instructions were never used. It also shows that 44.6% to 87.8% of the instructions were used 1% or less !

Naturally, the ideal frequency distribution of use would have a uniform distribution. But, the analysis showed that 31 of the 76 instructions for the MC68000 could be eliminated from the instruction set without affecting the overall microprocessor performance.

1.2.6 CALLING INTO QUESTION CISC MICROPROCESSORS

We have shown that the design of microprocessor instruction sets was based on evolution rather than revolution. Most of them are simply extensions of earlier sets. One important reason for this is the need to be compatible with older computers. Another reason is the complexity of the design task itself. This complexity forces a heuristic approach : instruction set designers must make heuristic decisions because they lack data on how instructions will be used.

Most CISC instruction sets were developed when assembler programming was of primary importance. Because earlier microprocessor architects were mainly electronic engineers, they generally did not know precisely how their instructions would be used. As a consequence, they found it safer to follow an existing design than to create a new set from scratch. This approach leads to an increase in instruction set complexity which increases the hardware complexity and therefore reduces the overall performance by increasing the number of clock cycles required (CPI) and the length of each cycle (T). In most CISC designs, the sequencer and control units take nearly 50% of the chip surface, compared to 5% for a pure RISC design.

However, following recent advances in compiler technology, new computers and workstations assume that high-level languages will be used, in contrast to older architectures. The goal is then to design the architecture so that compilers not assembly language programmers have an optimal working environment. As a consequence, most compiler research teams began to work in the field of instruction set and microprocessor design in order to match optimizing compilers with target instruction sets.

Finally, most foundations of the CISC approach are not now justified by the recent technological advances. The advantage of RISC architectures comes because they can achieve significant reduction in the number of clock cycles required per instruction

(CPI). This simplification, obtained by simpler instruction sets, increases the instruction count (I), but by a factor that is much smaller than the improvement in the average number of clock cycles per instruction. The next section gives an historical and technical survey of the earlier RISC designs.

1.3   RISC PIONEERS

1.3.1 AN OLD IDEA

The two first sections have introduced the idea that RISC was not a revolution, but rather the formalization of a set of design criteria guided by technological evolution. We will see later that the main principle of the RISC methodology is to integrate in hardware only those features that measurably improve performance. In other words, RISC can be seen as a style of computer architecture emphasizing simplicity and efficiency. This approach, which can be called "small is beautiful", follows Von Neumann's advice on instruction set design in 1946 :

We wish to incorporate into the machine in form of circuits only such logical concepts as are either necessary to have a complete system or highly convenient because of the frequency which they occur.

Von Neumann's advice shows that the foundations of the RISC philosophy are not new. RISC designs trace their roots to the first electronic computers. Like RISC, these early computers were direct-execution machines that had simple and easy-to-decode instruction sets. The idea of microprogrammed architectures appeared first in 1951, described by Wilkes. But, the first commercial computer based on a microcode was the IBM 360 in 1964, because of the lack of efficient memories. It was the first computer to have an architecture, that is, an abstract structure with a fixed set of machine instructions, separate from a hardware implementation.

Then, minicomputer designers warmly embraced microcode as a way to build cost-effective machines. They especially needed to reduce hardware costs and boost performance. Small microcode stores were built from ROM and microstate machines were moved to large microcode stores and to complex hardware units and sequencers, to achieve those goals. Improvements to integrated circuits around 1970 made microcode memory even faster, encouraging the growth of microprograms. For example, the DEC VAX 11/780 has more than 400,000 bits of microcode.

In fact, microcode design became a high art in the hand of computer architects. One of the biggest problems with microcode is that it is rarely bug-free. Negative consequences of such approach were increased design time, more design errors, etc. [4].

18

1.3.2 THE CRAY-1 SUPERCOMPUTER

Some computer architects do not hold the opinion that microcode improves performance. Seymour Cray has acheived recognition as a pioneer of RISC architectures. He believed that complexity was bad and continued to build the fastest supercomputers in the world by using simple instruction sets. Most of the design features of the CDC 6600 and the CRAY-1 computers recall the foundation of the RISC design philosophy [5]. In this way, the CRAY-1 supercomputer is one of the precursors of modern RISC architectures. In 1975, Seymour Cray made the following remarks about his studies :

"Registers made the instructions very simple ... That is somewhat unique. Most machines have rather elaborate instruction sets involving many more memory references in the instructions than the machines I have designed. Simplicity, I guess, is a way of saying it. I am all for simplicity. If it's very complicated, I can't understand it".

1.3.3 THE IBM 801 COMPUTER

The same year (1975), a group of researchers led by George Radin at IBM's Thomas J. Watson Research Center started work on a computer based on concepts developed by John Cocke.

John Cocke was an advocate of simple instructions for designing efficient compilers. The IBM team looked at many millions of lines of compiled code. They discovered that elaborate instructions are helpful to human assembly-language programmers, but high-level language compilers largely ignore them. The researchers determined that most of the code produced by compilers consisted mainly of load, store, branch, add and compare instructions. All these simple instructions had direct micro-instruction equivalents. Further, the IBM researchers observed that many of the more complex instructions available on most microcoded computers did not require extra hardware and were implemented only as microcoded routines. John Cocke concluded that high-performance processors really did not need to include a microcode ROM with an associated state machine controller. It is more efficient to design a simple instruction set that enables the execution of one instruction per clock cycle.

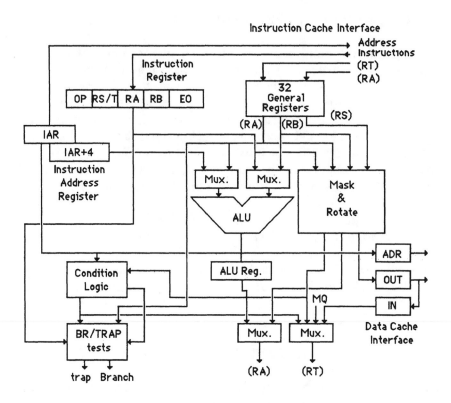

Fig.1.5 IBM 801 Architecture.

These findings guided the design of IBM's experimental 801 computer. Built from off-the-shelf ECL (Emitter-Coupled Logic) and completed in 1979, the IBM 801 was a 32-bit minicomputer with single-cycle instructions, 32 registers, separate cache memories for instructions and data, and delayed branch instructions [6]. The IBM 801 is now generally recognized as the first intentional RISC machine. However, the term RISC had not been coined and in 1980 rumours of the IBM 801 project spread even without formal disclosure by IBM.

At the same time, the RISC (Reduced Instruction Set Computer) and MIPS (Machine without Interlocked Pipeline Stages) projects started respectively at Berkeley (University of California) and Stanford.

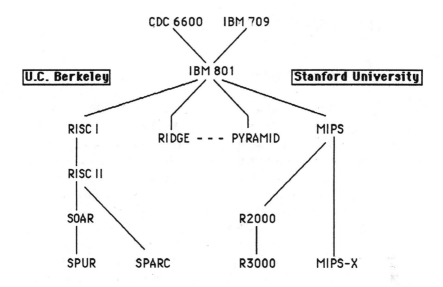

Fig.1.6 RISC Architecture Genealogy.

1.4 THE BERKELEY RISC PROJECT

1.4.1 THE RISC-I PROJECT

The term RISC was coined first as part of David Patterson's 1980 course in microprocessor design at the University of California at Berkeley. In 1980, the "Reduced Instruction Set Computer " (RISC) project was started with the goal of investigating an alternative to the more general trend which increases the complexity of architectures commensurate with the increasing potential of implementation technologies. The hypothesis was that, since complex instructions are rarely used by programs, their inclusion into the processor's instruction set has more negative effects on overall performance than it has positive ones. Another important consideration was that a simplified architecture is important in a field of such a rapidly changing technology, because it leads to a short design and debugging time, thus allowing quick exploitation of new technologies. The Berkeley RISC architecture was defined at the end of 1980, after extensive architectural studies performed during a graduate course. These included the measurement of several program parameters, such as the number of statements, addressing modes, usage of local scalars and procedure nesting depth. Most of these measurements were done in the C language.

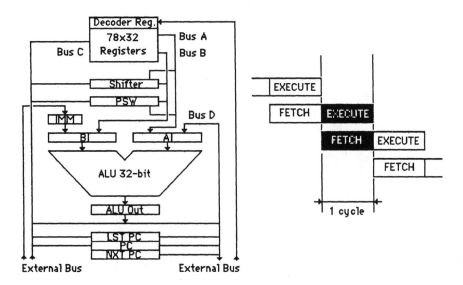

Fig.1.7 RISC-I architecture and pipeline.

Once the architectural design was finalized (summer 1980), a micro-architecture was defined to implement it. In early 1981, this definition was then adapted by a group of 5 graduate students who designed, laid-out, and debugged the circuit in only six months [7]. It was originally called "RISC I gold" and later on simply "RISC-I". The RISC-I chip was implemented in a 2 micron NMOS technology. The resulting integrated circuit was a 44500-transistor microprocessor which worked on the first silicon, in summer 1982. There was only a minor design error associated with the optional setting of condition codes on load and shift instructions. This problem was solved by modifying the RISC-I assembler. The fastest chip ran test programs at 1.5 Mhz (2 µsec. per instruction), that is slower than intended by about a factor of 4. This was mainly due to a lack of tools, at that time, that could find all the critical timing paths in simulation of the whole chip. The second factor, said Patterson, was inexperience : this was the first chip that any one of the Berkeley RISC team had built [8].

In order to meet the goals of simplicity and effective single-chip implementation, D. Patterson artificially placed the following design constraints on the architecture :

1. *Execute one instruction per cycle.*
    RISC-I instuctions should be about as fast and no more complicated than micro-instructions in current machines such as the PDP-11 or VAX.

2. *Make all instructions the same size.*
    This again simplifies implementation. Berkeley researchers intentionally postponed attempts to reduce program size.

3. *Access memory only with load and store instuctions ; the rest operate between registers.*
    This restriction simplifies the design. The lack of complex addressing modes also makes it easier to restart instructions.

4. *Support high-level languages.*
    The intent was to optimize the performance of RISC-I for use with high-level languages such as C or Pascal.

The selection of high-level languages for consideration in RISC-I was influenced by the large C user community and the resulting considerable expertise [9]. The idea was that given a limited complexity (number of transistors) that can be integrated into the

RISC chip, most of the processing of a high-level language such as C must be in software, but with hardware support for the most time-consuming operations.

To determine what constructs and instructions are used most frequently in programs, they looked at the frequency of classes of variables and the relative dynamic frequencies of high-level language statements. The most important observations were :

1. That integer constants appeared almost as frequently as arrays or structures.

2. More than 80% of scalars were local variables.

3. More than 90% of arrays and structures were global variables.

4. The procedure call/return is the most time consuming operation in high-level languages.

5. Nesting depth of procedure calls is greater than eight in less than 1% of the calls.

The resulting architecture designed to take advantage of these factors has 31 instructions, most of which do simple arithmetic, logical and shift operations on registers. The instruction set is divided into four categories : arithmetic and logical, memory access, branch and miscellaneous. The execution time of a typical RISC-I cycle is given by the time it takes to read and add two registers, and then to store the result back into a register. However, load and store instructions use two machine cycles in order to access the external memory. The conditional instructions are the same as used in the PDP-11. Innovative features of RISC-I are :

1. The register windows associated with procedure calls and returns.

2. The delayed branch.

The goal of the register windows is to make procedure calls and returns as fast as possible, in practice no larger than a few jumps. A procedure call/return generally involves two groups of time-consuming operations : saving/restoring registers on each call/return, and passing parameters/results to and from the procedure. The frequency of local variables justifies the use of registers for storing them. Baskett [10] and Sites [11] had already proposed that multiple banks of registers avoid register saving and restoring. This scheme was adopted by RISC-I and each procedure call allocates a new "window" and the return instruction restores the old set. Furthermore, the sets of registers used by different procedures overlap, in order to allow parameters to be passed in registers.

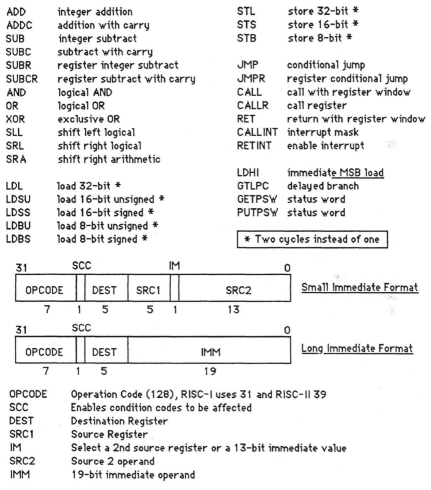

ADD	integer addition		STL	store 32-bit *
ADDC	addition with carry		STS	store 16-bit *
SUB	integer subtract		STB	store 8-bit *
SUBC	subtract with carry			
SUBR	register integer subtract		JMP	conditional jump
SUBCR	register subtract with carry		JMPR	register conditional jump
AND	logical AND		CALL	call with register window
OR	logical OR		CALLR	call register
XOR	exclusive OR		RET	return with register window
SLL	shift left logical		CALLINT	interrupt mask
SRL	shift right logical		RETINT	enable interrupt
SRA	shift right arithmetic			
			LDHI	immediate MSB load
LDL	load 32-bit *		GTLPC	delayed branch
LDSU	load 16-bit unsigned *		GETPSW	status word
LDSS	load 16-bit signed *		PUTPSW	status word
LDBU	load 8-bit unsigned *			
LDBS	load 8-bit signed *		* Two cycles instead of one

```
31        SCC         IM              0
 OPCODE  || DEST | SRC1 ||    SRC2      |   Small Immediate Format
   7     1   5     5    1     13

31        SCC                         0
 OPCODE  || DEST  |      IMM          |   Long Immediate Format
   7     1   5            19
```

OPCODE   Operation Code (128), RISC-I uses 31 and RISC-II 39
SCC   Enables condition codes to be affected
DEST   Destination Register
SRC1   Source Register
IM   Select a 2nd source register or a 13-bit immediate value
SRC2   Source 2 operand
IMM   19-bit immediate operand

Fig.1.8 RISC-I instruction set.

The register window technique used by RISC-I enables the execution of the full procedure call prologue or epilogue to execute in one machine cycle (see chapter 2 section 2.3.2 for a more detailed description of this mechanism).

Most microprocessors, like RISC-I, increase performance by prefetching the next instruction during the execution of the current instruction. This principle is called 2-stage pipelining. However, pipelining introduces difficulties for branch instructions, since the instruction cycle is just long enough to execute the following sequence of operations : read a register, do an ALU operation and store the result back in a register. The solution implemented in RISC-I was to refine jumps so that they do not take effect until after the following instructions. D. Patterson refers to this as the delayed jump technique. The delayed jump allows RISC-I never to break the regularity of the pipeline execution. We will describe more carefully the delayed jump technique in chapter 2 (section 2.2.4).

BENCHMARK	RISC-I		MC68000		VAX 11/780	
	N	T	N	T	N	T
STRING SEARCH	144	.46	.8	2.8	.7	1.3
BIT TEST	120	.06	1.2	4.8	1.2	4.8
LINKED LIST	176	.10	.7	1.6	1.2	1.2
BIT MATRIX	288	.43	1.1	4.0	1.0	3.0
QUICKSORT	992	50.4	.7	4.1	.9	3.0
ACKERMAN(3,6)	144	3200	-	-	.5	1.6
PUZZLE(SUBSCRIPT)	2736	4700	-	-	.5	2.0
PUZZLE(POINTER)	2796	3200	.9	4.2	.5	1.3
RECURSIVE QSORT	752	800	-	-	.6	2.3
SED(BATCH EDITOR)	17720	5100	-	-	.6	1.1
TOWERS HANOI(18)	96	6800	-	-	.8	1.8
AVERAGE			.9±.2	3.5±1.8	.8±.3	2.1±1.1

N: Sizes of C programs compiled for the RISC-I and size ratios for the MC68000 and VAX 11/780

T: CPU time in milliseconds for RISC-I and time ratios for the MC68000 and VAX 11/780

Fig.1.9

RISC-I, MC68000 and VAX 11/780 relative performances.

Because RISC-I was intended to be programmed in high-level languages, the compiler always inserts a no-operation (NOP) after a jump. Then, an optimizer tries to rearrange the sequence of instructions to do the equivalent operations while making use of the instruction "slot" where the NOP appears. A large set of performance evaluations were performed to compare RISC-I with other available microprocessors or minicomputers : MC68000,

Z8002, VAX-11/780, PDP-11/70, etc. Even at 1.5 Mhz, with one minor error corrected by an assembler patch, RISC-I executes C programs faster than the other microprocessors and minicomputers. We should notice also that RISC-I programs were, at worst, a factor of two larger than programs for the other machines, since no size optimization were performed. But, the most important figure of merit was its execution time. In parallel with the design of "RISC-I gold", the Berkeley researchers started, during the winter of 1982, the definition of a more ambitious micro-architecture for the same processor architecture. This was originally called "RISC-I blue" and latter on "RISC-II".

1.4.2 THE RISC-II PROJECT

In parallel with the design and test of RISC-I, Katevenis and Sherburne started the implementation of a second NMOS chip called RISC-II. RISC-II was completely functionally correct and worked very close to its predicted speed, that is a 330 ns cycle time.

PERIOD	ACTIVITY	PEOPLE
Winter 80	RISC idea	Patterson, Séquin
Spring 80	Architectural Studies	Patterson, 15 grad. stud.
Summer 80	Architecture Definition	Patterson, 4 grad. stud.
Summer/ Fall 80	Compiler, Assem., Simul.	Campbell, Tamir
Summer/ Fall 80	RISC-I Micro-Architecture	Katevenis
Winter 81	RISC-II Micro-Architecture	Katevenis
Winter/Spring 81	RISC-I Design & Layout	Fitzpatrick, Foderaro, Peek, Peshkess, VanDyke
Summer 81/Spring 82	RISC-I fabrication	MOSIS, XEROX
Summer 82	RISC-I tested	Foderaro, VanDyke
Spring/Summer 82	RISC-I board	VanDyke
Winter 81/Winter 83	RISC-II Design & Layout	Katevenis, Sherburne
Spring 83	RISC-II fabrication	MOSIS, XEROX
Summer 83	RISC-II tested	Katevenis, Sherburne
1981/1982	RISC/E ECL Paper Design	Beck, Davis, et al.
Spring/Fall 82	I-cache Design & Layout	Hill, Lioupis, Nyberg, Sippel
Spring 83	I-cache fabrication	MOSIS, XEROX
Summer 83	I-cache tested	Lioupis, Hill
Fall 82/Fall 83	CMOS RISC Layout Study	Takada
Winter 83	RISC-II microcomputer	Lioupis, Campbell

Fig.1.10 - History of the RISC project.

Even though RISC-II was faster than RISC-I, it occupied 25% less silicon area and had 75% more registers. This is the consequence of a careful attention to performance during the circuit design and layout. As we said in the previous paragraph, RISC-II executed the same instruction sets as RISC-I, but differs in its hardware micro-architecture. The main difference was a larger number of register windows : 138 registers organized as 8 windows (6 + 6 registers for parameter/result passing and 10 for locals) compared with 78 registers organized as 6 register windows for RISC-I (4 + 4 registers for parameter/result passing and 6 registers for locals).

The second important feature of RISC-II was the pipeline organization. RISC-I has a simple two-stage pipeline, overlapping instruction fetch and execution, and includes the delayed-jump technique. In RISC-II, a third pipeline stage was used : instruction fetch, read operands and execute, write back the result into the register file.

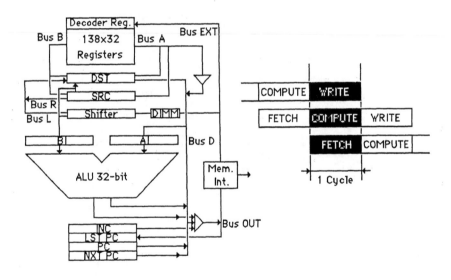

Fig.1.11 RISC-II architecture and pipeline.

Like RISC-I, RISC-II implemented the delayed-jump scheme for branch instructions and temporarily suspended the pipeline only during load and store instructions. This is the consequence of the use of a single memory port as we will discuss later (chapter 2 section 2.3.5).

RISC-I and RISC-II were the real pioneers of the modern computer design methodology, claiming a new relationship between hardware and software. With the Berkeley RISC projects, computer architects learned to design high-performance single chip microprocessors by minimizing the hardware required while optimizing speed by passing non-run-time tasks off to software optimizers.

1.4.3 THE SOAR PROJECT

David Patterson's researchers have not only worked on the RISC-I and RISC-II projects. In 1983, they also designed a VLSI instruction cache [12] and a high-speed version of RISC-I using a 100K ECL technology called "Big RISC" [13].

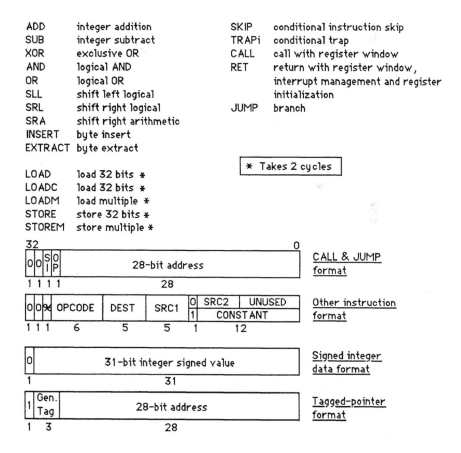

ADD	integer addition	SKIP	conditional instruction skip
SUB	integer subtract	TRAPi	conditional trap
XOR	exclusive OR	CALL	call with register window
AND	logical AND	RET	return with register window,
OR	logical OR		interrupt management and register
SLL	shift left logical		initialization
SRL	shift right logical	JUMP	branch
SRA	shift right arithmetic		
INSERT	byte insert		
EXTRACT	byte extract		

LOAD	load 32 bits *
LOADC	load 32 bits *
LOADM	load multiple *
STORE	store 32 bits *
STOREM	store multiple *

* Takes 2 cycles

Fig.1.12 SOAR instruction set and data formats.

The same year, David Patterson and his team also started the SOAR project which stands for Smalltalk On A Risc. One of the goals of this project was to answer the following question : are reduced instruction set computers good for languages like Lisp or Smalltalk? SOAR was certainly the first attempt to apply the RISC approach for symbolic processing. Like RISC-II, SOAR inherits directly from work done on the Berkeley RISC project, but also from other studies like the IBM 801 and the MIPS microprocessor.

The main distinctive feature of SOAR was the support for dynamic type checking through tagged data types. This technique was initially proposed on the Burroughs 5000, and thereafter used on the Symbolics 3600 Lisp machine [14]. SOAR supported two data types : 31-bit signed integers and 28-bit pointers. This allowed SOAR to start arithmetic and comparison operations immediately while simultaneously checking the tags. Most often, both operands of instructions are integers and the correct result is available after one cycle. If not, the operation is aborted and SOAR traps to routines that carry out the appropriate computation for the data types. Each SOAR instruction contains a bit that either enables or disables tag checking. We will discuss the run-time data-type checking technique more precisely with the KIM20 microprocessor later. Following the RISC methodology, the basic theme of the SOAR architectural additions was to allow the normal case to run fast in hardware and to trap to software in the infrequent complicated cases [15 16].

A first version of the SOAR microprocessor was implemented using a 4 micron NMOS technology. The resulting chip used 35,700 transistors, dissipated about 3 watts and ran about 400 ns per instruction. A second version of the chip was designed during 1984-1985, using a more efficient CMOS technology [17-18]. The SOAR project showed that, with the addition of a few hardware features, namely tags and traps, RISC was a good approach for an efficient execution of symbolic processing languages like Smalltalk. SOAR was the first "tagged-RISC" architecture, which influenced the design of the SPARC and KIM20 architectures, and other studies such as those done by Texas Instruments [19].

1.4.4 THE SPUR PROJECT

In 1985, following RISC-II and SOAR, SPUR (Symbolic Processing Using RISC) was started at the University of California at Berkeley to conduct parallel processing research [20]. The SPUR development was part of a multi-year effort to study hardware and software issues in multiprocessing, in general, and more precisely on parallel programming using Lisp. It extends the work done on RISC-II and SOAR with some special support for two emerging standards : Common-Lisp [21] and the IEEE 754 1985 Floating Point Arithmetic [22]. However, unlike dedicated Lisp machines, SPUR processors were general-purpose processors with some support for Lisp. The SPUR project consisted of the design of a workstation and research efforts in integrated circuits, computer architecture, operating systems and programming languages.

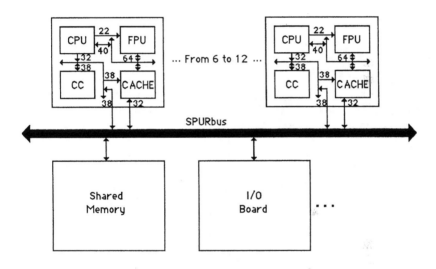

Fig.1.13 SPUR architecture.

SPUR contains 6 to 12 high-performance processors, that are connected to each other, to standard memory, and to input/output devices with a modified Nubus. SPUR supports sharing between cooperating processes with a global, shared memory. System performance is improved by placing 128 kbytes caches on each processor to reduce bus traffic, memory contention, and effective memory access-time. The caches are supplemented with hardware that guarantees that copies of the same memory location in different caches always contain the same data.

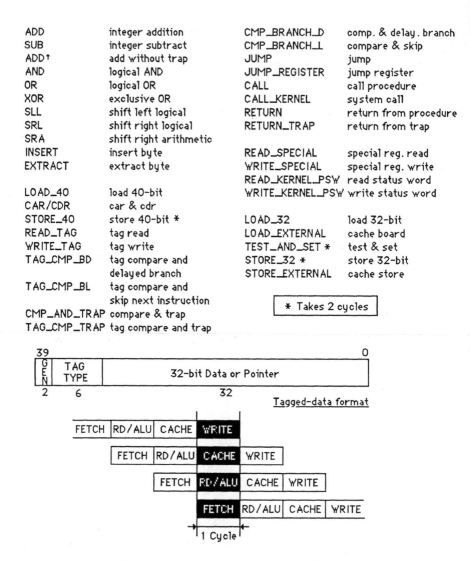

ADD	integer addition	CMP_BRANCH_D	comp. & delay. branch
SUB	integer subtract	CMP_BRANCH_L	compare & skip
ADD†	add without trap	JUMP	jump
AND	logical AND	JUMP_REGISTER	jump register
OR	logical OR	CALL	call procedure
XOR	exclusive OR	CALL_KERNEL	system call
SLL	shift left logical	RETURN	return from procedure
SRL	shift right logical	RETURN_TRAP	return from trap
SRA	shift right arithmetic		
INSERT	insert byte	READ_SPECIAL	special reg. read
EXTRACT	extract byte	WRITE_SPECIAL	special reg. write
		READ_KERNEL_PSW	read status word
LOAD_40	load 40-bit	WRITE_KERNEL_PSW	write status word
CAR/CDR	car & cdr		
STORE_40	store 40-bit *	LOAD_32	load 32-bit
READ_TAG	tag read	LOAD_EXTERNAL	cache board
WRITE_TAG	tag write	TEST_AND_SET *	test & set
TAG_CMP_BD	tag compare and	STORE_32 *	store 32-bit
	delayed branch	STORE_EXTERNAL	cache store
TAG_CMP_BL	tag compare and		
	skip next instruction		
CMP_AND_TRAP	compare & trap		
TAG_CMP_TRAP	tag compare and trap		

* Takes 2 cycles

```
39                                                          0
┌─┬─────┬──────────────────────────────────────┐
│G│ TAG │                                      │
│E│     │       32-bit Data or Pointer         │
│N│ TYPE│                                      │
└─┴─────┴──────────────────────────────────────┘
 2    6                  32
```
                                    Tagged-data format

```
┌───────┬───────┬───────┬───────┐
│ FETCH │RD/ALU │ CACHE │ WRITE │
└───────┴───────┴───────┴───────┘
    ┌───────┬───────┬───────┬───────┐
    │ FETCH │RD/ALU │ CACHE │ WRITE │
    └───────┴───────┴───────┴───────┘
        ┌───────┬───────┬───────┬───────┐
        │ FETCH │RD/ALU │ CACHE │ WRITE │
        └───────┴───────┴───────┴───────┘
            ┌───────┬───────┬───────┬───────┐
            │ FETCH │RD/ALU │ CACHE │ WRITE │
            └───────┴───────┴───────┴───────┘
            ├───────┤
             1 Cycle
```

Fig.1.14 SPUR instruction set and pipeline.

The SPUR processor is implemented on a single board with about 200 standard chips and three custom 2-micron CMOS chips : the cache controller (CC), the CPU and the Floating Point Unit (FPU). The CC chip handles cache accesses by the CPU, performing address translation, accessing shared memory and maintaining cache consistency. The CPU chip is based on the RISC-II design, but differs because of the addition of a 512-byte instruction buffer, a fourth execution pipeline stage, a coprocessor interface and support for Lisp tagged data. The FPU chip supports the full IEEE 754 standard for binary floating point arithmetic without microcode control.

All these three chips use four-phase nonoverlapping clocks with a cycle time of 100 to 150 nanoseconds. Initial results with small Lisp benchmarks showed that a single SPUR processor was comparable to the VAX 8600 and the Symbolics 3600 [23].

Not far from the University of California at Berkeley, Professor John Hennessy was also one of the early other academic stalwarts of RISC. In 1981, he started the MIPS project at Stanford University.

1.5 THE STANFORD MIPS PROJECT

1.5.1 THE MIPS MICROPROCESSOR

One of the major differences between the MIPS project and other RISC projects, was that MIPS traces its roots to the development of optimizing compilers. Thus, the Stanford optimizing compiler research was strongly coupled with the design of advanced RISC hardware technology. In 1981, John Hennessy started the MIPS project : a general purpose 32-bit microprocessor designed for the efficient execution of compiled code [24].

The MIPS instruction set comprises 31 instructions divided into four major groups : a rich set of load and store instructions, arithmetic and logicial operations, control flow instructions and others. The MIPS pipeline has five stages, that is Instruction Fetch (IF), Instruction Decode (ID), Operand Decode (OD), Operand Store (OD) or Execution (SX) and Operation Fetch (OF). Most architectures have special hardware that makes sure that operations are executed in the right order if conflicts occur. In contrast, the MIPS processor does not have pipeline interlock hardware, and the executed code must be free of any pipeline conflicts (MIPS = Microprocessor without Interlocked Pipeline Stages).

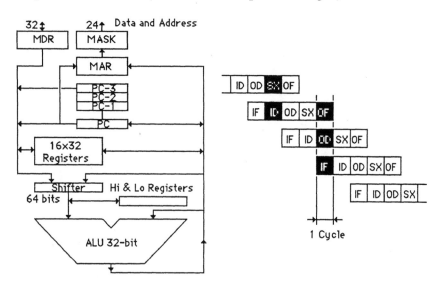

Fig.1.15 MIPS architecture and pipeline.

Like the Berkeley RISC, MIPS employs delayed branches to avoid a complex instruction prefetch unit and to simplify the pipeline design. Unlike RISC, MIPS has no "return" or "call subroutine" instructions, but there are macros (ret and jsr) which are expanded by assembler using jump instructions. This organization creates a two level hierarchy : the top level is the target of the compilers and the other level is implemented by hardware. The top level is also called the visible instruction set, since it is known by compilers. The hardware level instruction set is hidden. Therefore, the assembler is rather called a reorganizer and must transform instructions from the top level to the hardware level (machine code). One major advantage of this approach is that if a future hardware implementation differs from the original one, for example a longer pipeline, then only the reorganizer is affected. The main task of the reorganizer is to employ machine specific optimizations, to reorder instructions for delayed branches, and to resolve pipeline conflicts at compilation time [25 26].

ADD	integer addition	BRA (1)	condition branch
AND	logical AND	BRA (2)	unconditional branch
IC	insert byte	JMP (1)	direct jump
OR	logical OR	JMP (2)	jump register
RLC	combined rotate	JMP (3)	indirect jump
ROL	rotate	TRAP	trap
SLL	shift left logical		
SRA	shift right logical	LD (1)	register load
SRL	shift right arithmetic	LD (2)	indexed load
SUB	integer subtract	LD (3)	shifted base register load
XC	extract byte	LD (4)	direct load
XOR	exclusive OR	LD (5)	immediate load
		MOV	move registers
SAVEPC	save PC	ST (1)	register store
SET	set register to 1	ST (2)	indexed store
	if condition true	ST (3)	shifted base register store
	else 0	ST (4)	direct store

Fig.1.16 MIPS instructions set.

The MIPS processor was designed during 1981 1982 and implemented in NMOS 2-micron technology in 1983. It had a cycle time of 250 ns and fetched one instruction every 500 ns. The chip had 84 pins and included nearly 24,000 transistors.

Due to its 5-stage pipeline, the MIPS control logic covered almost double the area of the Berkeley RISC, and MIPS included only 16 registers compared to 138 for RISC-II. However, the main tendency in the MIPS design was to shift complexity from hardware to software : (1) complexity is paid only once during compilation and the resulting hardware is simpler and more efficient, (2) design effort is concentrated on compilers and the reorganizer rather than on constructing a complex hardware engine, which is hard to design, implement and debug [27].

In 1984, John Hennessy founded MIPS Computer Systems in Sunnyvale (California) and worked on a new architecture called R2000. Another path of continuation was the design of the MIPS-X microprocessor at Stanford.

1.5.2 THE MIPS-X MICROPROCESSOR

After the original MIPS projects, John Hennessy temporarily left Stanford to help form MIPS Computer Systems. He still works for the firm as chief scientist, while keeping his position at Stanford. After MIPS succeeded in making a fast simple chip, the Stanford group turned to symbolic processing, much as the Berkeley group did, but their path diverged. While Patterson's team designed SOAR and SPUR, the Stanford team went for raw speed. During the summer of 1984, the original MIPS design team plus about half a dozen new students began investigating architectures for a new high performance microprocessor.

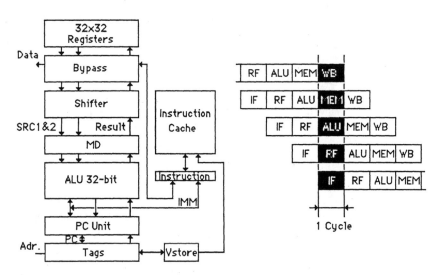

Fig.1.17 MIPS-X architecture and pipeline.

The resulting design, called MIPS-X borrows heavily from the original RISC and MIPS design, though most closely resembles the latter for obvious reasons. However, MIPS-X differs from MIPS in a few important areas [28] :

• all MIPS-X instructions implement a single operation and execute in a single clock cycle,

• instructions are all fixed format and every instruction is 32 bits long,

• simple and efficient support for coprocessors is provided,

• support for its use as the base processor of a shared memory multiprocessor is provided,

• MIPS-X contains a large on-chip instruction cache,

• the processor is fabricated in a 2-micron CMOS technology.

MIPS-X is heavily pipelined so that one instruction can be issued in every cycle. Each instruction is divided into five pipeline stages : Instruction Fetch (IF), Instruction decode and register Fetch (RF), ALU or shift operation (ALU), wait for data from memory on a load and output data for a store (MEM), write back the result into the destination register (WB) [29].

In this scheme, a delay occurs because the result of a previous instruction is not available to be used by the current instruction. An example is a compute instruction that uses the result of a load instruction. This mean that there is a delay of two instructions from a load instruction until the result can be used as an operand by the ALU. Besides the delays that can occur because one instruction must wait for the results of a previous instruction to be stored in a register or be bypassed, there are also delays because it takes time for a branch instruction to compute its destination (delayed branch technique). MIPS-X has two branch delay slots after every branch instruction. Like the original MIPS, MIPS-X requires the use of a reorganizer to find useful instructions to fill delay slots. Like MIPS, MIPS-X is a pipelined processor that has no hardware interlocks. Therefore, the software system is responsible for keeping track of the timing of the instructions.

The MIPS-X instruction set includes 40 instructions that can be divided into four different types : memory and coprocessor instructions, branch instructions, compute instructions, and compute immediate instructions. MIPS-X has 32 general-purpose registers and does not implement register windows as the Berkeley RISC does.

LD	load	ADD	integer addition
ST	store	DSTEP	divide step
LDF	floating-point load	MSTART	1st multiply step
STF	floating-point store	MSTEP	multiply step
LDT	load without cache	SUB	integer subtract
STT	store without cache	SUBNC	subtract without carry
MOVFRC	move from coprocessor	AND	logical AND
MOVTOC	move to coprocessor	BIC	clear bit
ALUC	coprocessor operation	NOT	logical NOT
		OR	logical OR
ADDI	immediate add	XOR	exclusive OR
JPC	jump PC	MOV	move registers
JPCRS	jump and restore state	ASR	shift right arithmetic
JSPCI	indexed jump and save PC	ROTLB	byte left rotate
MOVFRS	move from special reg.	ROTLCB	byte left rotate with complement
MOVTOS	move to special register	SH	shift
TRAP	software exception	NOP	no operation
HSC	halt and destruct (!)		
BEQ	branch if equal		
BGE	branch if greater or equal		
BHS	branch if higher or same		
BLO	branch if lower		
BLT	branch if less than		
BNE	branch if not equal		

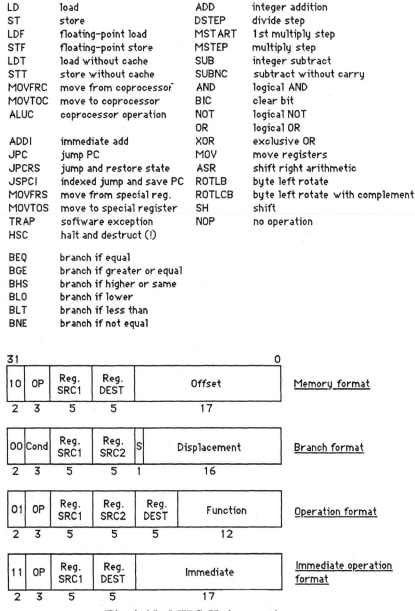

Fig.1.18 MIPS-X instruction set.

In contrast, MIPS-X includes a 2 kbytes on-chip instruction cache. This cache satisfies 90% of all instruction fetches and reduces the memory bandwith of the processor by a factor of 2.5 [30].

The processor was designed to run at a clock rate of 20 Mhz, executing an instruction every cycle, yielding a peak performance of 20 MIPS.

The first implementation was fully functional and ran at 16 Mhz. The slower speed was caused by a slow path involving branches that was fixed in the next revision. The Stanford team also designed a 25 Mhz version based on a simple shrink of the part to a 1.6 micron CMOS technology. With its on-chip cache, MIPS-X contains nearly 150,000 transistors on an 8 x 8.5 mm die.

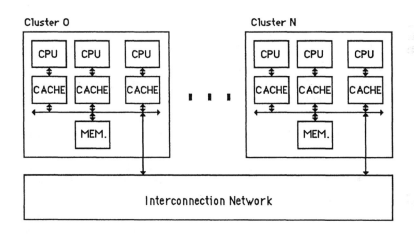

Fig.1.19 Multiprocessor architecture using MIPS-X.

MIPS-X demonstrated the power of keeping a VLSI processor simple, obtaining an effective throughput of over 10 MIPS while using a conservative technology. The key was to shift complexity from hardware to software and to use the "free silicon" where it made the most difference : an efficient on-chip instruction cache [31-32].

After the design of the MIPS-X microprocessor, the Stanford team started to work on a microprocessor architecture in order to break the frontier of 100 MIPS. The main effort was to work on distributed architectures, organized as multiple MIPS-X clusters connected to each other through a communication network. The major problem in such an architecture is to solve the cache coherence problem without affecting the overall performance [33].

1.6 FUTURE RESEARCH DIRECTIONS

1.6.1. UNIVERSITIES CONTINUE TO EXPLORE RISC

Although the RISC approach was first explored in universities, it has since had a huge impact on commercial computer architectures. Even designers who are not embracing it are borrowing from it. With a raft of new pure and not-so-pure RISC products appearing, there is no doubt that RISC has out grown the stage of an academic exercise. At the same time universities and research laboratories continue to explore the RISC idea, in order to design very high-performance microprocessors. Following RISC and MIPS, a large number of projects were started : PIPE (Parallel Instructions and Pipelined Execution) from Wisconsin University [34], RIMMS (Reduced Instruction Set Architecture for Multi-Microprocessor Systems) from Reading University [35], and more.

By continuing to reduce the number of instructions, D. Tabak and his team designed a special architecture based on a single instruction, called SIC (Single Instruction Computer) [36]. The single instruction implemented was MOVE, because it is the instruction most often used in many programs. A prototype of a SIC computer, named CMOVE, was fabricated at the University of Ben Guréon in 1982 [37] for specific control applications. The main features of the CMOVE architecture were the following :

1. The system has a single instruction, with no opcode and opcode decoding with the following general structure : <MOVE from SOURCE to DESTINATION>, where SOURCE represents the address of the source location in memory, and DESTINATION represents the address of the destination in memory.

2. The instruction is executed in two machine cycles : "from" and "to".

3. There are four addressing modes for each of the two operands : direct, immediate and indexed S or X (S and X are index registers).

4. CMOVE includes two memories, one for storing programs and the second for data.

5. The CPU contains no ALU. All operations are performed within external circuitry and I/O processors.

Another new architecture was proposed by Phil Koopman [38]. He defined the concept of WISC architecture (Writable Instruction Set Computer). The idea was to take advantages of both RISC and CISC architectures, by using a writable instruction store on a stack-based microprocessor.

The major goal of research on RISC architecture is to improve the overall performance of computing systems. A careful analysis of new research shows two main directions :

1. The design of high-speed microprocessors using high-performance technologies, such as ECL or GaAs (Gallium Arsenide).

2. The study of parallel microprocessors including "on-chip" parallelism using multiple functional units and multi-microprocessor architectures.

The next paragraphs describe some projects of both research directions.

1.6.2 TEXAS INSTRUMENTS GaAs RISC CHIP

Gallium Arsenide (GaAs) can be used in place of silicon because it has several key advantages, including radiation hardness and less temperature sensitivity. However, its main advantage is its speed. Because electrons travel faster in GaAs, circuits built using this technology can be faster than the same circuits on silicon. Disadvantages of GaAs are that it is harder to work with than silicon and that chip makers have less experience with it. However, the state of the art in GaAs technology has recently (1991) produced parts that have near 100,000 gates or memory cells. Although the GaAs technology has not yet reached far enough to produce CISC processors, it can be used to implement simple and efficient RISC ones [39].

A RISC microprocessor architecture is well suited to implementation in GaAs because of its low hardware requirements. In spring 1984, Texas Instruments and Control Data, under DARPA sponsorship, began a one-year project to develop a GaAs RISC microprocessor. The system was a chip set consisting of a CPU, a

FCOP (Floating Point Coprocessor), a MMU (Memory Management Unit) and a cache. The streamlined architecture minimizes latencies between instructions while allowing for parallel operation between the CPU and the FCOP. The MMU manages the cache to provide a high hit rate. The initial performance goal was a peak throughput of 200 MIPS [40].

In order to make it possible to successfully build a fully functional chip, they had established that a maximum gate count of 10,000 was necessary. Also, in order to obtain the fastest possible machine cycle, interaction between GaAs chips had to be kept to a minimum to preserve the inherent speed of the GaAs gates. This made it necessary to put entire logical functions on one chip. To place the CPU on a single chip, Texas Instruments and Control Data had to eleminate control gates as much as possible while implementing as many on-chip registers as possible to reduce off-chip activity.

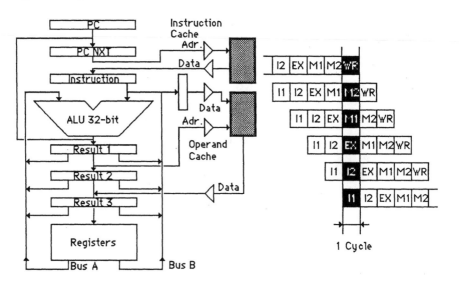

Fig.1.20 Texas Instruments GaAs RISC architecture and pipeline.

The instruction set was developed based on simulation statistics and previous work done on the Berkeley RISC and Stanford MIPS projects. It defined a core instruction set at an intermediate level between the hardware-dependent GaAs microprocessor system instruction set and a high-level language. Like MIPS, once a program is compiled to the core instruction set, a hardware-dependent translator transforms the code to the machine instruction set and performs any machine-dependent optimizations. However, the architecture has some hardware interlocks and data dependencies between register-to-register instructions are resolved in hardware. The instruction set was divided into three parts corresponding to the three elements of the GaAs microprocessor system : 29 CPU instructions, 31 FCOP instructions and 6 MMU instructions.

The initial pipeline was designed with a four-stage scheme. However, the cache memory access could not support a 5ns memory cycle required by the four-stage pipeline, so researchers decided to implement a pipelined memory accessed over two cycles and a six-stage pipeline. The latter consisted of instruction fetch cycle 1 (I1), instruction fetch cycle 2 (T2), ALU execute (EX), memory access cycle 1 (M1), memory access cycle 2 (M2) and write register file (WR).

The resulting GaAs RISC microprocessor showed a peak throughput of 200 MIPS, but this was reduced by 32 percent because of the NOP instruction required, and then reduced by another 32 percent because of the memory bandwidth limits. This resulting in an average net performance of 91 MIPS.

1.6.3 MCDONNELL DOUGLAS GaAs RISC CHIP

During the same period (1986-1987), McDonnell Douglas also started the design of a 32-bit RISC microprocessor based on GaAs enhancement JFET direct coupled FET Logic (DCFL). This circuit called MD484 was strongly influenced by the Stanford MIPS design.

The microprocessor architecture and implementation were driven by the constraints of the GaAs process. So that the microprocessor would be buildable in the near term, a strict transistor budget was established at less than 25,000 transistors. The microprocessor included 32 32-bit registers and the instruction set was very close to the original MIPS one. One of the most difficult design decisions was the choice of the number and type of execution pipeline stages. The decision centered on the problem of extending the execution pipeline into the memory and pipelining memory references. Increasing the number of stages to five or six, with the extra stages added to the memory access stages, would allow more time for memory accesses and therefore make the memory system easier to build. However, a long pipeline scheme increases branch delays and load latencies. The performance loss due to NOP insertion was from 20 to 30 percent for a six-stage pipeline and approximately half of that for the five-stage pipeline

43

relative to the four-stage. McDonnell Douglas researchers concluded that the four-stage pipeline was the ideal minimum [41].

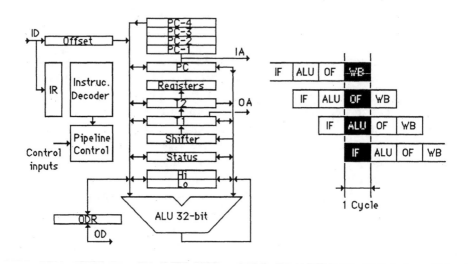

Fig.1.21 McDonnell Douglas GaAs RISC architecture and pipeline.

For efficient execution of floating point arithmetic, McDonnell Douglas also designed an optional Floating Point coprocessor optimized to perform floating-point arithmetic on either single precision (32-bit) or double precision (64-bit) data in the IEEE format. In 1987, the CPU chip was fabricated and tested fully functional.

An instruction execution cycle time of 16.5 ns has been measured giving an operation rate of 60 MIPS. Power dissipation was 4.7 W. The McDonnell Douglas team then started to work on transistor parameter improvements to attain greater than 100 MIPS operation [42].

1.6.4 OTHER GaAs RISC RESEARCH PROJECTS

Other projects were conducted in the field of high-performance GaAs RISC processors [43]. In 1989 RCA designed a 32-bit microprocessor architecture intended for implementation using GaAs VLSI [44]. However, the RCA 32-bit GaAs machine handles the problem in a way which was not the same as those from McDonnell Douglas or Texas Instrument/Control Data. For example, the instruction format chosen uses one and two-word instructions in contrast with most RISC machines. A second major difference was the pipeline design which was preceded by a number of experiments and simulations in order to quantify the value of alternate approaches. It was finally decided to invest most effort in the compiler technology and to base the architecture on a pipelined-memory structure. The resulting pipeline was nine-stage with two latency periods of 2 wait cycles, the first one related to the instruction fetch, and the second one related to the operand fetch for a load operation.

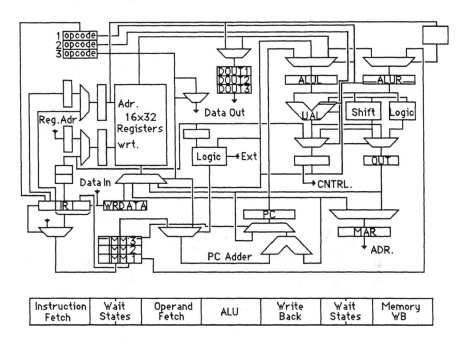

Instruction Fetch	Wait States	Operand Fetch	ALU	Write Back	Wait States	Memory WB

Fig.1.22 RCA GaAs RISC architecture and pipeline.

There are a number of computer design problems with high-speed technologies such as GaAs. The first problem is the limitation on the complexity of the logic functions that can be integrated, even if GaAs has reached the VLSI level. The second major problem is the relative high ratio of off-chip memory access time to on-chip data-path time. SODIMA S.A. has proposed a 32-bit four-stage architecture suitable for integration using GaAs Standard cell technologies [45]. SODIMA's team also designed a two-level cache architecture based on a small high-speed cache (4 Kbytes 3 ns access-time and a larger but slower cache (128 Kbytes 25 ns access-time) in order to obtain an average net performance of 100

45

MIPS and a peak throughput of 200 MIPS for instructions stored in the first cache level [46].

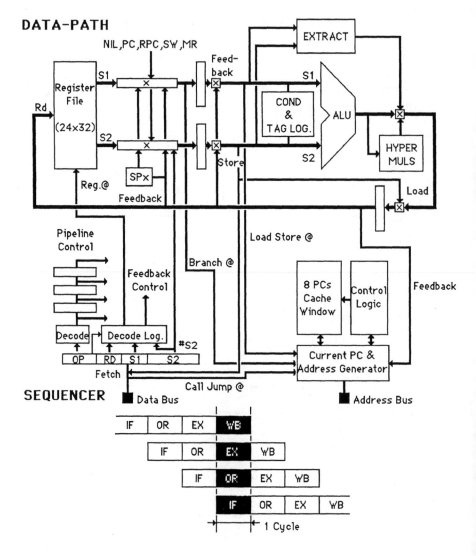

Fig.1.23 SODIMA GaAs RISC architecture and pipeline.

1.6.5 THE SUPERSCALAR APPROACH

As we have seen in section 1.1.4, the cornerstone of RISC can be understood with a simple equation, in which the CPU performance depends on the clock rate, the instruction count for some

46

benchmark of interest and the average number of cycles per instruction.

In the previous sections (6.2 to 6.4), we have described the first approach for improving RISC performance : that is, implementing a simple and efficient RISC architecture using a high-speed technology such as Gallium Arsenide. The aim of this approach is roughly to increase the clock rate parameter while keeping the other parameters close to standard RISC values. Since technology improvements will continue to be important, this approach will allow more and more powerful chips.

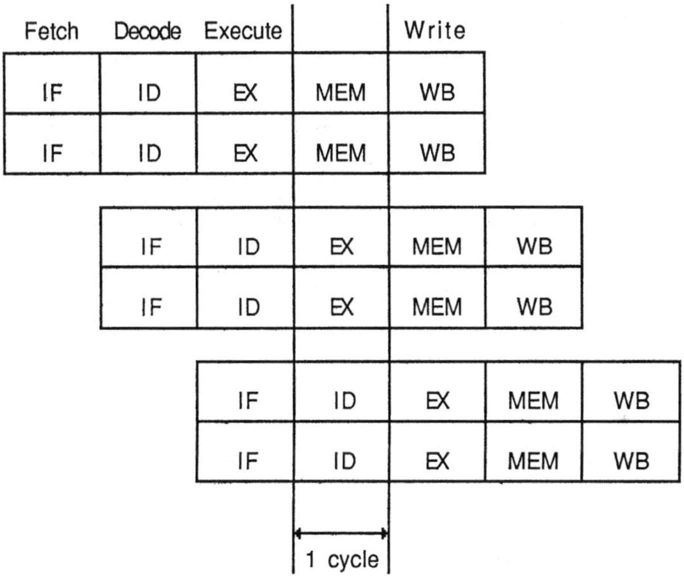

Fetch	Decode	Execute			Write			
IF	ID	EX	MEM	WB				
IF	ID	EX	MEM	WB				
		IF	ID	EX	MEM	WB		
		IF	ID	EX	MEM	WB		
			IF	ID	EX	MEM	WB	
			IF	ID	EX	MEM	WB	

1 cycle

Fig.1.24 Superscalar pipeline example.

However, technology and small architectural changes that allow higher clock rates cannot support alone the growth rate of 50-100% that RISC machines have recently demonstrated. Therefore, the second way to improve performance must arise from architectural enhancements, by increasing the amount of parallel execution of instructions. In such a framework, we can divide research efforts into three different architectural approaches [47].

1.   Superscalar architectures.

2.   Superpipelined architectures.

47

3. VLIW architectures.

The first one tries to issue multiple instructions, perhaps two or three, on every clock cycle. Superscalar processors can have clocks very close to that of a RISC and maintain a smaller average number of clock cycles required per instruction. They achieve that by issuing several independent instructions in the same clock cycle : one integer compute operation and a floating-point operation for example. However, if the instructions in the instruction stream are dependent, only the first of these in sequence will be issued. Generally, this will require that the processor is able to fetch and decode 64-bit instructions. Ideally, a superscalar machine will pick up two instructions and issue them both if the first one is an integer and the second is a floating-point instruction. If they do not fit this pattern, then they are issued sequentially in order.

The major difficulty with superscalar architectures is the increased effective latency of operations, and in order to fully exploit such architectures, advanced compiler scheduling techniques are needed. The second problem is the waste of code space and fetches when the program cannot be reorganized in such a way to provide the required mix of integer and floating-point instuctions.

1.6.6 THE SUPERPIPELINED APPROACH

The superpipelined approach is characterized by an increase in the number of pipeline stages.

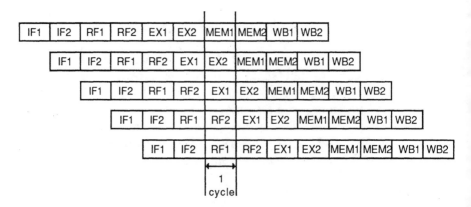

Fig.1.25 Superpipelined machine pipeline example.

A superpipelined RISC generally has about ten pipeline stages and all functional units are pipelined. In fact, superpipelined machines are not fundamentally different from earlier RISC designs, though the compiler may be much more sophisticated. Such a machine has a slightly higher number of cycles per instruction than classical RISC architectures, because the deeper pipeline increases the pipeline delays and potential losses from instruction dependencies. However, its main advantage is in clock rate, which is significantly higher. Most of today's supercomputers are superpipelined machines, designed using high-speed logic.

1.6.7 THE VLIW APPROACH

As we have seen in section 6.5, superscalar machines can issue two or three instructions per clock cycle. The VLIW approach extends this idea to 6, 7 or more.

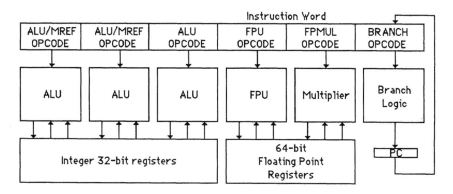

Fig.1.26 Very Large Instruction Word architecture.

VLIW is an acronym for Very Long Instruction Word, because it packages multiple operations into one very long instruction [48]. An example of a VLIW architecture might include three integer operations, two floating points, two memory references and a branch. Thus, the VLIW processor uses multiple independent functional units and instructions are characterized by a length generally higher than 100 bits. To keep all functional units busy at each cycle, a straightline code sequence must be reorganized and scheduled using a technique called "trace scheduling" [49]. If all works well, such an architecture can issue seven or more operations per cycle. The major disadvantages are the limitation of hardware resource compared to the complexity of multiple functional units, and the code size explosion when a program does not offer enough parallelism at the instruction level.

1.7 RISC VERSUS CISC

Finally, what is the major difference between a RISC microprocessor and a CISC one ? As we have seen in this chapter, RISC refers to a new design methodology that indicates a new relationship between hardware and software, rather than a set of technical features. In fact, the effects of the RISC approach on computer design is far more than just a collection of methods to run the CPU faster. In this sense, the term "Reduced-Instruction Set Computer" is somewhat misleading. The real goal of RISC design definitely is not to arbitrarily reduce the number of instructions. Rather, the main objective is to create a high-speed computer by making the compiler system match the hardware. Another way to compare RISC and CISC is to refer to the CPU performance equation established in section 1.1.4. The main goal of CISC designs was to reduce the number of instructions for executing programs (I). Rather, RISC tries mainly to reduce the average number of clock cycles per instruction (CPI). Both architectures want also to increase the clock-rate by using high-speed technologies, however RISC provides a greater performance improvement since its reduced complexity enables it to be fabricated earlier in such technologies.

Other microprocessor architects join the RISC faithful or not, they have been influenced by the RISC methodology : as an example, the Motorola's 68030 has already acquired some of its features [50]. The force of RISC is that it is based on a true design methodology pushed by advances in compiler technology. Within RISC, teams of hardware engineers and compiler architects work together to forge a unified design : one that will minimize the hardware complexity by integrating in hardware only such instructions that are justified by their occurrence in program trace analysis. We will see in the next chapters that this idea enables us to build high-performance microprocessors for dedicated application fields such as symbolic processing.

The next chapter lays out the main features of the RISC design methodology.

2

Principles of the RISC design methodology

2.1 THE RISC METHODOLOGY

2.1.1 COMPUTER DESIGN APPROACHES

There are three basic approaches for designing a microprocessor architecture. Most of commercially available CISC processors have been designed using a bottom-up approach in order to meet the compatibility requirement with earlier versions, and also in order to reduce the complexity of designing a new architecture from scratch. This approach starts from the architectural features, that is the earlier instruction set, and works upwards to the applications they can support efficiently by adding new instructions or functionalities. The second approach is called middle-approach, because it starts from a language definition and works down towards the architectural basis. This approach has been extensively applied in the past for designing language-based machines, such as the Symbolics 3600 Lisp machine [51]. Such a machine is designed to execute efficiently the computational model of the Lisp language. It incorporates special mechanisms in hardware to implement primitive operations of the language it must support. The Symbolics 3600 is stack-oriented, uses a tagged architecture and its performance improvement was mainly due to an efficient microcoded implementation of the time-consuming Lisp primitives. The third possible approach is called top-down since it begins by a detailed analysis of a dedicated application domain, in order to define the best-adapted architecture.

The next figure gives a comparison diagram of the three basic design approaches and lays out the underlying abstract levels : the application level, the knowledge representation level, the language level, the computing model level and the hardware architecture level.

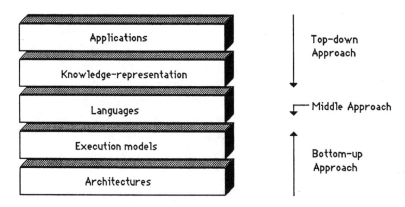

Fig.2.1 The three basic design approaches.

In practice, the choices made at each level of the hierarchy are not necessarily independent or exclusive. Furthermore, there is no pure top-down or bottom-up approach. For example, a top-down approach must take into account existing architectures and implementation constraints. As a result most microprocessor designers iteratively use the top-down and bottom-up approaches.

2.1.2 A TOP-DOWN APPROACH

The RISC methodology is based on a top-down approach guided by a set of architectural design criteria. The major goal is to reduce the semantic gap between the hardware machine and the application level, while maximizing the execution speed. Therefore, the first step in the RISC design methodology is to make a detailed and careful analysis of application codes in order to discover the most frequent operations. This analysis must be done on a large amount of program code related to the selected application field. Examples of the latter were mainly in the past : C programming, symbolic processing and signal processing. Then, the study of the highly frequent operations enables the designer to determine the instruction set architecture. The next step is then to verify that each instruction can fit in the basic RISC architecture model without increasing the cycle time : the real keys to enhanced performance are single-cycle execution and keeping the cycle-time as short as possible. Remember that the choice of a given implementation technology and related software tools also significantly influence the design.

A gate array is simpler to design but does not allow a high performance implementation. In contrast, a custom design enables enhanced performance but requires a longer and harder study. A standard cell is an intermadiete choice between these two alternatives. However, recent advances in silicon compilers enables the designer to use an optimizing tool for each functional module of the architecture : a data-path compiler for the data-path, a state-machine compiler for the control unit and the sequencer, a RAM or register-file compiler for the register file. These new CAD software techniques significantly reduce the design time and potential errors.

2.1.3 THE RISC METHODOLOGY

We have underlined that the RISC design flow is based on a top-down approach. This paragraph lays out the five basic steps of the methodology. They are the following :

1. Statistical analysis of typical application code in order to find the highly frequent operations.

2. Definition of the instruction set architecture. The latter must include only simple instructions unless there is a good reason for complexity.

3. Design of the data-path with related operators (ALU, shifters, etc.) in order to efficiently execute the selected instructions.

4. Add other instructions only because they measurably improve performance and do not break the pipeline scheme or increase the cycle time. Otherwise, these functions must be implemented in software as a sequence of simpler instructions.

5. Verify the instruction set performance and completeness by running application code on a software simulator. If some problems remain (poor performance and/or the compiled code is too large), return to step 1.

The five steps roughly underline the RISC top-down approach. In order to design the resulting architecture, the designer must keep in mind a coherent set of characteristics that are typical of RISC implementations. Although none of these are required for an architecture to be called RISC, this list describes the main RISC features that enhance performance through single-cycle execution and keeping the cycle-time as short as possible (optimized F and CPI parameters see section 1.1.4 in chapter 1).

2.1.4 RISC DESIGN CRITERIA

The following characteristics are typical of pure RISC architectures and most designers agree on them. The real key to enhanced performance relies upon a top-down approach strongly-coupled to the optimization of the cycle-time and the number of clock cycles required per instruction. However, the following implementation features provide the computer architect with some guidelines that help to converge using the design methodology. We can summarize these characteristics into nine main points:

1. Relatively few instructions and single-cycle operations for every instruction.

2. Few addressing modes and a fixed instruction format.

3. Hardwired control without microcode.

4. Migration of complex functions to software.

5. Only Load and Store instructions should reference external memory.

6. Each instruction must fit a pipelined model that allows parts of several operations to be processed at the same time.

7. Delayed-branches enable conditional and unconditional jumps to execute without flushing the pipeline.

8. The architecture must have at least 32 general-purpose registers and large cache memories.

9.   The architecture must be tailored for a dedicated application field and must support high-level languages.

The major tenet of RISC states that much of the static runtime complexity can and should be handled prior to runtime by an optimizing compiler. Then, the resulting hardware architecture must be quite simple to ensure single-cycle execution for every instruction and small clock cycles. Note that all these features, particularly pipelining and high-performance memories, have been used in supercomputer designs for many years. Remember that the main advance of RISC was to integrate all these ideas into a single architecture model, coupled with a coherent top-down methodology.

   The next sections will describe more precisely all these points through the study of the two major tasks of a RISC architecture design : (1) the instruction set definition and (2) the pipeline design.

2.2 A REDUCED AND HOMOGENEOUS INSTRUCTION SET

2.2.1 INSTRUCTION GROUPS

We have emphasized that the instruction set architecture must be the result of a careful analysis of application codes in order to select only highly frequent operations. In practice, instruction sets can be sub-divided into a few instruction groups. For most RISC processors, there are three basic instruction groups :

1. Compute instructions.

2. Control instructions.

3. Memory access instructions.

Compute instructions generally include arithmetic, logical and shift operations. These instructions compute a result that is a function of two source operands and then place the result in a register.

Control instructions require more attention because their implementation depends both on the characteristics of application codes and the selected pipeline organization. However, in most cases, the control group relies mainly on conditional and unconditional branches, explicit call and return operations or jump-and-link operations. Control transfers are usually delayed until after execution of the next instruction, so that the pipeline is not emptied every time a control transfer occurs.

Memory access instructions include only load and store operations. However, in most designs, load and store come in multiple flavours : they differ to enable operations on byte (8-bit), unsigned-byte, half-word (16-bit), unsigned-half-word, word (32-bit), unsigned-word and sometimes 64-bit words. Another solution, simpler for hardware implementation, but less efficient, is based on having only word store and load instructions, plus byte extract and insert instructions. Load and store instructions are the only operations that violate the single-cycle constraint, because of the time required to access the memory while fetching the next instruction. We will see later that a solution to this problem exists, but requires extra buses and hardware.

These three basic instruction categories are in most cases extended with two more additional groups :

1.   Application-specific instructions.
2.   Miscellaneous instructions.

The first group is dedicated to the selected application domain or a given high-level language. For example, we will see in chapter 4 a set of instructions designed to efficiently support symbolic processing. In most general purpose microprocessors, this group is omitted, since standard applications do not require any other instructions. The second group includes instructions to read and write the contents of various control registers, such as the processor status word, the cache controller or the memory management interface. It can also include generic coprocessor operations that enables optional coprocessors to execute concurrently with the RISC integer unit. The obvious application of this is for floating-point calculations. According to the architecture, the integer unit and the floating-point unit (or FPU coprocessor) may or may not be implemented on the same chip.

2.2.2 A REGISTER-ORIENTED INSTRUCTION SET

In order to meet the challenge of single-cycle execution, the RISC approach specifies two complementary points :

1.   Load-Store, register-to-register intensive design, all computational instructions involve registers. Memory accesses are made only with load and store instructions.

2.   A large register file reduces a program's need to load and store operands to and from external memory.

Because access to external memory is slower than access to processor registers (100 200 ns access time for a typical external memory compared to 10 50 ns for registers in common CMOS technology), these two points strive to keep all data in registers for as long as possible. A large register set allows a program to keep operands readily available and reduces memory-bandwith requirements. The load-store design explicitly limits the access to external memory. The Berkeley researchers argue that a computer does 70% operand accesses and 30% operations : for each operation, one or two source operands are required and the result is placed into another operand. This example clearly shows how important it is for a computer system to have quick access to operands.

Therefore, the fastest storage device is a register, not only because it is small and on the same chip, but also because addressing is made with a much shorter address than for an external memory or a cache system. Since at each cycle the RISC processor must fetch a new instruction, every access to external memory for loading or storing a value potentially breaks the pipeline execution and introduces latencies. This is the reason why RISC tries firstly to keep as many of its operands as possible in register and, secondly, tries to limit external memory references. These points imply also that the compute instructions operate on registers rather than on external memory. Thus the resulting instruction formats must rely mainly on register addressing for source and destination operands.

2.2.3 INSTRUCTION FORMATS

One of the major criteria for designing a RISC architecture is to simplify the overall design by making all instructions the same size with a few simple fixed formats. Adherence to these points facilitates the implementation of both single-cycle operation and hardwired control with a relatively small investment in design time and silicon real estate. In most RISC architectures, all instructions are the same length, typically 32-bit, and have just a few ways to address memory : from one to four instruction formats. For example, the Berkeley RISC microprocessors are based on two main formats :

1. The register format.
2. The immediate format.

These two formats are 32-bit long. The register format generally include the operation code (OpCode), a destination register, a first source register and a second source register or a small immediate value. This format enables instructions to use two registers or a register and a constant to compute an operation, and then to place the result in a destination register. The second format enables instructions to include an operation code, an explicit or implicit destination register, and long immediate value. This format is generally used to calculate the memory address involved in control-transfer instructions (call, jump, etc.) or memory access instructions.

2.2.4 FEW INSTRUCTIONS AND ADDRESSING MODES

Two commonly practiced RISC attributes are the following for designing the instruction set :

1. A relatively small number of instructions : less than 100.
2. A small number of addressing modes : one or two.

These two points, like the instruction format and the register-intensive approaches, facilitate both the implementation of single-cycle operation and a short clock cycle. They simplify the design of the control circuitry : less complexity can normally run faster overall. If the number of instructions is greatly influenced by the study of the application code, it is generally not the case for addressing modes. In most RISC architectures, all compute instructions operate on registers (section 2.2.2). Thus, only the load and store operation can access operands in memory and move them to or from registers. We can show that a single addressing mode, which matches well with the RISC philosophy, is quite versatile and permits one to synthesize many other simple addressing modes :

$$Rd <- -> M [Rs + S2]$$

Rd is a register, M an index, Rs a source register and S2 a second source register or constant. This single addressing mode enables the following more conventional addressing modes :

1. Absolute or direct for global scalar access :
    M [Rs + imm].

2. Register indirect for pointer reference (*p) :
    M [Rs + Rs2].

3. Indexed for structure field access (p ->field) :
    M [Rs + offset]
    or linear byte array (a[i]) :
    M [Rs + Rs2].

Notice that this kind of versatile addressing mode of the memory access instructions can also be used for the control-transfer instructions (jump, call, return) in addition to the classical PC-relative addressing mode.

2.2.5 AN EXAMPLE : THE DoD CORE MIPS

The study done by Thomas Gross and Robert Firth at the Software Engineering Institute of Carnegie Mellon University is a good illustration for the design of a RISC instruction set [52]. This work was sponsored by the U.S. Department of Defense (DoD) in order to define a generic instruction set architecture for MIPS-based microprocessors. By instruction set architecture, they mean those facets of the architecture that are important for the code generator or are seen by an assembly language programmer. Therefore, all hardware implementations of this virtual machine must be able to execute the defined instructions, either directly or after translation into a suitable sequence of machine instructions. It is assumed that the assembler or a low-level optimizer is able to map the assembly instructions into machine instructions. We call the instruction set interpreted by the hardware implementation the "low-level" or "hardware" instruction set. Since it is hidden from the compiler writer, we refer to this instruction set also as the "invisible" instruction set to contrast it with the core instruction set which is "visible".

For most instructions, the mapping from core instruction level to low-level instructions is a direct translation into the corresponding machine instruction. However, this arrangement allows the same assembly language to be used for different hardware implementations, while providing a uniform interface to all implementations. We can summarize the objectives of the DoD CORE MIPS instruction set architecture by the three following points :

1. The most frequent instructions map one-to-one into machine instructions for a single-cycle RISC-style machine.

2. More complex core instructions can be expanded by the assembler into a sequence of simpler machine instructions. The goal is to provide a framework for a machine instruction set that can be easily decoded and executed.

3. The expanded instructions might use resources in addition to those visible at the core instruction set level.

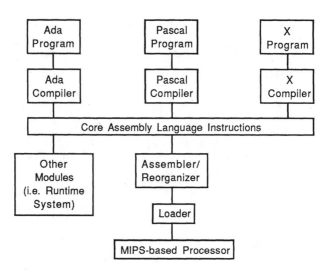

Fig.2.2 Core-MIPS compilation environment.

The second purpose of the core instruction set is to define a target for compiler writers. In this framework, several distinct steps are required to translate a high-level language for execution by a processor.

Compilers translate high-level languages into the MIPS core instruction set. This activity is independent of the choice of processor. Then, the translation from the core instruction set to the hardware instruction set is called assembly or reorganization. The latter knows the exact implementation of the target processor and translates the instructions accordingly.

The core instruction set uses at least sixteen 32-bit general purpose registers and four 64-bit floating-point registers. The register space is organized into different classes : stack pointer, frame pointer, link register, function return register, temporary registers, argument registers, expression evaluation registers and floating-point registers. The instruction set includes ALU instructions, shift instructions, load and store instructions, branch and jump instructions and floating-point operations. Most of these instructions are available in two- and three- operand formats. the two-operand form uses the first operand, source1, as destination. The three-operand format sets the destination register to the result of the specified function applied to two sources : source1 and source2.

destination <--- source1 op. source2

Either source1 or source2 can be specified as a 32-bit immediate value, with the remainder specified as a register. The core instruction set makes no decision on the formats that are supported by the hardware processor as long as all instructions can be translated by the assembler to the formats implemented in hardware. In all cases, the implementor should use dynamic instruction frequency data to guide his choices.

Here is a simple example of such a translation [53] with the MIPS M/500 machine. The MIPS M/500 native instruction set limits the size of immediate operands to 16 bits. Therefore, when a 32-bit constant value is needed, it is loaded in 16-bit halves. The "lui" instruction loads the upper half of the register while the "ori" instruction OR's in the lower half.

```
add      $4, $5, 0x20FF00   ; $x are virtual registers
```

is tranlated by the assembler into :

```
lui      at, 0x20           ; at, a0, a1 are real registers
ori      at, at, 0xFF00
add      a0, a1, at
```

ABS	Absolute value (integer)	BRA	Branch-destination
ADD	Integer addition	BRC	Condition, souce1, source2,
DIV	Integer division		branch-destination
MOD	Modulo		
MUL	Integer multiplication	JMP	Branch-destination
NEG	Negate (integer)	JMP	Register
REM	Remainder		
SUB	Integer subtraction	CAL	Call-target, link-location
AND	Bitwise "and"		
NOT	Bitwise "not"	TRAP	Trap-code
OR	Bitwise "or"		
XOR	Bitwise "exclusive or"	FPLDS	Load single-precision floating-point value
MOV	Register move		into floating-point register
		FPLDD	Load double-precision floating-point value
ADDU	Unsigned integer addition		into floating-point register
DIVU	Unsigned integer division	FPSLDI	Load integer into floating-point register
MODU	Unsigned modulo	FPDLDI	Load integer into floating-point register
MULU	Unsigned integer		(double-precision)
	multiplication	FPSTS	Store single-precision floating-point value
		FPSTD	Store double-precision floating-point value
REMU	Remainder unsigned	FPRSSTI	Round short format floating-point value
SUBU	Unsigned integer subtraction		and store
		FPDSSTI	Round double precision floating-point value
SLL	Shift left logical		and store result
SRL	Shift right logical	FPTSSTI	Truncate short format floating-point value
SRA	Shift right arithmetic		and store result
ROL	Rotate left	FPRDSTI	Truncate double-precision floating-point
ROR	Rotate right		value and store result
		FPSADD	Short floating-point addition
SDL	Shift double word left logical	FPSDIV	Short floating-point division
SDR	Shift double word right logical	FPSMUL	Short floating-point multiplication
SDA	Shift double word right	FPSSUB	Short floating-point subtraction
	arithmetic		
RDL	Rotate double word left	FPDADD	Floating-point addition
RDR	Rotate double word right	FPDDIV	Floating-point division
		FPDMUL	Floating-point multiplication
LDBS	Load byte sign-extended	FPDSUB	Floating-point subtraction
LDBU	Load byte unsigned		
LDHS	Load halfword sign-extended	FPDABS	Absolute value of a floating-point number,
LDHU	Load halfword unsigned		full (double) precision
LDW	Load word	FPSABS	Absolute value of a floating-point number,
			short precision
STB	Store byte	FPDSQRT	Floating-point square root, full (double)
STH	Store halfword		precision
STW	Store word	FPSSQRT	Floating-point square root, short precision
LDA	Destination, general_address	FPMOV	Move data from one floating-point register
			to another

Fig.2.3 Core-MIPS instruction list.

2.3   A STREAMLINED ARCHITECTURE

2.3.1 BASIC PROCESSOR ORGANIZATION

Von Neumann divided a computer into four basic components that still remain today : the processor, the memory, the inputs and outputs. The processor or CPU (Central Processing Unit) is the core of the computer. It can be in turn divided into two basic components :

1.   The computation part.
2.   The control part.

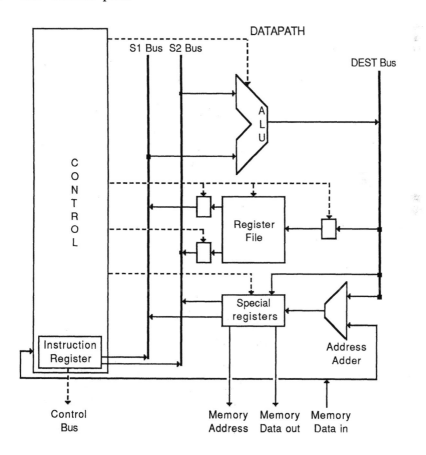

Fig.2.4 Basic processor organization.

The computation part of a processor is called the data-path. It mainly consists of the registers organized in a register file, the execution units such as the Arithmetic and Logical Unit (ALU), shifters, etc., and the communication paths between them. From the software perspective, it contains most of the essential blocks of the processor.

The control part of a processor mainly consists of the sequencer and the logic for fetching and decoding instructions. The sequencer is one of the most important units of a processor, because it is responsible for scheduling all basic operations done by the processor. At each step (clock cycle), the sequencer controls the execution of the pipeline.

2.3.2 THE DATA-PATH

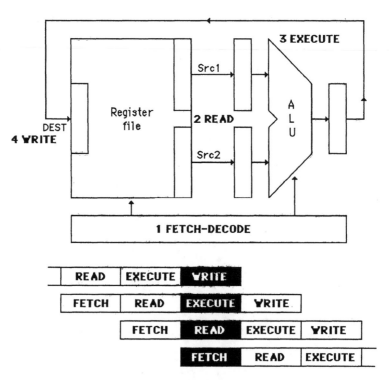

Fig.2.5 Simple RISC data-path.

The two main elements of the data-path are the register file and the ALU. The data-path uses three buses for routing information between registers and the ALU : Src1, Src2 and DEST. Src1 and Src2 are used to read information from the register file and send them to the corresponding inputs of the ALU. DEST takes the result of the computation done by the ALU and enables it to be written-back to the register file. Because it takes too long to read operands from the register file, operate on them in the ALU and store them back, latches are added on the two outputs of the register file and on the input.

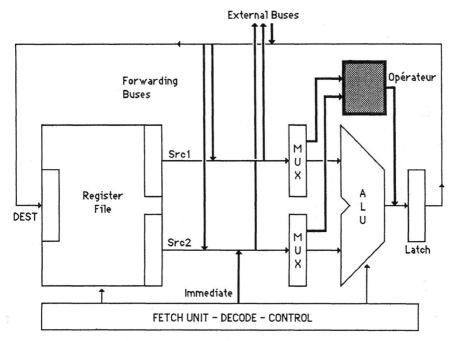

Fig.2.6 Enhanced RISC data-path.

These latches are called pipeline registers, since they are directly controlled by the sequencer in order to store new values at each clock cycle, following the pipeline execution model. We can easily deduce from this that the clock cycle time of the processor is determined by the slowest circuits that operate during a clock cycle period. In most RISC architectures, the data-path contains three critical paths :

1. The time required to read the two operands from the register file.

2. The time to compute the appropriate operation in the ALU, shifter or other functional unit.

3. The time required to store back the result into the register file.

Thus, the designer must take care when implementing the register file and the operators.

2.3.3 HARDWIRED CONTROL

In 1951, Maurice Wilkes first developed a scheme to implement flexible control units. His solution was to turn the control unit into a miniature computer. He called his invention microprogramming. For each fetched instruction, the control unit executes a sequence of micro-instructions stored in the microprogram memory. Microprogram memory is sometimes called ROM (Read Only Memory), because most CISC processors use ROM for their control stores. Micro-instructions specify all the control signals for the data-path, plus the ability to conditionally decide which micro-instruction should be executed next. However, advances in memory performance now makes microcode generally no faster than a sequence of hardwired instructions. In such a framework, moving software into microcode does not make it better or faster, it just makes it harder to design and modify : microcode adds a level of complexity and raises the number of clock cycles required per instruction.

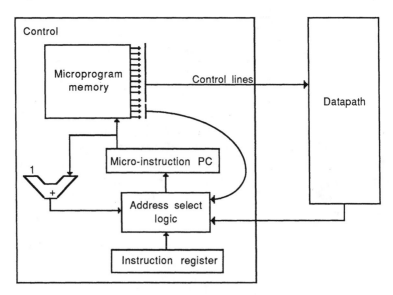

Fig.2.7 Microcoded control in CISC processors.

Given an instruction set description, the first step is to define what control is required to tell the data path what to do every clock cycle. This is typically specified by a finite-state machine, where each state corresponds to one clock cycle. Then, the straight forward hardware implementation of such a state machine is a table. The latter can be basically designed using a Read Only Memory or implemented in a Programmed Logic Array (PLA).

Because of the simplicity and performance of the underlying hardware, hardwired control minimizes the average number of clock cycles required per instruction and the clock cycle time. In most RISC architectures decoding the incoming instruction is particularly easy, because of the simple instruction format with fields of fixed size and position. As an example, the RISC-II control section occupies only 10% of the chip area, compared to 68% for the Motorola MC68000.

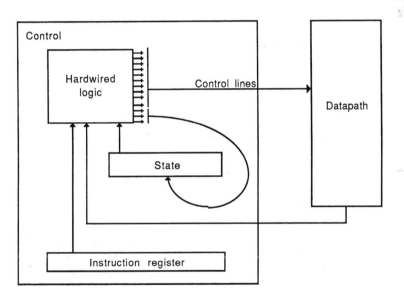

Fig.2.8 Typical RISC hardwired control.

2.3.4 PIPELINING

Most RISC architectures are based on a large pipeline in order to break up the instruction fetching, decoding and execution phases. Pipelining is an implementation technique that allows the execution of multiple instructions at the same time. Each instruction is divided in "pipe stage" or "pipe segment" and are connected one to the next to form a pipeline. At every clock cycle, a new instruction begins, and another one ends : some of the stages of the execution of each instruction are overlapped. The throughput of a pipeline is determined by how often an instruction exits the pipeline. Because the pipe stages are hooked together, all the instruction stages must be ready to proceed at the same time. The time required between moving instructions down the pipeline is one machine cycle and its length is determined by the time required by the slowest pipe stage. Therefore, the designer generally try to balance the differents stages. However, in most RISC designs, the slowest pipe segment is the first one, that is the one that accesses the program memory in order to fetch the instruction. As we have seen in section 2, most RISC instructions can be executed within the same amount of time (i.e. a machine cycle), adhering to the following execution pattern :

1. Fetch and decode the instruction.
2. Read source1 and source2 operands from the register file.
3. Perform an arithmetic, logical or shift operation on these operands.
4. Write back the result into the register file.

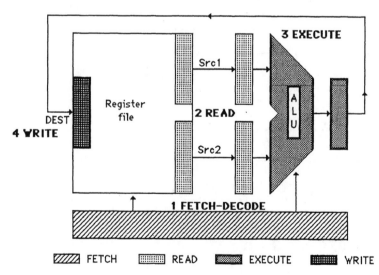

Fig.2.9 Four-stage pipeline model.

The other basic operations are in step 2, to get the PC or an immediate value instead of a register, and in step 4, to use the result as an effective address for a memory access. Load and store, the only instructions containing a data memory access, require an additional cycle for completion. They will be discussed in section 4. Another important operation is also the instruction fetch that begins every instruction execution pattern. These simple execution patterns lead to simple pipeline schemes. As examples, let us look at the RISC-I and RISC-II pipelines.

RISC-I has a simple two-stage pipeline, overlapping instruction fetch and execution, and includes the delayed-branch scheme (see the next section). It is assumed that an instruction-fetch memory cycle takes roughly the same amount of time as a register read-operate-write cycle.

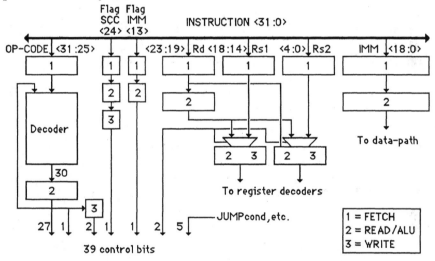

Fig.2.10 Decoding unit in RISC-II.

As we have seen in previous sections, this scheme requires a two-port register file, in order to simultaneously get source1 and source2. Next, the operation is performed on the two sources, while the register file remains idle. After the operation has completed, the result can be written into the specified register while the operational unit remains idle. Thus, the register file must have at least 3 buses : two for simultaneous reads and one for write. In RISC-II, a third pipeline stage was introduced, and the write-back of the result was delayed until that stage. Internal forwarding is used to resolve register interdependencies among subsequent instructions in the pipeline, in contrast with the MIPS design. This is done by two equality comparators that detect the conditions : register source of the second instruction is equal to the destination

71

register of the first instruction. When these occur, the result of the first operation is automatically forwarded from the temporary latch where it is kept, for use by the second instruction in lieu of the stale contents of the destination register of the first instruction. The requirements that this pipeline scheme places on the data-path are radically different from the previous ones. Here, the register file is kept busy all the time. It performs the destination register write immediately after the reads of the source register. The register-write operation is done in parallel with the compute phase instead of sequentially after it as the two-stage pipeline requires.

The next chapter will describe all the pipeline schemes used in commercial processors. They differ from the original Berkeley RISC designs by the number of pipe stages and their respective use. The next section describes the delayed branch scheme used in most RISC architectures in order to solve the problem of flushing the pipeline when executing a branch or jump instruction.

2.3.5 DELAYED-BRANCH

We have described in the previous section the problem of interlocked pipe stages due to the use of the same register as the destination of one instruction and the source of the following instruction. This problem is called a data hazard. There is a second cause that can disrupt the pipeline : control hazards. In a conventional pipelined processor, a branch or jump to another area in a program generally cannot be done in only one machine cycle. Thus, these instructions invalidate the pipeline and force the controller to flush the pipe. Fetching instructions that are subsequently flushed from the pipeline before they can be executed can waste as much as 20% of the computer's memory bandwidth. Instead of flushing the next instruction from the pipeline, and thus wasting one cycle after every control transfer instruction, most RISC architectures employ the delayed-branch scheme. The basic idea is that the transfer of control to the destination address takes effect with a delay of one instruction. Thus, an instruction immediately after a branch, jump, call or return is always executed and belongs to the block preceding the transfer-instruction. The compiler puts a no-operation at that place: this instruction is then called a delay-slot. Then, an optimizer tries to move a suitable instruction to replace the no-operation. This can be done when the transfer instruction does not depend on that instruction. The processor always executes the instructions that immediately follow the control transfers, so it will produce identical results whether the processor executes the calculations before or after executing the transfer instruction. Measurements done at Berkeley have shown that a good optimizer is able to remove about 90% of the no-operations following unconditional transfers and 40 to 60% of those following conditional branches. Thus, while a conventional pipeline could lose nearly 20% of the cycles, such a technique enables only about 6% of them to be lost.

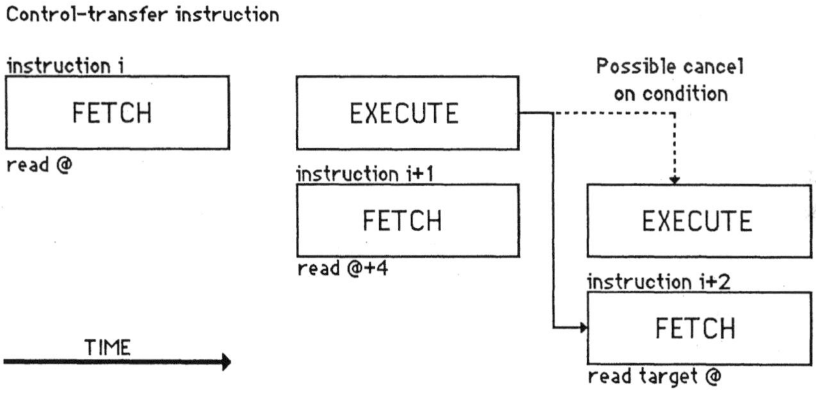

Control-transfer instruction

Fig.2.11 Delayed-branch scheme on RISC-I.

The delayed-branch scheme is quite simple for small pipelines and requires only a small amount of additional hardware. However, the complexity of delayed-branch is directly affected by the length of the pipeline. A delay of only one clock cycle is very acceptable, and easily optimized, but machines can require more. This will cause an increase in the penalty and a larger percentage of wasted time.

2.3.6 ADVANCED PIPELINE TECHNIQUES

We have seen that, in some cases, for example when there is a data dependency, the basic pipeline can be disrupted. In the basic RISC approach, the software is responsible for rescheduling the instructions in order to minimize these problems. This approach is currently called "static scheduling". This approach has the advantage of solving the pipe problems at compile time and therefore minimizes the hardware cost. The other solution is to rearrange the instructions during execution, using hardware. This approach is called "dynamic scheduling". The latter has the advantage of handling some cases when dependencies are unknown at compile time and can significantly simplify the compiler. The main drawback is an increase in the complexity of the hardware. The three major techniques employed are the following :

1. Scoreboarding.
2. Tomasulo algorithm.
3. Dynamic hardware prediction for branch.

The goal of the scoreboard is to maintain an execution rate of one instruction per cycle by executing an instruction as early as possible. Every instruction goes through the scoreboard, where a picture of dependencies is constructed. It then determines when the instruction can access its operands, begin execution or write the result into the destination register. This can be done by updating a tag-bit associated with each potential conflicting resource : registers, operators, etc. This structure is repeated for each instruction that has been issued or is pending issue. Based on this data structure, the scoreboard controls the instruction execution step by step, dynamically resolving data hazards. The scoreboarding technique was probably first used in 1964 when CDC delivered the 6600 [54].

Robert Tomasulo was credited another technique for dynamic scheduling, used in the IBM 360/91 [55]. However, Tomasulo's scheme shares many ideas with the scoreboarding technique.

There are mainly two significant differences. First, hazard detection and execution control are distributed in each functional unit, instead of a centralized control in a scoreboard. Second, results are passed directly to functional units rather than going through the registers. The two previous techniques are useful for overcoming data hazards. In order to solve control hazards, the basic RISC approach relies mainly on the delayed-branch scheme, that is a software-oriented approach. the simplest dynamic hardware solution is to try to predict the branch using a branch-prediction buffer [56]. The latter is a small memory buffer indexed by the lower portion of the branch instruction address. The memory contains a bit that says whether the branch was recently taken or not. This buffer is only useful to reduce the branch delay when it is longer than the time to compute the possible target address. In these cases, the branch prediction is known at the same time, as the instruction has already been decoded. However, it may have been put in the buffer by another branch that has the same low-order address bits. In this case, it is assumed to be correct and fetching begins in the predicted direction. If it turns out to be wrong, then the prediction bit is inverted. An enhanced version of this technique uses two bits in order to solve the problem of taken-untaken branches, for example in a loop. In the two-bit scheme, a prediction must miss twice before it is changed.

In the previous sections, we have seen a variety of software-based static and hardware-based dynamic techniques used to reduce data and control hazards in pipelined RISC architectures. Advanced pipeline techniques have also been designed in order to allow multiple instructions to issue in a single clock cycle [57]. The most simple technique to increase the number of instructions per clock cycle is called "Loop Unrolling". This is done by simply replicating the loop multiple times, then scheduling the unrolled loop. It is normally done early in the compilation process. Then, it can be effectively executed by a superscalar or VLIW architecture in order to attempt to issue multiple operations in a single cycle (see sections 1.6.5 to 1.6.7 in chapter 1). This scheme has the effect of increasing code size.

2.4 THE MEMORY BOTTLENECK

2.4.1 MEMORY BANDWITH REQUIREMENTS

Since a RISC microprocessor tries to fetch one instruction every clock cycle from the program memory, a data load or store cannot occur without stopping the pipeline if there is only one external bus. In this framework, designers try at the same time to reduce accesses to external memory, while increasing the memory bandwidth. This has been done on most RISC architectures by :

1. Implementing a large register set in order to reduce a program's need to store operands in external memory.

2. Using large and high-speed cache memories for both data and program accesses.

3. Employing separate data and program bases to enable data accesses without disrupting the pipeline.

2.4.2 OVERLAPPING REGISTER WINDOWS

A unique feature contributing to the high performance of the Berkeley designs was their overlapping register windows. Instead of just having a large set of general-purpose registers, they organized register files as rotating groups of multiple register banks. Data from the measurements made at Berkeley indicate that about 80% of all memory accesses are made to local scalars, and about 20% of them access all other kinds of objects. For most of the time, all these objects can be coded in a single machine word and accessed with direct addressing. Thus, allocating them into registers is the obvious way of providing a fast access to them and reducing memory accesses. One major problem of keeping local variables in registers is that they have to be saved on every procedure call and restored from memory on every return. Measurements have shown that this is the main source of the very high cost of procedure calls and returns, in terms of execution time. Argument passing and result returning are the second main source of cost. Statistically, a procedure call roughly occurs once every eight-level statements. However, measurements done on the locality of the nesting-depth show that if sufficient storage is provided, instead of only one in classical processors, then register saving and restoring costs can be reduced dramatically. In 1980, Halbert and Kessler proposed a large register set with multiple overlapping windows for their RISC architecture [58].

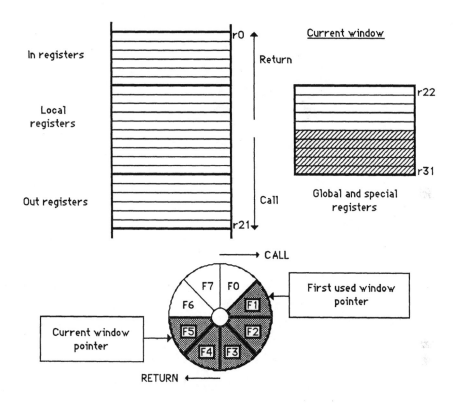

Fig.2.12 Overlapped register windows.

Figure 2.12 shows the organization of a register file into fixed-size, overlapping windows. The window changes every time a procedure call or return is executed. Thus, every procedure has its own window. The compiler allocates the local variables of each procedure into the "local" registers, so that no other procedure has access to them : saving and restoring these registers are then not necessary. If the number of local variables is greater than the available registers, then they can be stored on the execution stack in main memory, as usual. The register windows also provide "overlap" registers for argument and result passing, that are visible by adjacent windows. The absolute procedure nesting-depth is of course virtually unbounded. In fact, the register windows are only a cache of the usual execution stack in main memory.

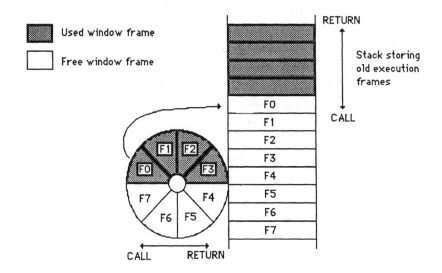

Fig.2.13 Overlapped register windows as execution stack cache.

Measurements show that the locality of procedure nesting-depth allows the use of only 8 windows in more than 90% of calls. Thus, the register windows are used for the few most recent procedure calls, for the top of the execution stack. Older records may have to be saved in memory when the nesting-depth increases, and the windows which they occupy need to be reused for younger procedures. Later on, as the depth decreases, these records have to be restored into the register file. The register windows are not an infinite stack, but rather a circular cache buffer for the top of the execution stack. The rest of the stack is maintained in memory as usual.

2.4.3 CACHE MEMORIES

It is well known that the use of a cache in a memory hierarchy has considerable influence on the overall performance of a computer system. It is the basic solution used to reduce processor-memory traffic. Cache memory is therefore becoming an integral part of RISC-based computers. Cache memories are used to hold temporarily those portions of the contents of main memory which are currently in use. Information located in a cache memory may be accessed in much less time than that located in main memory : in most cases a main memory can be accessed in 200 to 600 nanoseconds, while a cache uses high-speed static RAM and can be accessed in 25 to 100 nanoseconds. Since a RISC architecture performance is already limited in instruction execution rate by cache memory access time, the absence of any cache memory at all would produce a very substantial decrease in execution speed [59]. The success of a cache memory architecture has been clearly explained by the reference to the property of locality [60]. The latter has two aspects : temporal and spatial. Over short periods of time, a program distributes its memory references nonuniformly over its address space, and which portions of the address space are favoured remain largely the same for long periods of time. The temporal locality property means that the information which will be in use in the near future is likely to be in use already. This type of behaviour can be expected from program loops for example. The spatial locality property means that portions of the address space which are in use generally consists of a fairly small number of individually contiguous segments of that address space. In other terms, it means that the next instruction references of the program are likely to be near the current ones. This type of behaviour is mainly due to the fact that instructions are mostly executed sequentially. Optimizing the design of a cache memory underlines four major points :

1. Maximizing the probability of finding a memory reference's target in the cache (i.e. hit-ratio).

2. Minimizing the time to access information that is needed in the cache (i.e. cache access time).

3. Minimizing the delay due to a miss (main memory access and cache update).

4. Minimizing the overheads of updating main memory, or in general maintaining consistency of information.

Basically, a cache memory is placed between the CPU and the main memory. It consists of a data buffer that holds instruction or data, a tag buffer which is a small associative memory that contains the address of the stored instructions or data, and the cache controller. On each memory access, the address generated by the CPU is compared to those stored in the tag buffers. If it is present (i.e. there is a hit) the instruction or data is directly fetched from the data buffer. If a miss occurs (i.e. none of address tags in the cache match the CPU-generated address), then the CPU must fetch the instruction from the main memory at its lower speed. Then, the cache controller removes some instructions or data from the cache and loads these new ones. If the data to be removed from the cache has been modified, and main memory has not yet been updated, then the data or instructions are copied back to main memory. Therefore, cache memory designs mainly differ by :

1. The cache fetch algorithm which is used to decide when to bring information into the cache (when it is needed, before it is needed, etc.).

2. The cache placement algorithm for storing information in the cache and the tag scheme (direct-mapped, two-way associative, etc.).

3. Line-size that is the size of information transferred from and to the main memory (generally a few machine words).

4. The replacement algorithm (FIFO, last-recently used, random, etc.).

5. The main-memory update algorithm employed when the CPU performs a write (copy-back, write-through, etc.).

6. Cache size and access-time.

7. Instruction or data cache.

Cache memory systems have been extensively studied and used in microprocessor architectures. The reader can refer to [61] for more details about the one used in the MIPS-X design and to [12] for the U.C. Berkeley studies. More detailed information on cache memories can be found in the paper of Alan Jay Smith [59].

2.4.4 THE HARVARD ARCHITECTURE

The Harvard architecture solves the problem of disrupting the pipeline when executing data memory accesses. The Harvard architecture was coined first early after the Second World War by the researchers of the University of Harvard when they designed the Mark-I computer, one of the first electronic computers. The idea is quite simple : employing separate data and instruction buses to improve the total bandwidth of the processor. The resulting architecture is then able to fetch one instruction every clock cycle, while accessing the main memory for load and store operations. Dual buses also make it possible to incorporate dual cache memories in the architecture : one for instructions and the other one for data. The major drawback of the Harvard model is its hardware cost in terms of input/output pins : for a 32-bit microprocessor it requires up to 128 pins without control and power lines (32 data lines and 32 data-address lines, 32 instruction lines and 32 associated address lines). Some Harvard designs try to reduce the number of I/O pins by multiplexing address lines for instruction and data buses. This defeats some of the benefits of the pure Harvard approach.

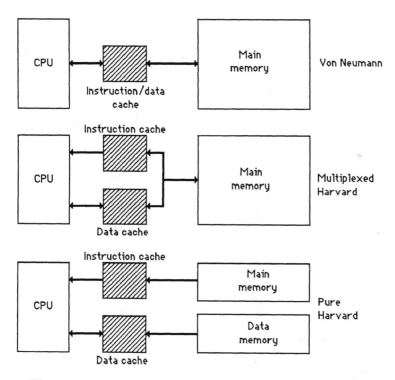

Fig.2.14 Harvard architecture versus Von Neumann.

2.5 CONTROVERSIES

2.5.1 THE INCREASE OF CODE SIZE

In this chapter, we have seen that the basic idea of the RISC approach can be summarized by the simple idea of integrating in hardware only the useful and highly frequent operations. Following the RISC researchers at Berkeley and Stanford, many companies have designed their own RISC architectures. RISC-based approaches to computer design have come of age and are being incorporated into mainstream products. However, there has been an ongoing debate on the viability of RISC architectures as compared to existing CISC architectures. One of the strongest objections and points of criticism of RISC systems is the increase of the binary code size. Since a RISC microprocessor has a small set of simple instructions, it generally requires two, three or more instructions to emulate instructions with enhanced addressing modes or extended functionalities.

We have seen in chapter one, that the RISC approach enables an average number of clock cycles per instruction to be between 1.3 and 1.7, compared to between 4 and 10 for CISC microprocessors. Given the same clock speed, this would make the instruction execution rate about 3 to 6 times faster than CISC. If it is assumed that RISC must execute 20% to 40% more instructions, they are about 2 to 5 times faster than the CISC machines.

However, since RISC designers eliminate the more rarely used instructions it is not expected that programs should be significantly longer than corresponding CISC ones. Thus, an increase in the size of binary object code is generally due to the following points :

1. A fixed-size for instruction formats is not optimal, since in many instructions some bit-fields are not used.

2. The processor was not designed using a pure RISC approach, as described in this chapter (i.e. mainly in the instruction set design).

3. The microprocessor is not well-suited for the application (i.e. the highly frequent instructions of the application are not efficiently provided by the processor.

In the following sections, some of the other contested points are discussed in order to list advantages and disadvantages.

2.5.2 A SHORT CYCLE-TIME

The obvious advantage of short cycle-times is a faster execution speed, especially if one instruction can be issued every clock cycle.

The disadvantage is that a short cycle-time does not allow the implementation of complex operations or addressing modes, even if they occur frequently. However, recent advances in VLSI technology enables the designer to integrate more complex functions using high-speed technologies (see section 6, chapter 1).

2.5.3 SINGLE-CYCLE EXECUTION

The main performance advantage of RISC architectures arises from issuing one instruction every clock cycle.

The main disadvantage is the relative simplicity of the instruction set needed to achieve this. In most cases, one clock cycle does not allow implementation of complex operations, especially if the clock cycle-time is short. However, studies made on compilers demonstrated that complex instructions are unnecessary because of their low occurrence in most application programs. The few ones required can be therefore simply emulated using a sequence of hardwired RISC instructions.

2.5.4 LOAD/STORE ARCHITECTURE

This tenet simplifies the architecture and especially the pipeline model. In addition it reduces the memory processor traffic, which is one of the major performance bottlenecks.

The drawback is that the instruction set cannot include high-level memory-based operations, such as string search, graphic operations, etc.

2.5.5 A LARGE REGISTER SET

A large register set enables most instructions just to operate between registers. Thus, memory access operations are minimized and the overall performance is maximized. When configured as multiple overlapped register windows, it improves the performance of procedure calls and returns, which are frequent in high-level languages.

A large register set, especially when implemented as overlapped register windows, increases the complexity of the register address decoder and the time required to access registers. Since this time is on one of the main critical paths, it may increase the clock cycle-time. Another drawback is the time required for saving/restoring the processor context in real-time applications.

2.5.6 CACHE MEMORIES

Cache memories make it possible to implement high-performance computers with large main memories at an attractive cost.

There are no major drawbacks of using cache memories. However, it generally complicates the design of the pipeline in order to take into account the cache-miss problem. In addition, some real-time applications do not allow the use of caches, because of cache flush problems during critical execution phases (interrupts, context-switch, etc.).

2.5.7 DELAYED-BRANCHES

The delayed-branch scheme permits a streamlined architecture with no latencies or pipe flush problems due to branch instructions.

The disadvantages of the delayed branch technique is the systematic insertion of no-operation calls after every control-transfer instruction. It implies the use of a code reorganizer at compile time, which complicates the design of the compiler and generally complicates the design and debug of assembly language programs.

2.5.8 HARDWIRED CONTROL

Hardwired control enables very efficient fetch and decode phases at a small hardware cost. Thus, the chip area dedicated to the realization of the control unit is considerably reduced compared to CISC processors. As a result, the designer is able to incorporate a larger number of operating resources (registers for example).

The disadvantage is that it does not allow implementation of complex operations like multi-cycle instructions. The latter require specific state machines or microcoded control (multiple-register save or restore instructions for example).

2.5.9 MIGRATION OF COMPLEX FUNCTIONS TO COMPILERS

Only those features that measurably improve performance are implemented in hardware. Complex instructions are implemented as sequences of simple instructions at compile-time.

The disadvantage is that it may makes compilers more complex and therefore harder to design. However it clearly enables the design of efficient and simple (run-time) processors. Obviously it is simpler to design and maintain software than hardware.

2.6 RISC VERSUS CISC

Performance is the main reason to use RISC processors. The arrival of this new design methodology indicates a new relationship between hardware and software design. RISC computers promise to speed up computer systems. However, despite the publicity given to RISC CPUs, there are concrete reasons why CISC machines will continue in 32-bit systems. At the time we wrote this book, much embedded-system programming is still written in assembly language. Although there are benefits to using single-cycle RISC instruction sets, register windowing and Harvard instruction sets to simplify timing calculations, and high-level languages for reliability, even here. RISC-compiler writers insist that software engineers will be forced to shift to compiled, high-level languages if their companies adopt RISC processors. Thus, adopting RISC forces them to shift software-engineering methodologies from assemblers to compilers :

1. Programmers would have to abandon assembly language and instead write in high-level language.

2. Programmers would not be able to hand-tune or debug assembled programs.

The shift from assembly to high-level language is good news, but it cannot be effective in a short time, since many software engineers must learn to use these new tools. The second problem is that a typical algorithm coded for a commercially available RISC CPU will require between 20% to 40% more code than the same algorithm coded for a CISC CPU. In engineering workstations, such a difference in code density is not relevant, since the program can probably be 30% larger and still fit in 8-Mbyte of main memory. In addition, virtual memory systems allow programs larger than the available physical memory to be executed. But in space-or cost-constrained embedded systems, the difference in memory size may be important, although memory chip density has also increased.

However, the makeup of the 32-bit market is changing rapidly. From a virtually nonexistent position in 1983, the RISC share of the 32-bit microprocessor market is expected in 1992 to reach about 25 30% (Dataquest Inc.).

Although RISC computer design is often perceived as unconventional, in fact it adheres strictly to most computer design commandments. The force of the RISC approach is a clear top-down design methodology with architectural guidelines derived from some of the fundamental concepts of supercomputer design and validated by carefully analyzing millions of lines of existing computer code.

This chapter has described the fundamental principles of the RISC methodology. Readers who want to go further in the study of the RISC technology should refer to the three following books :

1.   Reduced Instruction Set Computer for VLSI
     Manolis G.H. Katevenis
     The MIT Press, 1983

     The U.C. Berkeley thesis on RISC-I and RISC-II design.

2.   The MIPS-X Microprocessor
     P. Chow
     Kluwer Academic Publishers, 1989

     The Stanford University thesis on the MIPS-X design.

3.   Computer Architecture : A Quantitative Approach
     J.L. Hennessy, D.A. Patterson
     Morgan Kaufman Publishers, 1989.

     A complete course on computer architecture by the two RISC pioneers Professor J.L. Hennessy (MIPS project at Stanford University) and Professor D.A. Patterson (U.C. Berkeley RISC project).

The next chapter gives an overview of the major commercially available RISC microprocessors. For each of them, we give a detailed description of the architecture, pipeline model and instruction set. The chapter ends with comparative architectural and performance tables, providing a good decision tool for system designers who want to select the right architecture for their application.

3

Overview of RISC microprocessors

3.1   RISC PRODUCTS

Since the term "RISC" was coined by Professors D.A. Patterson and
C.H. Sequin at U.C. Berkeley, new vendors such as SUN
Microsystems and MIPS Computer Systems have proposed
commercial RISC-based products. This effect has provided
opportunities and resulted in major changes in the industry
structure.

In 1983, Ridge Computer Inc. released the RISC32C, the first
RISC system to be actively promoted as such. Three months later,
Pyramid Technology Corp. followed with the announcement of the
90x. A few month after SUN's SPARC announcement, major
computer suppliers announced their own RISC architecture. Today,
all major computer vendors, SUN, HP, DEC, IBM, etc. base their high-
performance workstations and mainframes on the RISC technology.
The general opinion seems to be that RISC leads CISC by a factor of
two in performance and that the RISC versus CISC war is over. The
RISC idea has had a huge impact on computer architecture. Even
designers who are not embracing it are borrowing from it.

The two main market segments of RISC microprocessors are
the following :

1.   RISC chip-set for high-performance engineering workstations.
2.   RISC microcontrollers for embedded applications.

The commercial impact of the RISC technology is mainly the
consequence of its success in the workstation market. Because of its

performance and price, RISC streamlined architectures meet the requirements of most of the scientific/engineering and UNIX-based segments. The market share of such systems is growing rapidly, first at the expense of conventional CISC microprocessor-based systems, and later cut at the expense of proprietary superminicomputers [62].

The second historical market segment of microprocessors is the microcontrollers market for embedded applications. Microcontrollers usually must manipulate a large amount of data quickly. This is done at the expense of many of the features found in general-purpose data-processing architectures. These kind of applications include keyboards, graphics terminals, laser-printer controllers, floppy-disk drive controllers, SCSI controllers, etc. The system designer can use specialized RISC processors to perform specific tasks. Signal processing is a special subset of these kind of applications. It requires small controllers such as those used as protocol processors in modems or as format controllers for personal computer disk drives. Signal processing can also require large number-crunching processors for telephone switching systems, for graphic controllers in high-resolution workstations, or for speech recognition and synthesis [63].

In this chapter, we will describe the main RISC microprocessors available as chip-set products or as the kernel of a computer system. Among all the existing commercial products, we have selected the SPARC architecture from SUN Microsystems, the MIPS R3000 from MIPS Computer Systems, the AMD 29000 from Advanced Micro Devices, the Power architecture from IBM, the Fairchild Clipper, the MC88100 from Motorola, the i960 and i860 from Intel, the ARM microprocessor from Acorn and VLSI Technology, and the Inmos Transputer. After a brief overview of other RISC products, we will conclude this chapter by giving a non-exhaustive comparative study of the previously-listed products. It includes three architectural tables, a performance table and an application field table.

89

3.2 THE SPARC ARCHITECTURE FROM SUN MICROSYSTEMS INC.

SUN Microsystems has designed a RISC architecture, called SPARC™, and has implemented that architecture within the SUN4™ family of workstations and servers. SPARC stands for Scalable Processor ARChitecture, emphasizing its ability to produce large as well as small machines. SPARC systems have an open architecture : the design specification is published and other vendors are able to produce microprocessors implementing the design. In the beginning (1987), the first SPARC integer-unit implementation was base on a Fujitsu 1.5 micron CMOS gate array. This implementation code-named Sunrise by SUN, is represented by the original 16.67 Mhz Fujitsu chip from Fujitsu Microelectronics (San Jose, CA). This chip was the one used in the first SUN4 workstations [64-65]. After Fujitsu, came announcements from Cypress Semiconductor and Bipolar Integrated Technology. The Cypress design (0.8 micron CMOS) differs from Sunrise in a few important details : the chip runs faster (33 Mhz), has eight register windows instead of seven, and has more integrated cache control logic. In addition, the processor is able to handle a true floating-point coprocessor, rather than an autonomous slave coprocessor [66-67]. For both implementations, the cache memory, the memory management and Floating-Point Unit must be supported in external chips. This reduces the cost of the integer unit and increases the variety of ways the architecture can be used. The Cypress chip was second sourced by Texas Instruments, LSI Logic, and more recently Philips and MHS.

Beyond the near-20-MIPS performance range of the Cypress implementation [68] lies Prisma, a board-level SPARC with MSI Gallium Arsenide parts running at a 250-Mhz cycle rate. The success of the SPARC architecture was so important that every month seems to add new names to the list of vendors.

The SPARC architecture has more similarities to Berkeley's RISC-II architecture than to any other RISC architecture (in particular, note that Professor D.A. Patterson has co-authored papers on the SPARC definition [69]). Like the RISC-II architecture, it uses register windows in order to reduce the number of memory accesses. In addition, the SPARC instruction set includes tagged-instructions which are derived from SOAR. Changes to the original RISC-II design, including extensions for multiprocessors, floating-point and tightly coupled coprocessors, were made with the guidance of an operating system/compiler/hardware team. The SPARC architecture was defined at SUN Microsystems in this framework over the period 1984 to 1987.

A SPARC processor is basically divided in two parts : an Integer Unit (IU) and a Floating-Point Unit (FPU). Although not a formal part of the architecture, most SPARC chip-sets provide a Memory Management Unit (MMU), and a data/instruction cache. The IU and FPU operate concurrently. The IU extracts floating-point operations from the instruction stream and places them in a queue for the FPU. The SPARC architecture also specifies an interface for the connection of an additional coprocessor [70-71].

The SPARC architecture defines 55 basic integer and 13 floating-point instructions, a few more than earlier RISC designs. The instructions fall into five basic categories :

1. Load and store instructions. These are the only way to access memory. They use two registers or a register and a constant to calculate the memory address involved. Half-word accesses must be aligned on 2-byte boundaries, word accesses on 4-byte boundaries, and double-word accesses on 8-byte boundaries. The alignment restrictions greatly speed up memory access.

2. Arithmetic/logical/shift instructions. These instructions compute a result that is a function of two source operands and then place the result in a register. They perform arithmetic, tagged arithmetic, logical, or shift operations. Tagged arithmetic is useful for implementing Artificial Intelligence languages.

3. Coprocessor operations. These include floating-point calculations, operations on floating-point registers, and instructions involving the optional coprocessor. Floating-point operations execute concurrently with IU instructions and with other floating-point operations when necessary. This architectural concurrency hides floating-point operations from the applications programmer.

4. Control-transfer instructions. These include jumps, calls, traps, and branches. Control transfers are usually delayed until after execution of the next instruction, so that the pipeline is not emptied every time a control transfer occurs. Thus, compilers

should be augmented with an optimizer to manage delayed branching.

5. Read/write control register instructions. These include instructions to read and write the contents of various control registers. Generally the source or destination is implied by the instruction.

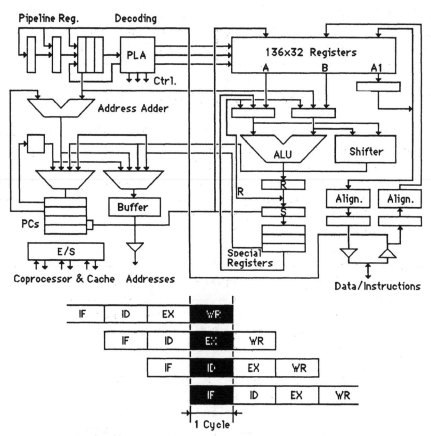

Fig.3.1 SUNRISE SPARC Architecture.

All instructions are 32 bits wide. The first format holds a 30-bit word displacement for the PC-relative CALL instruction. Thus a PC-relative call or an unconditional branch can be made to an arbitrarily distant location in a single instruction (note that there is also a register-indirect call encoded via a format 3 instruction). The return address of the CALL is stored into out register 7.

Format 2 defines two instructions types : SETHI and branches. SETHI loads a 22-bit immediate value into the high 22 bits of the destination IU register and clears its low 10 bits. SETHI, in conjunction with a format 3 instruction, is used to create 32-bit constants (note that the immediate fields of formats 2 and 3 overlap by three bits). Format 2's 22-bit word displacement defines the ±8-Mbyte displacément for PC-relative conditional branch instructions.

LDSB(A)	load signed 8-bit *	ADD(cc)	integer addition
LDSH(A)	load signed 16-bit *	ADDX(cc)	addition with carry
LDUB(A)	load unsigned 8-bit *	TADDcc(tv)	tagged addition
LDUH(A)	load unsigned 16-bit *	SUB(cc)	integer subtract
LD(A)	load 32-bit *	SUBX(cc)	subtract with carry
LDD(A)	load 64-bit *	TSUB(tv)	tagged subtract
LDF	load single *	MULScc	multiply step
LDDF	load double *	AND(cc)	logical and
LDFSR	load status *	ANDN(cc)	logical and negate
LDC	load coprocessor *	OR(cc)	logical or
LDDC	load double coprocessor *	ORN(cc)	logical or and negate
LDCSR	load coprocessor status *	XOR(n)	exclusive or
STB(A)	store 8-bit *	XNOR(n)	not exclusive or
STH(A)	store 16-bit *	SLL	shift left logical
ST(A)	store 32-bit *	SRL	shift right logical
STD(A)	store 64-bit *	SRA	shift right arithmetic
STF	store single *	SETHI	set MSB of a register
STDF	store double *		
STFSR	store FP status *	RDY	read Y register
STDFQ	store double FP queue *	RDPSR	read status word
STC	store coprocessor *	RDWIM	read window mask
STDC	store double coprocessor *	RDTBR	read trap base register
STCSR	store status *	WRY	write Y register
STDCQ	store double copro. queue*	WRPSR	write status word
LDSTUB(A)	atomic load 8-bit *	WRWIM	write window mask
SWAP(A)	swap register *	WRTBR	write base trap regist.
		UNIMP	unimplemented instr.
SAVE	next window	IFLUSH	cache flush
RESTORE	previous window	FPop	floating-point operation
Bicc	conditional branch	CPop	coprocessor operation
FBicc	FP conditional branch	*	2 to 4 cycles instead of 1.
CBccc	CP conditional branch		
CALL	procedural call	A	alternate space
JMPL	jump and link	cc	code condition
RETT	return from exception	tv	overflow trap
Ticc	conditional trap		

OP	30-bit displacement

CALL format (1)

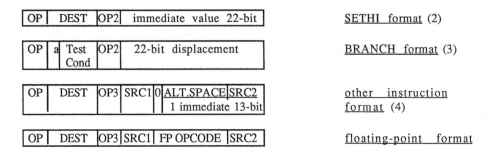

OP	DEST	OP2	immediate value 22-bit	

SETHI format (2)

OP	a	Test Cond	OP2	22-bit displacement

BRANCH format (3)

OP	DEST	OP3	SRC1	0	ALT.SPACE	SRC2
				1	immediate 13-bit	

other instruction format (4)

OP	DEST	OP3	SRC1	FP OPCODE	SRC2

floating-point format

Fig.3.2 SPARC instruction set.

Format 3, which has specifiers for two source registers and a destination register, encodes the remaining instructions. Like Berkeley's RISC and SOAR, if the i bit is set, a sign-extended 13-bit immediate substitutes for the second register specifier. The upper 8 bits of this field are used as an opcode extension field for the floating-point instructions and as an "address space identifier" for the load/store instructions.

A unique feature contributing to the high performance of the SPARC design is its ovelapping register windows. It may contain from 40 to 520 registers depending on the implementation. These are partitioned into 2 to 32 overlapping register windows plus 8 global registers (Sunrise has 7 windows and the Cypress implementation has 8 windows). At any one time, a program can address 32 general-purpose registers : the 8 "ins", 8 "locals", and 8 "outs" of the active window and the 8 globals. The active window is identified by the 5-bit Current Window Pointer (CWP). Decrementing the CWP at procedure entry causes the next window to become active and incrementing the CWP at procedure exit causes the previous window to become active. Thus, these operations are not part of the call/return instructions and must be explicitly executed (save and restore instructions). SUN's team argue that for large C programs, dynamic trace data shows that about 20% of executed SPARC instructions are loads and stores, including the window overflow/underflow processing overhead. This compares to about 30 to 40% of executed instructions for RISCs without register windows [72 73].

The Sunrise implementation can be basically decomposed into four logic blocks : the register file, the data-path (or execution unit), the instruction fetch unit, and the control unit. The register file has two read ports and a single write port. The uniform format of instructions allows reading both sources of any instruction and writing the result of a previously fetched instruction into the register file, through the write port. The entire process occurs in a single cycle. The execution unit consists of a fast 32-bit carry-look-ahead ALU which performs all arithmetic and logical operations, a 32-bit barrel shifter, condition-code-generation logic, load-and-store-alignment logic, and related pipeline registers required to save the operands and intermediate results. Like RISC-II and unlike the MIPS design, all arithmetic and logic instructions use the execution unit for a single cycle to complete their execution, even if dependencies exist between the operands and results of consecutive instructions. This is done by two additional bypass paths incorporated into the main data-path. The instruction fetch unit contains the four Program Counters : one for each pipe stage (in case of exceptions), and instruction/data-address-generation circuitry. This unit also includes the circuitry for the special registers. The control unit implements the main state machine, instruction pipeline, instruction decoder, Processor Status Register (PSR), circuitry for exception/trap handling and the interface to the cache and FPU. The control unit maintains a copy of the instructions that execute in different stages of the pipeline. The control unit is responsible for generating and dispatching the majority of the control signals for other units.

The processor has a four-stage pipeline. Each stage of the pipeline performs a subset of operations that are needed to complete the execution of an instruction. All operations performed in a given pipeline stage occur in one full clock cycle. The four stages are the following : the Instruction Fetch stage (IF), the Instruction Decode stage (ID), the Execution stage (EX), the Write stage (WR) (see fig.3.1).

During the Instruction Fetch stage, the address of an instruction is sent out. Once the instruction is fetched, it enters the processor's pipeline at stage completion. In the Instruction Decode stage, the instruction is decoded and source operands are read from the register file. The source operands are passed to the execution unit and the instruction fetch unit for later execution. This stage also generates the next instruction address, including the branch target address for control transfer instructions. The Execute stage performs arithmetic and logical operations on the ALU. The results of the operations are saved into temporary registers before they are actually written into the register file. In the Write stage, the processor either writes the results into the register file or prohibits any changes in the state of the processor. This last stage aborts if an exception is raised during the execution of the related instruction. In order to keep the pipeline full at all times, the

Sunrise implementation includes a dual-instruction buffer. This buffer prefetches instructions during the execution of multiple-cycle instructions and so speeds up the execution by utilizing the data bus more efficiently.

The initial goal for the Sunrise implementation was to reach a typical cycle-time of 50 ns or less. The worst-case cycle-time for the resulting implementation was approximately 60 ns, allowing the design of a system with a 16.67 Mhz clock rate. Both Fujitsu and Cypress implementations provide the instruction set with most instructions executing in a single cycle. A small subset of instructions takes more than one cycle to complete. The multiple-cycle instructions use one or more internal (single-cycle) instructions to complete their execution. They are the following : load (2 cycles), load double (3 cycles), store (3 cycles), store double (4 cycles), Atomic Load and store (4 cycles), floating-point operations (2 cycles + Cf), jump and Rett (2 cycles), and untaken branch (2 cycles).

Based on this informations and a conservative instruction-mix ratio, the average number of clock cycles required per instruction is approximately 1.42 for the Fujitsu chip and 1.59 for the Cypress chip. The latter uses an equivalent of approximately 12000 2-input nand gates plus a custom design 3-port register file.

It seems likely that from here, the different implementations of the SPARC architecture will diverge, as the special needs of each market are reflected in the architectures. Fujitsu has designed the SPARC-H based on a Harvard architecture, and modified branch and load/store instructions. Cypress focus on increasing throughput and integrating peripheral functions. The Cypress chip was specified at 20 MIPS at 33 Mhz, first tests performed by Cypress indicate that clock frequencies of 56 to 60 Mhz are in reach. Early 1991, Solbourne Computers and Matsushita announced a 64-bit implementation of SPARC. The chip includes nearly 1 Million transistors providing : the IU, FPU, MMU, a 6-kbyte instruction cache, a 2-kbyte data-cache, a bus controller and error correction circuitry.

Based on a superscalar scheme and a Harvard model, this implementation called KAP enables 40 MIPS/20 Mflops peak at 40 Mhz. It is known that SUN Microsystems is also working on a multiprocessor implementation of the SPARC architecture, providing the ability to design high-performance low-cost computer boards based on standard CMOS technology, compared with costly and hard-to-produce high-speed technology.

96

3.3 THE R3000 ARCHITECTURE FROM MIPS COMPUTER SYSTEMS

As we have seen in the first chapter, John Hennessy of Stanford University was one of the early academic stalwarts of RISC. He founded the Stanford MIPS project. Then, he temporarily left Stanford to help form MIPS Computer Systems at Sunnyvale (CA). He still works for the firm as chief scientist while keeping his position at Stanford (Director of the Computer System Laboratory). MIPS has introduced a series of RISC boards and systems rooted in the Stanford MIPS experience, but it uses wholly new designs. One of the first commercial RISC chip-sets was created by MIPS Computer Systems. The first MIPS RISC chip set included two chips: the R2000 RISC processor and the R2010 floating-point units. A few months later, MIPS announced the R3000/R3010 chip set, a new higher-performance machine. These two chips are architecturally identical to the original R2000/R2010, only the electrical and performance characteristics differ. Therefore, the description in this section applies to both series of machines.

The MIPS R3000 Integer Unit consists of two tightly-coupled functional units implemented on a single chip;. The first one is a full 32-bit RISC CPU. The second one is a system control processor called CP0, containing a Translation Lookaside Buffer (TLB) and control registers to support a 4 Gbyte virtual memory subsystem and separate 4 to 64-kbyte caches for instructions and data [76].

Instead of overlapping register windows, the R3000 processor provides only 32 general-purpose 32-bit registers, a 32-bit Program Counter and two 32-bit registers that hold the results of integer multiply and divide operations. All R3000 instructions are 32 bits long and there are only three instruction formats in order to simplify instruction decoding. More complicated and less frequently used operations and addressing modes are synthesized by the compiler using sequences of simple instructions. The three formats are the following :

1. The I-type format for instructions including a 16-bit immediate operand.

2. The J-type format for jump instructions including a 26-bit target address.

3. The R-type format for register-oriented instructions like most arithmetic and logical operations.

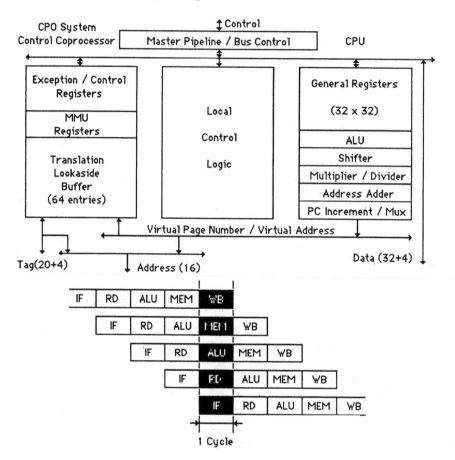

Fig.3.3 R3000 architecture.

Based on these three formats, the R3000 instruction set can be divided into the six following groups :

1. Load/Store instructions move data between memory and general registers. They are all I-type instructions, since the only addressing mode supported is base register plus 16-bit, signed immediate offset.

2. Computational instructions perform arithmetic, logical and shift operations on values in registers. They occur in both R-

type (both operands and the result are registers) and I-type (one operand is a 16-bit immediate) formats.

3. Jump and Branch instructions change the control flow of a program. Jumps are always to a paged absolute address formed by combining a 26-bit target with four bits of the Program Counter (J-type format, for subroutine calls) or 32-bit register addresses (R-type, for returns and dispatches). Branches have 16-bit offsets relative to the program counter (I-type). Jump and Link instructions save a return address in Register 31.

4. Coprocessor instructions perform operations in the coprocessors. Coprocessor Loads and Stores are I-type. Coprocessor computational instructions have coprocessor-dependent formats.

5. Coprocessor 0 instructions perform operations on the System Control Coprocessor (CP0) registers to manipulate the memory management and exception handling facilities of the processor.

6. Special instructions perform a variety of tasks, including movement of data between special and general registers, system calls, and breakpoints. They are always R-type.

The R3000 CPU can operate with up to four tightly-coupled coprocessors, designated CP0 through CP3. CP0 is the System Control Coprocessor. It is incorporated on the R3000 chip and supports the virtual memory system and exception handling features. The R3000 chip has an addressing range of 4 Gbytes and provides the logical expansion of memory space by translating addresses composed in a large virtual address space into available physical memory addresses. Virtual Memory mapping is assisted by the Translation Lookaside Buffer (TLB). It is a fully-associative memory buffer containing 64 entries, each of which maps a 4 kbytes page, with controls for read/write access, cachebility, and process identification. The TLB allows each user and the kernel to access up to 2 Gbytes of virtual address space. The floating-point instructions supported by the R3010 are all implemented using the CP1 operation instructions of the R3000 instruction set. The basic operations are load/store and from/to the FPU registers, moves between FPU/IU registers, floating-point operations and comparisons.

The pipelined architecture of the R3000 consists of five primary steps : Instruction Fetch (IF), Read Operands (RD) from registers while decoding the instruction, perform the required operation (ALU) on instruction operands, access memory (MEM), and write back results to register file (WB). Each of these steps requires approximately one machine cycle, because some operations lap over into another cycle while other operations require only 1/2 cycle. To achieve an instruction rate approaching one instruction per machine cycle, the five-instruction pipeline operates on five instructions at a time, in an overlapped fashion. The R3000 architecture enables most instructions to execute in a single cycle. However, there are two categories of instructions whose special requirements could disrupt the smooth flow of instructions through the pipeline :

1. "Delayed" Load instructions.
2. "Delayed" Jump and Branch instructions.

LB	load byte	MULT	multiply
LBU	load byte unsigned	MULTU	multiply unsigned
LH	load halfword	DIV	divide
LHU	load halfword unsigned	DIVU	divide unsigned
LW	load word		
LWL	load word left	MFHI	move from HI
LWR	load word right	MTHI	move to HI
SB	store byte	MFLO	move from LO
SH	store halfword	MTLO	move to LO
SW	store word		
SWL	store word left	J	jump
SWR	store word right	JAL	jump and link
		JR	jump to register
ADDI	add immediate	JALR	jump and link register
ADDIU	add immediate unsigned	BEQ	branch on equal
SLTI	set on less than immediate	BEN	branch on not equal
SLTIU	set on less than immediate unsigned	BLEZ	branch on less than or equal to zero
ANDI	and immediate	BGTZ	branch on greater than 0
ORI	or immediate	BLTZ	branch on less than zero
XORI	exclusive or immediate	BLTZAL	branch on less than 0 and link
LUI	load upper immediate		
		BGEZAL	branch on greater than or equal to zero and link
ADD	add		
ADDU	add unsigned	LWCz	load word from coprocessor
SUB	subtract	SWCz	store word to coprocessor
SUBU	subtract unsigned	MTCz	move to coprocessor
SLT	set on less than	MFCz	move from coprocessor
SLTU	set on less than unsigned	CTCz	move control to coprocess.

AND	and	CFCz	move control from coproc.
OR	or	COPz	coprocessor operation
XOR	exclusive or	BCzT	branch on coprocessor z
NOR	nor		true
		BCzF	branch on coprocessor z
SLL	shift left logical		false
SRL	shift right logical		
SRA	shift right arithmetic	MTC0	move to CP0
SLLV	shift left variable	MFC0	move from CP0
SRLV	shift right logical variable	TLBR	read indexed TLB entry
SRAV	shift right arithmetic	TLBWI	write indexed TLB entry
	variable	TLBWR	write random TLB entry
		TLBP	probe TLB for matching
SYSCALL	system call		entry
BREAK	break	RFE	restore from exception

Fig.3.4 R3000 instruction summary.

```
31                          0
 OP  RS  RT    IMMEDIATE        I-type  (immediate)
 6   5   5        16
 OP          ADDRESS            J-type  (jump)
 6            26
 OP  RS  RT RD SHIFT  FONC      R-type  (register)
 6   5   5  5   5      6
```

Fig.3.5 R3000 instruction formats.

These two categories of instructions require a delay, or latency, of one clock cycle. The technique used in the R3000 is to continue execution despite the delay. Loads, Jumps and Branches do not interrupt the normal flow of instructions through the pipeline. That is, the processor always executes the instruction immediately following one of these instructions. Instead of having the processor deal with pipeline delays, the R3000 turns over the responsibility for dealing with delayed instructions to software. Thus, an assembler can insert an appropriate instruction immediately following a delayed instruction and has the responsibility of ensuring that the inserted instruction will not be affected by the delay.

One important feature of the MIPS architecture is the relationship between the hardware machine and compilers [74]. The MIPS compilers not only translate language statements to machine instructions, but also control and structure the execution environment. The speed and efficiency of program execution is substantially determined by the quality of the complier. The MIPS

101

compilers have been developed in close coordination with the hardware architecture. The development of the optimizing compiler technology included in the MIPS compilers began at Stanford in the mid 1970s with a research project aimed at creating an optimizer to work in an intermediate-language form independent of any particular high-level language. The MIPS contribution to optimizing compiler technology began with that Stanford work, and subsequently has grown significantly along with its integration with advanced RISC hardware technology. The MIPS compiler suite can be divided into three levels. The first one includes the high-level language-specific front-ends which translate source code into the MIPS Intermediate code. The second level provides all the optimizations that can be done on the intermediate code : local optimization, global optimization, program and library optimization. Finally, the second level generates the MIPS assembler code. The third level includes the assembler, linker and loader. The assembler converts assembly language statements into machine code. In most assembly languages, each instruction corresponds to a single machine instruction. However, some MIPS assembly language instructions can generate several R3000 machine instructions. This approach provides a more regular assembler language that generates optimized code for certain short sequences and also results in assembly programs that can run without modification on future machines, which might have extended machine instructions. The assembler performs "peephole" optimization and pipeline scheduling-filling delay-slots with useful instructions, reorganizing the machine code, etc. After assembly, the linker and loader operates to generate the final executable code. The MIPS assembler code is very close to the CORE-MIPS instruction set architecture, since MIPS Computer Systems has previously enrolled in the DoD CORE ISA standard (chapter 2 section 2.2.5).

The R2000 RISC CPU first shipment occurred in 1985, based on a near 100000 transistor 2 micron CMOS chip. The R2000 chip was designed with the execution of UNIX in mind, enabling 12 MIPS at 16.7 Mhz, that is an average number of clock cycles per instruction of between 1.39 and 1.50. The R3000 design was initially available in 1988 as a second-generation RISC processor. Based on a 1.2 micron CMOS technology, the R3000 is able to execute 20 MIPS at 25 Mhz, which represents an average number of clock cycles per instruction of 1.25. The floating-point performance of the R3010 with the R3000 measured by the Linpack benchmark is 7 MFLOPS single precision and 4 MFLOPS in double precision calculations.

MIPS focus on advanced compiler optimizing techniques has also resulted in efficient code generation. The code size for any given program generated for the R3000 is comparable in size to that for the same program compiled for more traditional CISC microprocessors. Some programs are actually smaller in code size for the R3000 and typically will be within 15% of the code size of a CISC program. This is contrary to the argument that CISC programs are significantly smaller due to the more complex and robust instruction set of the CISC machine [75 76 77].

Like the SPARC architecture, the MIPS R3000 chip set is available from multiple vendors : Integrated Device Technology Inc. (Santa Clara), LSI Logic Inc., Performance Semiconductor Corp. (Sunnyvale), Siemens, NEC, Sony and others. Unlike SUN Microsystems that sells directly its own SPARC-based workstations, MIPS Computer Systems bases its strategy on a strong partnership with computer vendors : Digital Equipment, Tandem Computers, Bull, Nixdorf, Sony are among 13 computer makers using the MIPS design. In 1989, MIPS Computer Systems announced a 55 MIPS/10.3 MFLOPS performance implementation of the MIPS architecture, based on the R6000/R6010 ECL chip set running at 67.7 Mhz. The machine uses a multilevel cache : a 64-kbyte primary instruction cache, a 16-kbyte primary data cache and a 512-kbyte secondary cache [78]. In the beginning of 1991, MIPS Computer Systems announced the R4000 64-bit RISC processor, fully compatible with earlier versions. The R4000 is designed using a 1.1 million transistor 1-micron CMOS chip. It includes on the same chip a superpipelined integer unit, a system control coprocessor, a floating-point unit, an 8-kbyte instruction cache and a 8-kbyte data cache. The R4000 includes special circuitry for connecting a secondary external cache (128 kbytes up to 4 Mbyte). The R4000 is able to deliver 50 MIPS at 50 Mhz due to its superpipelined architecture.

3.4 THE AM29000 ARCHITECTURE FROM ADVANCED MICRO DEVICES

In 1987, Advanced Micro Devices (Sunnyvale) announced another RISC product, called Am29000. Aimed at single-cycle execution, the 25 Mhz Am29000 achieves processing speeds of about 17 MIPS for C programs, with burst rates up to 25 MIPS [79]. The Am29000 design tries to optimize performance on two levels. On one, it has a large register set, with 192 registers. These registers can be configured as a run-time stack cache, mapping activation environments onto the stack, as procedures are called, or as a set of eight banks with 16 registers each. For instructions, it counts on the availability of fast static RAM in order to perform an instruction every cycle. A special design feature in the Am29000 is the branch target cache that holds up to 128 instructions. Organized in sets of four words, these are the targets of the last 32 recently taken branches. Aimed at reducing pipeline loss for loop-type branches, the cache lets the pipeline fill without delay for repetitive branches.

Microprocessors are usually used in general-purpose CPU applications or in embedded controller applications. The Am29000's features address problems unique to each of these target areas [80]. The Am29000 uses an ALU, a field shift unit and a prioritizer to execute most instructions. Each of these is organized to operate on 32-bit operands, and to provide a 32-bit result. Most operations are performed in a single cycle. In general, the processor meets its instruction bandwidth requirements via instruction prefetching. However, instruction prefetching is ineffective when a branch occurs. The Am29000 incorporates an on-chip Branch Target Cache to supply instructions for a branch, if this branch has been taken previously, while a prefetch stream is established. If branch-target instructions are in the Branch Target Cache, branches execute in a single-cycle. The Branch Target Cache of the Am29000 has an average hit rate of 60%. Branch conditions are based on Boolean data contained in general-purpose registers, rather than in arithmetic condition codes. Like the U.C. Berkeley design, the Am29000 always executes the instruction following a branch, referred as the delay slot. An optimizing compiler can then define a useful instruction for the delay slot in approximately 90% of branch instructions. The performance degradation of load and store operations is minimized by overlapping them with instruction execution. A load/store is performed concurrently with execution of instructions which do not have dependencies on the load or store operation. The optimizing compiler can schedule load/store instructions in the instruction sequence so that, in most cases, data accesses are overlapped with instruction execution. The Am29000 instruction set includes load- and store-multiple. These instructions allow the transfer of the contents of multiple registers to or from external memories or devices. This transfer can occur at a rate of one register per cycle. The advantage of these instructions is best seen in task switching, register-file saving and restoring, and block data moves. The load/store instructions are interruptible, so that they do not affect interrupt latency. The Am29000 instruction set contains 112 instructions. All instructions execute in a single cycle except for IRET, IRETINV, LOADM and STOREM. Most instructions deal with general-purpose registers for operands and results. However, in most instructions, an 8-bit constant can be used in place of a register-based operand. The instruction set is divided into 9 classes :

1. Integer Arithmetic : perform integer add, subtract, multiply, and divide operations.

2. Compare : perform arithmetic and logical comparisons. Some instructions in this class allow the generation of a trap if the comparison condition is not met.

3. Logical : perform a set of bit-wise Boolean operations.

4. Shift : perform arithmetic and logical shifts, and allow the extraction of 32-bit words from 64-bit double-words.

5. Data Movement : perform movement of data fields between registers, and the movement of data to and from external devices and memories.

6. Constant : allow the generation of large constant values in registers.

7. Floating-point : included for floating-point arithmetic, comparisons, and format conversions. These instructions are not currently implemented directly in processor hardware.

8. Branch : perform program jumps and subroutine calls.

9. Miscellaneous : perform miscellaneous control functions and operations not provided by other classes.

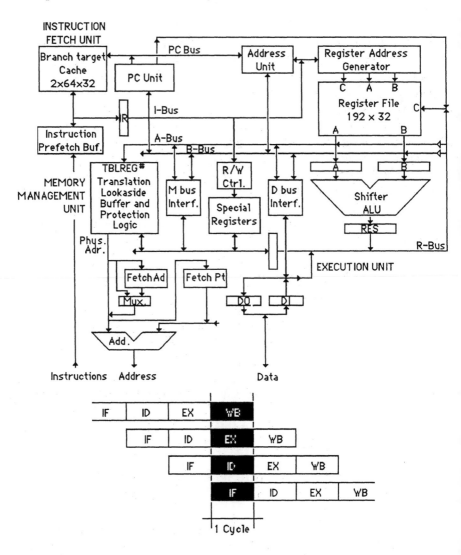

Fig.3.6 Am29000 architecture.

All instructions for the Am29000 are 32 bits in length, and are divided into four fields. These four fields contains 8 bits each and have several alternative definitions, except the first one which is reserved for the operation code. In certain instructions, one or more fields are not used and are reserved for future use. Unlike MIPS, pipeline interlocks are implemented by processor hardware.

Except for branches and loads, it is not necessary to rearrange programs to avoid pipeline dependencies.

The Am29000 implements a four-stage pipeline for instruction execution. The four stages are : fetch, decode, execute, and write-back. The pipeline is organized so that the effective instruction execution rate may be as high as one instruction per cycle.

During the fetch stage, the Instruction Fetch Unit determines the location of the next processor instruction, and issues the instruction to the decode stage. The instruction is fetched either from the Instruction Prefetch buffer, the Branch Target Cache, or an external instruction memory.

During the decode stage, the Execution Unit decodes the instruction selected during the fetch stage, and fetches and/or assembles the required operands. It also evaluated addresses for branches, loads, and stores.

During the execute stage, the Execution Unit performs the operation specified by the instruction. In the case of branches, loads, and stores, the Memory Management Unit performs address translation if required.

During the write-back stage, the results of the operation performed during the execute stage are stored. In the case of branches, loads, and stores, the physical address resulting from translation during the execute stage is transmitted to an external device or memory.

Most pipeline dependencies which are internal to the processor are handled by forwarding logic in the processor. For those dependencies which result from the external system, the Pipeline Hold mode ensures proper operation.

In a few special cases, the processor pipeline is exposed to software executing on the Am29000.

The Am29000 contains three main units : the Instruction Fetch Unit, the Execution Unit and the Memory Management Unit. The Instruction Fetch Unit fetches instructions and supplies instructions to other functional units. It incorporates the Instruction Prefetch Buffer, the Branch Target Cache, and the Program Counter Unit. All components of the Instruction Fetch Unit operate during the fetch stage of the processor pipeline. The Execution Unit executes instructions. It incorporates the Register File, the Address Unit, the Arithmetic/Logic Unit, the Field Unit and the Prioritizer. The register File and Address Unit operate during the decode stage of the pipeline. The ALU, Field Shift Unit and Prioritizer operate during the execute stage of the pipeline. The Register File operates during the write-back stage and can perform two read accesses and one write access in a single cycle. The Memory Management Unit (MMU) performs address translation and memory-protection functions for all branches, loads and stores. The MMU operates during the execute stage of the pipeline, so the physical address which it generates is available at the beginning of the write-back stage. It accept a 32-bit virtual byte-address and translates it into a 32-bit physical byte-adddress in a single cycle. Address translation in the MMU is performed by a 64-entry Translation Lookaside Buffer (TLB), an associative table which contains the most-recently-used address translations for the processor. If a translation for a given address cannot be performed by the TLB, a TLB miss occurs, and causes a trap which allows the required translation to be placed into the TLB.

The separate instruction and data buses of the Am29000 processor allow a Harvard architecture implementation, similar to bit-slice, for maximum bandwith. The processor can fetch and execute instructions and access data memory or device registers concurrently. The Am29000 incorporates two 32-bit buses for instruction and data transfers, and a third address bus which is shared between instruction and data accesses. This organization allows simultaneous instruction and data transfers at a much reduced pin count than with four separate 32-bit buses.

The Am29000 allows a program to communicate with an off-chip coprocessor for performing operations not directly supported by hardware : floating-point calculation for example. In addition to the coprocessor interface, the Am29000 also provides a timer facility for implementing a real-time clock or other software timing functions, and a trace facility allowing a trap to be generated after the execution of any instruction in the program being tested.

One of the main reasons for AMD's development of a RISC product is that RISC concepts hold special appeal for designers of embedded computer systems. Instead of relying on hard-to-microcode bit-slice architectures, they can turn to RISC architectures that they can tune at the compiler level for optimal applications performance. In the past, AMD was recognized as a leader in bit-slice microprocessors, with its Am2900, Am29100 and Am29300 families. The Am29000 marks a new venture for AMD, trying to keep its traditional market segments against new firms that were not conventional microprocessor players. AMD has a long tradition of supplying semi-conductor products that meet the requirements of the military market, and in 1988 about 15% of the beta-site requests for the chip were for defense-system applications.

The first commercial implementation of the Am29000 was in CMOS technology, with a 1.2 micron effective transistor-channel length. This technology allows the processor to operate at a frequency of 25 Mhz. AMD expects in the future to announce 33 Mhz (22MIPS), 42 Mhz (28 MIPS) and 55 Mhz (37 MIPS) implementations [81]. As part of the initial announcement, AMD has presented a complete chip set including the Am29027 Arithmetic Accelerator, the Am29069 for instruction and data caches, and the Am29041 data-transfer controller designed to act as a gateway between the Am29000 and a slower peripheral bus [82]. The Am29000 is a typical Berkeley-like RISC design, but with an increase in complexity due to enhanced hardware features building on AMD's past strengths.

ADD	add	FDIV	floating-point divide single precision
ADDC	add with carry		
ADDCS	add with carry signed	FEQ	floating-point equal to single precision
ADDCU	add with carry unsigned		
ADDS	add signed	FGE	floating-point greater than or equal to single precision
ADDU	add unsigned		
AND	and logical	FGT	floating-point greater than single precision
ANDN	and-not logical		
ASEQ	assert equal to	FMUL	floating-point multiply single precision
ASGE	assert greater than or equal to		
		FSUB	floating-point subtract single precision
ASGEU	assert greater than or equal to unsigned		
		HALT	enter halt mode
ASGT	assert greater than	INBYTE	insert byte
ASGTU	assert greater than unsign.	INHW	insert half-word
ASLE	assert less than or equal to	INV	invalidate
ASLEU	assert less than or equal to unsigned	IRET	interrupt return
		IRETINV	interrupt return and invalidate
ASLT	assert less than		
ASLTU	assert less than unsigned	JMP	jump
ASNEQ	assert not equal to	JMPF	jump false
CALL	call subroutine	JMPFDEC	jump false and decrement
CALLI	call subroutine indirect	JMPFI	jump false indirect
CLZ	count leading zeros	JMPI	jump indirect
CONST	constant		
CONSTH	constant high	JMPT	jump true
CONSTN	constant negative	JMPTI	jump true indirect
CONVERT	convert data format	LOAD	load
CPBYTE	compare bytes	LOADL	load and lock
CPEQ	compare equal to	LOADM	load multiple
CPGE	compare greater than or equal to	LOADSET	load and set
		MFSR	move from special register
CPGEU	compare greater than or equal to unsigned	MFTLB	move from translation look aside buffer register

109

CPGT	compare greater than	MTSR	move to special register
CPGTU	compare greater than unsigned	MTSRIM	move to special register immediate
CPLE	compare less than or equal to	MTTLB	move to translation look aside buffer register
CPLEU	compare less than or equal to unsigned	MUL	multiply step
		MULL	multiply last step
CPLT	compare less than	MULTIPLY	integer multiply unsigned
CPLTU	compare less than unsigned	MULTIPLY	integer multiply signed
CPNEQ	compare not equal to	MULU	multiply step unsigned
		NAND	nand logical
DADD	floating-point add double precision	NOR	nor logical
		OR	or logical
DDIV	floating-point divide double precision	SETIP	set indirect pointers
		SLL	shift left logical
DEQ	floating-point equal to double precision	SRA	shift right arithmetic
		SRL	shift right logical
DGE	floating-point greater than or equal to double precision	STORE	store
		STOREL	store and lock
DGT	floating-point greater than double precision	STOREM	store multiple
		SUB	subtract
DIV	divide step	SUBC	subtract with carry
DIVO	divide initialize	SUBCS	subtract with carry signed
DIVIDE	integer divide signed	SUBCU	subtract with carry unsigned
DIVIDU	integer divide unsigned		
DIVL	divide last step	SUBR	subtract reverse
DIVREM	divide remainder	SUBRC	subtract reverse with carry
DMUL	floating-point multiply double precision	SUBRCS	subtract reverse with carry signed
DSUB	floating-point subtract double precision		
EMULATE	trap to software emulation routine	SUBRCU	subtract reverse with carry unsigned
EXBYTE	extract byte	SUBRS	subtract reverse signed
EXHW	extract half-word	SUBRU	subtract reverse unsigned
EXHWS	extract half-word sign-extended	SUBS	subtract signed
		SUBU	subtract unsigned
EXTRACT	extract word bit aligned	XNOR	exclusive nor logical
FADD	floating-point add single precision	XOR	exclusive or logical

Fig.3.7 Am29000 instruction set.

31			0
OP	RC/constant	RA	RB/constant
8	8	8	8

Fig.3.8 Am29000 instruction format.

3.5   THE 88100 ARCHITECTURE FROM MOTOROLA

After down-playing RISC for years, Motorola is now marketing a RISC microprocessor of its own. Motorola was one of the major detractors of RISC in the beginning of the 1980s. In a special report of Business Week, Murray A. Goldman, vice-president of Motorola's Microprocessor Products Group conceded : *"Whether Intel and Motorola likes it or not, that's what the market wants"* [83]. Thus, in 1988, Motorola announced their new 88000 RISC microprocessor family including the MC88100 and the associated Cache Memory Management Unit (CMMU), the MC88200.

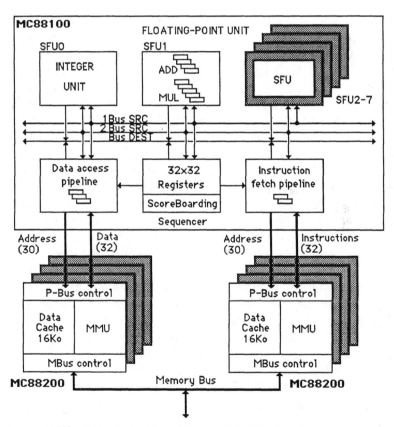

Fig.3.9 MC88100/MC88200 block diagram.

The MC88100 was designed in only 20 months and the MC88200 was completed in 11 months to meet several stringent design goals. The design was done entirely with the GDT software of Silicon

Compiler Systems in order to deliver the complete chip-set while meeting aggressive time-to-market goals [84]. The centerpiece of the MC88000 architecture is multiple pipelined function units that execute independently and concurrently. These units execute out of a register set with hardware-monitored interlocks, called scoreboarding (see chapter 2 section 2.3.6). In addition, separate data and instruction paths to memory (Harvard architecture) and combination cache-and-MMU chips completed the initial design goals.

The MC88100 provides register-to-register operation for all data manipulation instructions. Source operands are either located in source registers or are provided as an immediate value embedded in the instruction. A separate destination register stores the results of an instruction, which allows source operand registers to be raised in subsequent instructions. Register contents are read from or written to memory only through ld (load), st (store) and xmem. The xmem instruction provides an atomic load and store operation, which is useful for semaphore testing and multiprocessor synchronization. The MC88100 instruction set contains 51 instructions. All arithmetic, logical, bit-field and certain control-flow instructions execute in a single-clock-cycle. Memory-access and floating-point, data and instruction units implement execution pipelines so one multicycle instruction can be started in each clock cycle. Although these individual instructions may take more than one cycle to complete, effective one-cycle execution can be accomplished. All instructions are implemented directly in hardware, precluding the need for microcoded operations. Complex operations are handled in software by using advances in operating system and optimizing compiler technology. All instructions use simplified addressing modes and are implemented as single-word 32-bit instructions. The fixed instruction length eliminates the need for alignment circuitry, thereby decreasing instruction decode time. Formats are consistent across instructions, which allows for efficient decoding to occur in parallel with operand accesses. Branch address calculations and register usage checking also operate in parallel with decoding. All instructions can be fetched in a single-memory-access.

ADD	add	ID	load register from memory
ADDU	add unsigned	IDA	load address
CMP	compare	IDCR	load from control register
DIV	divide	ST	store register to memory
DIVU	divide unsigned	STCR	store to control register
MUL	multiply	XCR	exchange control register

| SUB | subtract | XMEM | exchange register with |
| SUBU | subtract unsigned | | memory |

FADD	floating-point add	BB0	branch on bit clear
FCMP	floating-point compare	BB1	branch on bit set
FDIV	floating-point divide	BCND	conditional branch
FLDCR	load from floating-point control register	BR	unconditional branch
		BSR	branch to subroutine
FLT	convert integer to floating-pt	JMP	unconditional jump
FMUL	floating-point multiply	JSR	jump to subroutine
FSTCR	store to floating-point control register	RTE	return from exception
		TB0	trap on bit clear
FSUB	floating-point subtract	TB1	trap on bit set
FXCR	exchange floating-point control register	TBND	trap on bounds check
		TCND	conditional trap
INT	round floating-point to integer		
		CLR	clear bit field
NINT	round floating-point to nearest integer	EXT	extract signed bit field
		EXTU	extract unsigned bit field
TRNC	Truncate floating-point to integer	FF0	find first bit clear
		FF1	find first bit set
		MAK	make bit field
AND	and	ROT	rotate register
MASK	logical mask immediate	SET	set bit field
OR	or		
XOR	exclusive or		

Fig.3.10 MC88100 instruction summary.

The MC88100 instruction set is divided into six categories :

1. Integer arithmetic instructions.
2. Floating-point arithmetic instructions.
3. Logical instructions.
4. Load-store-exchange instructions.
5. Flow-control instructions.
6. Bit-field instructions.

The MC88100 incorporates delayed-branching to reduce pipeline penalties associated with changes in program flow. The next instruction in the pipeline always executes while the branch target instruction is prefetched from memory. The execution of the instruction following the branch is under explicit software control through the value of a bit in the instruction encoding. When delayed branching is selected, the compiler must pick a useful instruction to be executed before the change of flow and places the instruction after the branch in the instruction stream.

The MC88100 is based on a Harvard model that uses a two-part nonmultiplexed memory access interface. Operand reads and writes from/to memory are performed through dedicated data address and data paths. Instruction fetches also occur over dedicated instruction address and data paths. These parts operate concurrently, eliminating bus contention between data accesses and instruction fetches. The MC88100 memory parts can interface directly to memory. However, most designs incorporate at least two MC88200 CCMMUs : one for data memory and one for instruction memory. Two to eight MC88200s can be easily incorporated into an MC88000 system, by using up to four for the data memory space and up to four for the instruction memory space.

The MC88100 is based on a multipipelined superscalar architecture that contains four execution units : the integer unit, the Floating-Point Unit, the data unit and the instruction unit. In addition, the MC88100 architecture can execute instructions concurrently with Special-Function Units (SFUs).

The SFUs are designed so that they can stand alone and can be added to or removed from a given implementation of the MC88000 family with no impact on the architecture. Multiple SFUs are connected to common buses and share data through general-purpose registers. The MC88000 architecture allows up to seven SFUs per implementation. The MC88100 Floating-Point Unit is implemented as SFU #1.

The MC88100 integer unit performs 32-bit arithmetic and logical operations and bit-field operations. All integer instructions are executed in one machine cycle. The Floating-Point Unit handles floating-point arithmetic and multicycle integer instructions such as multiply or divide. The FPU implements two pipelines, one for multiply operations and one for all other floating-point instructions. The divide instruction is the only floating-point operation that is not completely pipelined. A divide instruction iterates through one execution stage once for each bit of accuracy required in the result. The free-running multiply pipeline operates independently. The FPU requires more than one clock cycle per instruction. Floating-point instructions prevent subsequent instructions from using the results prematurely by setting a bit in the scoreboard register during their execution. The data unit executes the instructions that access data memory and controls the data memory interface. The data unit contains a dedicated calculation unit for address computation. Addresses are formed by adding the source1 register operand specified by the instruction with either a source2 operand or a 16-bit immediate value embedded in the instruction. Memory accesses are pipelined in the data unit using a three-stage pipeline : (1) Compute address, (2) drives the external data address bus ; if the access is a store operation, fetches data from registers and drives the external bus, (3) monitors the reply from the memory system ; if the access is a load operation, reads the data bus and writes the load result to the general-purpose register. The instruction unit prefetches instructions from memory, performs the first steps of instruction decode, and provides instructions to the appropriate execution unit via encoded internal control signals. The instructions prefetched from memory are dictated by program flow, which includes sequential accesses, execution of absolute jump, absolute and conditional branch instructions with displacement, and exception vectoring. Other tasks, such as partial instruction decoding and tasks related to subroutine returns and exception processing, are also performed.

The instruction unit maintains three instruction pointers that indicate the contents of the execution pipeline. The execute instruction pointer (XIP) points to the instruction currently executing in the integer unit, data, unit, or FPU. The next instruction pointer (NIP) points to the instruction currently being accessed from memory and decoded for execution. The fetch instruction pointer (FIP) points to the memory location of the next instruction to be accessed.

The instruction unit identifies and saves the return pointer for "jsr" and "bsr" instructions to the register file. The return pointer is written to a specific general-purpose register. The return pointer is either the contents of the NIP or FIP at the time the "jsr" or "bsr" instruction begins execution, depending on whether or not delayed branching is used.

The MC88100 contains a register file/sequencer that contains the general-purpose registers and performs overall internal control functions.

The register file contains 32 general-purpose registers, maintains concurrency control information, optimizes the operand/result internal bus utilization, and provides a means of separating instruction initiation from instruction completion.

Instruction execution begins sequentially but can finish in any order. All operands are read or written from/to registers or memory. The register file contains the scoreboard register, which maintains a bit for each of the general-purpose registers "in use" except r0 (r0 contains the constant zero and cannot be modified). All instructions that take longer than one clock cycle to execute

115

cause the scoreboard bit(s) corresponding to the destination register(s) to be set. If an instruction requires a register that is to be read or written to, the scoreboard register is checked for the availability of that register. If the source and/or destination registers are flagged as "in use" (defined as the destination register for a previous instruction still in execution), the execution of the requesting instruction is delayed until both the source and destination registers are flagged as available. The scoreboard register is checked on each clock cycle until the source and destination registers are available.

To increase instruction throughput, the MC88100 incorporates a register feed-forward capability. Feed-forward gates the contents of the destination bus onto the appropriate source bus so that, if an execution unit is waiting on the data, it receives the data at the same time that the register is updated. When both source registers required by an instruction are in use and may be modified by the previous instruction, both operands can be received by feed-forward. When the source operands are received, the destination register scoreboard bit(s) are set, and the instruction begins execution.

The sequencer performs the register writeback arbitration, performs exception arbitration, and generates control signals for the instruction unit and the internal buses.

The MC88100 has one bidirectional and two unidirectional 32-bit register buses that perform all internal data transfers. The source1 and source2 buses carry source operands to the integer unit, data unit, instruction unit, and FPU. All source data comes from the general-purpose register or from 16-bit immediate values embedded in the instruction. The bidirectional destination bus transfers data from the execution units to the general-purpose registers. The destination bus also transfers data to be stored from the register file to the data unit.

The four execution units allow the MC88100 to perform up to five operations in parallel :

1.   Access program memory.
2.   Execute an arithmetic, logical, or bit-field instruction.
3.   Access data memory.
4.   Execute floating-point or integer divide instructions.
5.   Execute floating-point or integer multiply instructions.

In addition, the floating-point, data, and instruction units themselves are pipelined and can complete an operation in every clock cycle :

1. Up to five floating-point add, subtract, compare, or convert instructions can execute simultaneously.

2. Up to six floating-point or four integer multiply instructions execute simultaneously.

3. Up to three data memory accesses can be in progress simultaneously :
    two memory accesses on the external bus,
    one address calculation.

4. Up to two instruction fetches can be in progress simultaneously.

The MC88000 chip set, operating at 20 Mhz can execute instructions at a sustained rate of 17 VAX-equivalent MIPS [85]. Floating-point operations are executed at a sustained rate of 7 MFLOPS. The MC88200 CMMU offers the combined functions of both a 16-kbyte cache and a segmented demand-paged memory management system [86]. The MC88100 chip set was designed using Motorola's high density CMOS (HCMOS) technology. The MC88100 contains near 165000 transistors and the MC88200 contains near 750000 transistors.

3.6 THE 80960 ARCHITECTURE FROM INTEL

The Intel 80960 is a good example of a 32-bit microprocessor that was introduced after RISC ideas become widely published. The processor has a load/store architecture, 3-operand instructions, a 512-byte instruction cache and a large register set. However, the 80960 also incorporates microcode. The microcode not only interprets complex instructions, it allows the processor to execute a power-on self--test without fetching instructions from memory. The 80960 family is designed to be the high-end follow-up to the company's 8- and 16-bit embedded microcontrollers. In the 80960 series, Intel is attempting to combine elements of RISC and CISC architectures, application specific designs, and its experience as a major supplier of single-chip microcontrollers. The family's first devices include the 20 Mhz 80960KA, a reduced implementation of the 80960 architecture, the 20 Mhz 80960KB incorporating an on-chip 32-bit Floating-Point Unit, and the 80960MC dedicated to military applications. The 80960K family supports operation in a 20 MIPS burst mode at 20 Mhz, and a near 7.5 VAX-MIPS equivalent [87 88 89].

In 1989, Intel announced the 80960CA, the second generation RISC 80960 microprocessor for real-time embedded control and the fourth following the KA, KB and MC implementations, all-code compatible. The 80960CA is a superscalar implementation of the 80960 architecture, requiring 575000 transistors on a 1 micron CMOS die. At 33 Mhz, the 80960CA executes 66 MIPS in burst native instructions. Assuming 50% cache hit and 50% efficient instruction stream, it executes 25 equivalent VAX-MIPS [90].

The 80960CA (also called i960CA) was the first processor commercially-available superscalar microprocessor, capable of the dispatch and execution of multiple independent instructions during each processor clock cycle [91-92].

The 80960 architecture presents a simple reduced instruction set to the user. It is a three-operand load/store architecture, indicating that most instructions operate on three register operands, two source operands and a destination, and that the only instructions that access memory are specific load and store instructions. The architecture defines 24 basic instructions, including the normal arithmetic, logical, and memory access instructions, and 16 extended instructions, including a combined compare-and-branch instruction, subroutine call and return

118

instructions, and atomic and synchronous memory access operations.

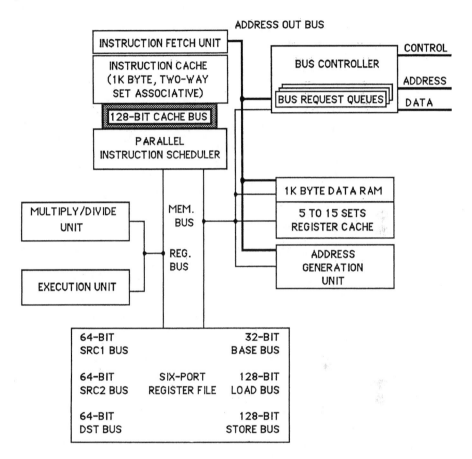

Fig.3.11 i960CA architecture.

All 80960 instructions fall into one of four main categories : Register (REG) format instructions, Memory (MEM) instructions, Control (CTRL), and Compare-and-Branch (COBR) instructions. Most general instructions are of the REG type, such as add, subtract, boolean, and bit manipulation instructions. Compare instructions are also of REG type, and are the only general-purpose instructions which set the condition codes. The COBR instructions are a variant of the REG-style compare instruction that combine a comparison operation with a conditional branch. These instructions are useful to reduce code size when a useful instruction cannot be placed in the delay slot after a comparison and prior to a branch instruction.

The load, store, and load address instructions are of the MEM type, and may access byte, half-word, word, double-word, triple-word or quad-word data. Conditional and unconditional branches as well as the call and return instructions are of the CTRL type. The instruction types are distinguished by the most significant three bits of the encoding, with the operation code occupying the remaining 5 of the uppermost bytes in each instruction. This allows extremely simple decoding of instructions.

The 80960 architecture defines a register file consisting of 32 general-purpose registers that are divided into two sets : global registers and local registers. The local register r0 through r15 represent the currently visible portion of a local register cache, where local registers from previous subroutine invocations are retained. Management of the local register cache is fully transparent to the user program, as the processor automatically flushes frames out to memory when the cache becomes full. The 80960CA allows user-control of the size of the local register cache, supporting up to 240 cached registers (15 frames). The 16 global registers are not affected by procedure calls and returns, and are used for parameter passing and, within a procedure, as temporary value registers.

The 80960CA microprocessor consists of the superscalar 80960CA core processor, a 1 kbyte instruction cache, 1.5 kbytes of on-chip SRAM and stack-frame cache, a four-channel DMA controller, an interrupt controller, and a pipelined burst bus controller with a programmable wait-state generator.

The core of the 80960CA processor consists of a single 6-ported register file, an instruction sequencer, and a set of independent parallel execution units that operate on data in the register file.

The 80960CA includes a 6-ported register file. Three ports are provided for use by the register-to-register functions units : two 64-bit wide ports for source operands and one 64-bit wide port for results. Three ports are also provided to the memory-access function units : a 128-bit wide load port, a 128-bit wide store port, and a 32-bit wide base-register access port. In addition to providing the 32 registers defined by the architecture, the register file generates literal values in the range 0 to 31 for use by instructions.

The register file provides 1.8 Gigabytes per second of interface bandwidth, allowing the simultaneous execution of register and memory operations. The 128-bit read and write ports to on-chip memory allow the 16 local registers to be loaded or stored to the on-chip local register cache in only four clock cycles. Because other operations can be overlapped with these memory operations, call and return operations take only these four clock cycles, establishing an entirely new register (and stack) context for the called procedure.

The operation of the parallel execution units is orchestrated by the parallel Instruction Sequence (IS), which decodes instructions fetched from the on-chip instruction cache and prefetch buffers and dispatches instructions to either the register (REG) or memory (MEM) execution units. The instruction sequencer on the 80960CA can issue two instructions during each clock cycle, and can execute a branch instruction internally, for a maximum instruction dispatch rate of three instructions per clock cycle.

The instruction sequencer does more than dispatch instructions. It dynamically detects dependencies between adjacent instructions that prevent those instructions from being executed in parallel. The IS uses the register scoreboarding technique to determine whether a particular register is already the target of a previously-issued multicycle instruction such as a multiply or a load.

The Instruction Sequence handles both conditional and unconditional branch instructions internally. Branch instructions are executed out-of-order and prefetching of branch destinations with the help of static branch prediction bits allows many branches to "disappear" from the instruction stream, being overlapped by other operations.

ADD	integer add	NOR	logical not-or
SUBTRACT	integer subtract	NAND	logical not-and
MULTIPLY	integer multiply	CLRBIT	clear bit
DIVIDE	integer divide	ANDNOT	and negate
MODULO	modulo	ORNOT	or negate
		XNOR	exclusive nor
CMP	compare	ALTERBIT	bit alteration
TEST	test	NOTBIT	negate bit
SHIFT	shift		
ROTATE	rotate	BRANCH	branch
AND	logical and	BRANCH-LINK	branch and link
OR	logical or	CALL	procedure call
XOR	exclusive or	RETURN	procedure return
NOT	negate		
SETBIT	set bit	MOVE	move
NOTAND	negate and	LOAD	load
NOTOR	negate or	STORE	store

Fig.3.12 80960 RISC core instruction set.

121

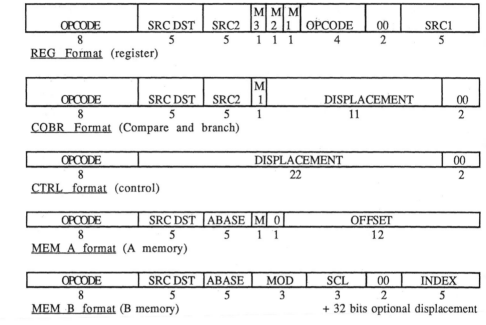

Fig.3.13 80960 RISC core instruction formats.

The 80960CA also pipelines fetch, decode, issues, execution, and result-return of instructions. The basic 80960CA pipeline is three stages : a fetch/decode stage in which four instructions are fetched, an issue stage in which instructions are issued to varous execution units and during which they fetch their operands from the register file, and a result-return stage during which results are written back into the register file.

Execution of individual instructions is performed by several independent execution units. Execution units fall into two classes, REG-side and MEM-side. REG-side units operate only on register operands (two source and one destination), and MEM-side units operate on memory-oriented instructions (loads, stores, and load effective address).

In the 80960CA, two execution units are provided on the register side of the machine, the (Integer) Execution Unit (EU) and the Multiply/Divide Unit (MDU).

All the instructions executed by the EU complete in one clock cycle. The MDU executes the multiply, divide, modulus and remainder instructions. MDU instructions take between 4 (mul) and 39 (div) clock cycles to complete.

The MEM-side of the 80960CA consists of the Address Generation Unit (AGU), the Local Register Cache (LRC) and on-chip

SRAM, a DMA controller, and the Bus Control Logic (BCL). The Address Generation Unit is used to produce a complete address from any of the 80960CA architecture's addressing modes :

1. Direct.
2. Register indirect.
3. Register + offset.
4. Scaled index.
5. Base + scale + displacement.

The 80960CA was designed to allow high-performance with a minimum of off-chip support components. To achieve this, several critical peripheral components were integrated with the 80960CA processor.

The 80960CA includes a 1.5-kbyte on-chip static RAM array. Part of this RAM is used as a Local Register Cache. The LCR can hold a user-selectable number (between 5 and 15) of set of local registers. This removes the need for accesses to main memory during most call and return operations. Thus, the 80960CA can be considered to have 256 registers, organized as non overlapping register windows.

The 80960CA implements a Multi-Function Bus Controller that allows easy interface to a wide variety of I/O devices and external memory types.

The 80960CA also includes a four-channel DMA (Direct Memory Access) controller and I/O processor. The DMA controller is autonomous from the main processor, allowing memory transfers to occur independently of program execution.

The 80960CA contains an on-chip interrupt controller. Unlike many RISC chips, which provide only a single interrupt, the 80960CA support up to 248 separate interrupt vectors at 31 different priorities, as well as a Non-Maskable Interrupt (NMI).

The latency of 80960CA interrupts is very low typical latency of the dedicated NMI vector is 700 nanoseconds, and typical latency of normal interrupts is only 1 microsecond at 33 Mhz.

Performance was a key consideration in the design of the 80960CA. However, the class of applications that were examined for performance characteristics differ somewhat from those often examined during the design of processors intended for non-embedded applications. The 80960CA achieves peak performance when executing algorithms that achieve a high hit-rate in the on-chip instruction cache. Applications dominated by moderately-sized computational loops can often achieve a sustained execution rate of

66 MIPS when inner loops of algorithms are unrolled and software pipelined, to maximize the opportunity to execute register and memory operations in parallel. The 80960CA obtains an additional performance boost because of its ability to execute branches out-of-order and by using branch-prediction information.

The 80960CA architecture is only the first of this generation of 960 processors. Numerous opportunities exist to continue to improve performance, and to provide additional functions. Because the core processor in the 80960CA is modular, it can be used as the basis for a variety of implementations that provide additional functional units, or different on-chip peripherals. Among the first proliferations is an implementation of the 80960 Numerics Architecture, providing fast floating-point addition and multiplication function units.

Additionally, advances in fabrication technology will soon allow the 80960CA to operate at 50 Mhz to 70 Mhz, bringing performance levels of up to 140 MIPS.

3.7 THE i860 ARCHITECTURE FROM INTEL

In parallel with the 80960 architecture, Intel announced a new RISC architecture optimized for floating-point and 3-D graphics. The i860 microprocessor, known previously as the N10, was one of the first single-chip microprocessors to integrate relatively large instruction and data caches, a TLB-based memory management unit, a pipelined RISC integer unit, a pipelined Floating-Point Unit, and a 3-D graphic unit. The i860 is capable of an impressive peak performance because of its parallel architecture : under the right circumstances, the integer core unit, the floating-point multiplier and the floating-point adder can each issue an operation every cycle. Thus, at 40 Mhz, the i860 can execute bursts at 40 native integer MIPS and 80 single-precision MFLOPS. In addition, the chip has a special graphics hardware unit, which has instructions that speed-up 3-D graphics algorithms, such as hidden-surface elimination and smooth-shading [93].

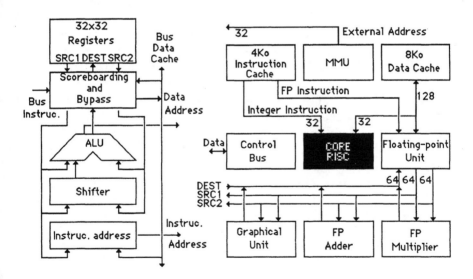

Fig.3.14 i860 architecture.

However, in most cases only one unit will be running at any given time. In some cases, during floating-point operations, an integer operation can be run at the same time if the compiler is able to plan it. The integer core is a true RISC architecture and nearly all integer instructions take only one cycle. The instruction set is deliberately kept simple to support single-cycle execution. Load/store architecture, in which only explicit load and store operations access memory and other instructions operate on registers, is crucial to single-cycle performance. There are related issues in programming. For example, an instruction should not use as a source a register that was used as a destination by the previous instruction, or a delay-slot will automatically result.

That is, there is no forwarding paths to solve pipeline interlocks. Unlike the MIPS academic design, the delay is automatically inserted to prevent problems. The i860 implements the delayed-branch scheme and can also execute the instruction only if the branch is taken, and skip it otherwise. The compiler system must attempt to structure the code so that the instruction to be executed is on the most-used side of the branch.

Like the MIPS R2000/R3000 and the Motorola 88100, the i860 has a flat, 32-word register file, with R0 as a fixed constant "zero". There are no "move" instructions. A register-to-register move is performed by using, for example, an "OR" with R0, with the result directed to the desired destination. Only load and store instructions access memory. A single addressing mode permits four useful variants : offset + register, register + register, register, and offset. This addressing mode is essentially the same as that offered by most RISC machines, and is considerably simpler than that of the 80960.

The core instruction set is complete by the standards set by other RISC architectures with three exceptions : there are no add or subtract with carry instructions, no integer multiply or divide, and no compare instructions. The omission of add and subtract with carry is partially solved by the long-integer add and subtract instructions in the floating-point set, and such instructions are rarely needed by high-level languages in any case. Integer multiply is performed by the Floating-Point Unit, and integer divide requires an iterative process using the floating-point reciprocal functions.

Like traditional machines, the i860 uses condition codes for storing information about relative values. Unlike other processors, however, it has just one condition code bit. This single condition code is set only by the integer arithmetic and logical instructions and the two floating-point compare operations.

Compare operations are performed using add and subtract instructions, with the result directed to R0. With the appropriate arithmetic instruction followed by a branch-on-CC instruction, all the usual compare-and-branch idioms can be synthesized.

126

The i860 includes a special floating-point register file, a 64-bit Multiplier unit and a 64-bit adder unit. Adder and multiplier instructions usually execute in three clocks, but take four clocks with some data combinations. The data types, instructions, and exception handling of the Floating-Point Unit support the IEEE floating-point standard. The register file can be viewed as 32 single-precision registers, 16 double-precision registers, or 8 128-bit registers.

Floating-point division is not performed directly. Instead, the i860 contains a small ROM that approximates the reciprocal of an operand, accurate to seven bits. A software routine is then required to increase the accuracy of the mantissa to full single or double precision. Floating-point square root is handled similarly.

Programming the units can be done in either scalar mode or pipelined mode. In scalar mode, an operation is started and allowed to complete before another operation can begin. A scalar instruction specifies the two source operands, its precision, and the destination for its result.

In pipelined mode, each instruction still specifies an operation, a precision, and the source operands for that operation. However, the destination specified by the instruction is the location for the result that will emerge from the pipeline when the operation specified by the instruction is started. Thus, a pipelined floating-point add/multiply instruction pushes a result out of the last stage of the adder/multiply pipeline, and this result is stored in the register specified by the destination field of the floating-point add/multiply instruction.

The Floating-Point Unit pipelines do not advance unless a new operation is started in that pipeline. Thus, unlike scalar floating-point instructions, pipelined floating-point instructions do not complete by themselves. This is because the pipeline does not know where to store the results that would be generated. Dummy pipelined operations must be inserted to flush the pipes at the end of a string of pipelined operations and before a scalar operation can be performed.

LD.X	load integer	FMUL.P	FP multiply
ST.X	store integer	PFMUL.P	pipelined FP multiply
FLD.Y	FP load	PFMUL3.DD	3-stage pipelined FP multiply
PFLD.Z	pipelined FP load		
FST.Y	FP store	FMLOW.P	FP multiply low
PST.D	pixel store	FRCP	FP reciprocal

127

Mnemonic	Description	Mnemonic	Description
		FRSQR.P	FP reciprocal square low
IXFR	transfer to integer to FP register		
FXFR	transfer FP to integer register	FADD.P	FP add
		PFADD.P	pipelined FP add
		FSUB.P	FP subtract
ADDU	add unsigned	PFSUB.P	pipelined FP subtract
ADDS	add signed	PFGT.P	pipelined FP greater than compare
SUBU	subtract unsigned		
SUBS	subtract signed	PFEQ.P	pipelined FP equal compare
AND	logical and	FIX.P	FP to integer convert
ANDH	logical and high	PFIX.P	pipelined FP to integer convert
ANDNOT	logical and not		
ANDNOTH	logical and not high	FTRUNC.P	FP to integer truncate
OR	logical or	PFTRUNC.P	pipelined FP to integer truncate
ORH	logical or high		
XOR	logical xor		
XORH	logical xor high	PFAM.P	pipelined FP add and multiply
TRAP	software trap	FFSM.P	pipelined FP subtract and multiply
INTOVR	software trap on integer overflow	PFMAM	pipelined FP multiply with add
BR	branch direct		
BRI	branch indirect	PFMSM	pipelined FP multiply with subtract
BC	branch on CC		
BC.T	branch on CC taken		
BNC	branch on not CC	FISUB.Z	long integer subtract
BNC.T	branch on not CC taken	PFISUB.Z	pipelined long integer subtract
BIE	branch if equal	FIADD.Z	long integer add
BINE	branch if not equal	PFIADD.Z	pipelined long integer add
BLA	branch on LCC and add		
CALL	subroutine call	FSCHKS	16-bit Z-buffer check
CALLI	indirect subroutine call	PFZCHKS	pipelined 16-bit Z buffer check
		FZCHKL	32-bit Z-buffer check
FLUSH	cache flush	PFZCHKL	pipelined 32-bit Z-buffer check
LD.C	load from control register		
		FADDP	add with pixel merge
ST.C	store to control register	PFADDP	pipelined add with pixel merge
LOCK	begin interlocked sequence	FADDZ	add with Z merge
		PFADDZ	pipelined add with Z merge
UNLOCK	end interlocked sequence	FORM	or with merge regist.

The W, X, Y and Z suffixes specify integer word size ; each suffix represents a different range of options. The P suffix specifies precision for the source and result, and can be ss (both single), sd (single source, double result), or dd (both double).

PFORM	pipelined or with merge register
MOV	integer reg-reg move
FMOV.Q	FP reg-reg move
PFMOV.Q	pipelined FP reg-reg move
NOP	core no operation
FNOP	FP no operation
PFLE.P	pipelined FP less than or equal

Fig.3.15 i860 instruction set.

Because the pipeline must be cleared before use and results must be stored correctly during and after pipelined operations, pipelining is effective only for repetitive operations on large arrays of data, such as those found in geometric tranformations. Successful implementation of pipelined operations does impose a burden on the compiler. When pipelining is in use, dual-operation instructions can also be used. These instructions run the floating-point adder and multiplier units simultaneously. Normally, the adder and multiplier each require two source operands and a destination, for a total of six operands. In dual-operation mode, only three operands are specified, and intermediate registers are used as additional inputs to the multiplier.

In dual-operation mode, the programmer needs to be concerned about making best use of the 8-kbyte data cache, since cache misses will adversely affect performance.

The graphics unit operates on 8-, 16-, or 32-bit pixels, although all data is handled 64 bits at a time. The pixel size is determined by a 2-bit field in the status register. The graphics units is supported by the floating-point for very fast operation. Rotational transformations of 3D wireframes or solids are among the computation-intensive routines that can benefit from pipelined floating-point operations, as well as dual-operation and dual-instruction modes.

The i860 is not a direct competitor to other RISC chip sets, because of its advantages for use as a stand-alone processor for a graphics workstation running UNIX. However, even if the i860 was a generation ahead in terms of integration, the general-purpose workstation market already has too many RISC architectures, and it was probably too late for the i860 to be a major player in this market segment. The i860 will be certainly more popular as a graphics/floating-point accelerator, used with another general-purpose RISC chip set.

The i860 was initially available in a 33 Mhz version, but Intel is quoting performance figures at 40 Mhz. Intel's VAX-MIPS rating for the i860, based on the Stanford integer suite, is 32.1 at 40 Mhz and 26.5 at 33 Mhz [94-95].

3.8 THE C400 ARCHITECTURE FROM INTERGRAPH

The Clipper was one of the earlier 32-bit microprocessors balancing RISC and CISC features. The original Clipper C100 architecture was designed 1982 by Fairchild and introduced in October of 1985. In September of 1987, the Advanced Processor Division of Fairchild was acquired by Intergraph Corporation. Residing securely at the heart of Intergraph's successful line of advanced graphics workstations, the Clipper architecture has continued to evolve through two new generations : the C300, announced in November of 1987 and now shipping in volume, and the C400 announced in September of 1990.

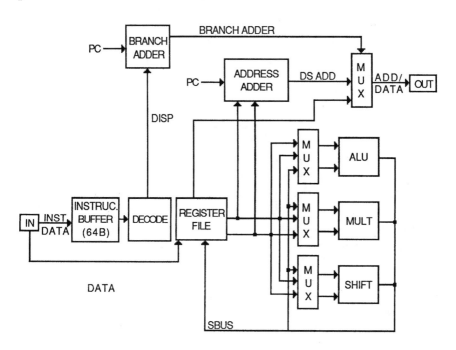

Fig.3.16 C400 architecture.

The original Clipper C100 processor differs from other commercial 32-bit microprocessors architecturally as well as mechanically. Its features include a balanced instruction set, high-bandwidth dual buses, caching, hardware-managed pipelining and resource allocation, concurrent processing units, and hardware-based operating system support [96].

The processor comes as a preassembled module. Physically, it comprises a set of three CMOS VLSI chips and a smaller CMOS clock generator, which partition processing and memory features to minimize interchip traffic. These chips include the combined CPU/Floating-Point Unit ; the two identical cache/memory management units (CAMMUs), one for data and the other for instructions ; and the clock generator chip, which distributes the required clock signal.

Clipper's instruction set fosters fast-executing compiled code from compilers that optimize register use. The RISC-like instructions are implemented in fast-acting hardwired logic ; most frequently-used instructions execute in one 30-nanosecond clock-cycle.

In accord with RISC philosophy, Clipper is essentially a load/store machine in which all arithmetic and logical instructions operate only on data in registers ; only loads, stores, branches, calls, and stack manipulations access memory. The hardware architecture provides thirty-two 32-bit registers, sixteen for the operating system and sixteen for user programs. To simplify and speed up decoding, all instructions are formatted as multiples of 16-bit parcels. The most frequently used instructions are shortest.

The instruction set includes 101 hardwired and 67 high-level macroinstructions that operate on the basic data types. Each instruction specifies the operation to be performed, plus the type and location of its operands. These operands can reside in memory, in a register, or within the instruction itself. To speed decoding, all instructions contain from one to four 16-bit parcels.

These instruction formats fall into two groups, those with addresses and those without. Instructions with addresses are those that must access memory, such as loads, stores, and branches. Instructions without addresses are the arithmetical and logical types and generally can execute in one clock cycle. Although instructions can have zero, one, or two operands, only one operand can access a memory address.

Clipper's instruction set consists of 10 functional categories. Load/store instructions transfer addresses, bytes, halfwords, words (32 bits), longwords, and floating-point quantities (single and double) between memory and registers. Scattered throughout these 10 categories are the 67 CISC-like macroinstructions. For example, all conversion and string instructions are macros ; except for push and pop, some stack operations are macros ; and some move, arithmetic, and control instructions are also macros. Except for format, however, the programmer should see no difference between macros and hardwired elemental instructions. In fact, each macroinstruction is implemented in the CPU's macroinstruction unit as a sequence of the hard-wired instructions.

Additional CISC-related features include a complete set of nine addressing modes for load/store instructions to facilitate access to the complex data structure elements. Clipper provides separate modes, with dedicated resources and unique privileges, for users and the operating system.

Pipelining in the CPU has three phases. Parallel and concurrent operations take place in each phase. In order of occurrence, the three phases are fetch, decode, and execute. The execute phase supports more concurrent operations than either of the others ; in essence, another level of pipelining.

In the first phase, instructions from the cache or from the macroinstruction unit are brought into the CPU's instruction buffer. This buffer holds two words, or up to four instructions.

Next, instructions are decoded into resource requests. In response to these requests, resource management logic makes allocations using its table of busy resources. This resource scoreboard keeps tabs on the status of currently executing instructions and on which of these are using particular resources. This detailed tracking lets the CPU restart instructions that have caused page faults and continue executing instructions after interrupts and traps. Therefore, unlike software-managed pipelines, programmed instructions, interrupts, and traps do not crash the pipeline.

The pipeline's final phase issues instructions for execution in either the CPU's three-stage integer-execution unit or its Floating-Point Unit. In the former, successive instructions (three integer and one floating-point) can execute simultaneously and are often overlapped.

The first integer-execution stage reads into the L register's operands from the general register file. Immediate operands move directly from the instruction buffer to the L registers via the J register.

The second stage performs arithmetic, logical, and shift operations on L register operands or on the previous operation's intermediate results. Results are stored in the A register.

The third and final stage sends the A register contents to the FPU, to the general register file for storage via the bypass loop as feedback to the A stage, or to the data CAMMU. The bypass loop immediately feeds back to the next instruction intermediate results of multi-instruction calculations. The bypass loop immediately feeds back to the next instruction inermediate results of multi-instruction calculations. The bypass loop's feedback action renders pipeline flushing, and its consequent program complications and performance degradation, unnecessary.

Clipper uses two buses between its CPU/FPU and the CAMMUs. Each bus is dedicated one to data and the other to instruction traffic. The two-bus system effectively more than doubles the single-bus bandwidth by eliminating bus arbitration. In addition to raising the bandwidth, the two buses and two CAMMUs increase the caching operation's efficiency.

Burst-mode transfers also enhance the bandwidth over the Clipper bus for information exchanges between the processor module and main memory. Clipper's closely integrated caches bridge the gap between its 30 ns CPU/FPU and the 500 ns main-memory systems that are implemented using 150 ns DRAMs. Each cache is in reality a two-level mechanism : the 4-kbyte main caches each contain a quadword buffer that is, in effect, a smaller high-speed virtual cache.

Based on the C100 design, Intergraph introduced the C300, that executes 15 MIPS and is implemented using a CMOS technology.

The C400 represents a significant increase in computational power over either of its two predecessors. Important features include :

1. Separate integer and floating-point units.
2. Single-cycle execution of all integer instructions.
3. Simultaneous issue of integer and floating-point instructions.
4. Simultaneous issue of branch instructions with any other instruction except stores.
5. 50 Mhz operation (scalable to 80 Mhz at half-micron geometries).
6. Upward compatibility with C100 and C300 binary software.

The integer processor contains separate functional units for integer ALU, Multiply, and Shift operations, as well as a five-ported file of thirty-two 32-bit wide registers. In addition, it contains a dedicated Address Adder, allowing load/store operations to be issued one clock early. The unit also contains a dedicated Branch Adder, allowing branches to execute early and in parallel with any other operation except stores.

A floating-point instruction can be issued to a separate IEEE-compatible Floating-Point Unit on the same clock cycle that an instruction is issued to one of the integer execution units. The FPU contains separate functional units for floating-point Add/Subtract, Multiply, and Divide, as well as its own five-ported file of 16 registers. To maximize the efficiency of double-precision operations, the floating-point register file is 64-bit wide ; as are all paths onto, off from, and inside the Floating-Point Unit.

The floating Add/Subtract, and Multiply functional units are both pipelined. A single-precision instruction can be issued to the Multiply unit on every clock, and a double-precision instruction can be issued to it on every other clock, with execution latencies of 5 and 6 clocks, respectively. Either single- or double-precision instructions can be issued to the Adder on every clock, with execution latencies fo 4 clocks each. The Divide unit is not pipelined. Its execution latencies are 16 clocks for single-precision, and 30 clocks for double-precision arithmetic.

Cache and memory-management functions for the C400 are implemented in discrete logic, thus providing maximum flexibility to the system designer [97].

To achieve a high-level of performance, the C400 combines two architectural features, discussed earlier and called "superscalar" and "superpipelined". A superscalar processor has the ability to issue more than one instruction in a single clock cycle. A superpipelined processor uses a more finely divided pipeline than a typical RISC machine, thus allowing the processor to run at a higher clock rate (see chapter 1, section 1.6). The objective behind each of these features is higher overall performance for the machine.

Since the two capabilities are not merely independent of each other, but actually serve to increase the utilization of different parts of the processor hardware, it is possible to combine both in a single machine. The C400 chipset has been designed for implementation in one micron CMOS technology. The CPU die is a modest 200000 square mils, with approximately 140000 transistors.

Fujitsu and Motorola both are serving as semi-conductor partners for these chips. Intergraph claims a 50 native MIPS integer performance with a perfect 1.00 CPI (Esprisse benchmark), and 21.1 MIPS at 0.9 CPI (Spice benchmark).

The vector performance measured on the Linpack benchmark results in 94 native MIPS and 33.3 Megaflops with a 0.53 CPI.

3.9 THE POWER ARCHITECTURE FROM IBM

In 1975, the 801 minicomputer [98] project at IBM Research in Yorktown Heights pioneered many of the architectural concepts used by Reduced Instruction Set Computers (RISC) including the RT™ System V [99-100]. The IBM second-generation RISC processor architecture was developed to support engineering, scientific and commercial application environments. The IBM second-generation RISC processor architecture is based on a logical view of the processor consisting of three independent functional units : a branch processor, a fixed-point processor, and a floating-point processor [101-102].

The instruction set includes 184 instructions that were divided between the functional units and defined to minimize the interaction and synchronization of these functional units. There are three main functional units :

1. the branch processor,
2. the Fixed-Point processor,
3. the floating-point processor.

The logical function of the branch processor is to process the incoming instruction stream from the instruction cache and feed a steady flow of instructions to the fixed-point and floating-point processors. The branch processor provides all of the branching, interrupt, and condition code functions within the system. It is designed to execute the seven different branch instructions and nine different condition register instructions. The branch processor logically also contains six special registers : the Machine State Register (MSR), the Save Restore Registers (SRR0, SRR1), the Condition Register (CR), the Link Register (LR) and the Count Register (CTR).

The branch processor supports seven branch instructions. All of the branch instructions have a special link bit, which, if set, will cause the address of the next instruction to be placed in the Link Register (LR) in the branch processor. This function is used to provide the return address on subroutine and supervisor calls.

Three of the four branch instructions are conditional. A conditional branch can be based on the value of any bit within the CR. The conditional branch instructions also have a count capability. The count feature is primarily used as the loop-closing instruction of an innermost do loop. When the count feature is enabled in a conditional branch, the CTR is decremented by 1 and tested to see if it is 0. The decrement and test of the CTR can be selected independent of or in concert with the test of a CR bit, thus providing a very powerful conditional branch capability.

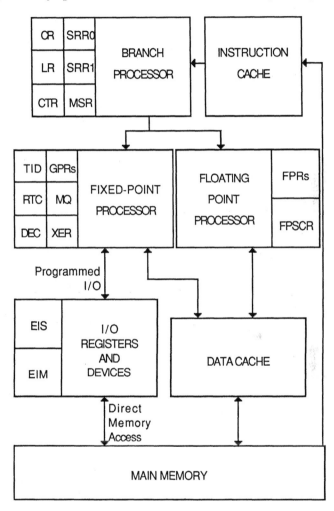

Fig.3.17 Power architecture.

In addition to the branch instructions, a set of nine condition register instructions are defined that allow all possible Boolean operations to be performed on any two bits within the CR and placed into a third bit in the CR. When the compiler encounters a compound Boolean expression in an if statement, it can generate a

137

series of compares and CR logical operations followed by a single branch instead of the equivalent series of compares and branches.

The common characteristic of all the branch processor instructions is that they have been defined in such a way that all the information and resources required to execute the instructions are available within the branch processor itself. All the information required to perform CR logical operations, to resolve conditional branches, to determine the target address of a branch, or to take an interrupt are predefined or are contained in the branch processor special registers. The logical independence of the branch processor, allow it to process the incoming instruction stream in advance, resolving all interrupts, branch, and CR operations. By doing so, the branch processor can then dispatch a steady stream of instructions to the fixed- and floating-point processors. This implies that for large sequences of meaningful code, the cycles required for handling branches are completely overlapped. This allows implementations to easily achieve a zero-cycle branch. This capability obviates the delayed-branch or branch with execute instructions which traditional RISC processors have used to minimize delays associated with branching.

The fixed-point processor (FX) is designed to support the execution of all 79 of the fixed-point arithmetic and logical operations as well as all 55 of the data reference instructions. All of the arithmetic and logical instructions include a Record bit, which the compiler can set to cause this instruction to return a condition code to CR. The FX has thirty-two 32-bit general-purpose registers and five special registers.

The 24 arithmetic instructions all provide an overflow enable bit, which controls whether this instruction will affect the overflow bits. This allows the compiler to deal with unsigned values, such as addresses, without spurious setting of the overflow bits. The arithmetic instructions include 14 add and subtract instructions, which provide complete support for addition and subtraction of constants and register values in both normal and extended precision. The arithmetic instructions include five instructions that support functions such as maximum, minimum, and absolute value without the need for a test and branch. In addition, five multiply and divide instructions are defined.

The FX supports 16 logical instructions that provide the capability to perform all bit-wise boolean operations between two registers and place the results in a third register. A powerful set of 26 rotate, shift, and mask instructions is provided for dealing with bit strings within a register or spanning multiple registers, as well as for performing simple multiplies and divides by powers of 2.

The FX architecture defines 13 instructions that deal with transferring information between the FX and branch processors. Included in these instructions are the four fixed-point compare instructions that compare two values and return a condition code to one of the eight fields in the CR register of the branch processor. Two trap instructions are provided that compare two values and force the branch processor to take a precise program interrupt.

The FX processor also handles all 55 data reference instructions. The architecture supports byte, unsigned half-word, signed half-word, and full-word data types in the FX GPRs as well as IEEE single-precision and double-precision data types in the floating-point registers. The addressing modes supported are absolute, indirect, base plus displacement, and base plus index. Automatic increment and decrement of the base register is supported by the update form of these data reference instructions.

The FX architecture has extensive support for misaligned operands and for dealing with character strings. In support of character string data, a set of five string instructions are provided for efficient copy and compare of character strings whose alignment is unknown.

The floating-point processor (FP) architecture supports the execution of all 21 of the floating-point instructions. Each of these instructions includes a record bit, which the compiler sets to cause this instruction to return a condition code. The FP has thirty-two 64-bit floating-point registers (FPRs) and a floating-point status and control register (FPSCR). The FPSCR contains all the appropriate status information required by the IEEE standard as well as control bits for the rounding and exception modes.

This second-generation RISC design is optimized to perform in numerically-intensive engineering and scientific applications as well as in multiuser commercial environment. A number of design choices were made for various environments.

To extend the performance beyond the capabilities of first-generation RISCs, a superscalar implementation is employed, which means that multiple instructions are issued and executed simultaneously. This requires independant functional units that can execute concurrently and a high instruction bandwidth to feed them. A high-level of concurrency is achieved by implementing separate branch, fixed-point, and floating-point units and by establishing a four-word interface to the I-cache arrays in order to be able to dispatch a maximum of four instructions per cycle. This satisfies the peak instruction demand : a branch, a condition-register instruction, a fixed-point instruction, and a floating-point instruction.

The overall architecture contains several semicustom chips : an instruction-cache unit (IC), a fixed-point unit (FX), a Floating-Point Unit (PF), four data-cache units (DC), a storage-control unit (SC), an input/output interface unit, and a clock chip. Every memory card contains two data multiplexing chips (D) and one control chip (R) for interleaving.

In addition to the branch processor, the ICU contains a two-way set-associative 8-kbyte I-cache with a line size of 64 bytes. It also has the cache directories and a 32-entry two-way set-associative TLB. Four instructions per cycle can be fetched from the I-cache arrays to the instruction buffers and to the dispatch unit, which can dispatch up to four instructions per cycle. Two of these are internal dispatches to IC (branches and condition register instructions) and two are external dispatches to FX and FP. There is no restriction on the combination of instructions that are dispatched to the FX and FP.

The architecture includes the D-cache which is a four-way set-associative 64-kbyte cache divided into four identical DCU chips of 16 kbytes each. The cache-line size is 128 bytes, and the cache is implemented as a copy-back cache to minimize the memory bus traffic.

The SC unit is the central system controller. All the communication between CPU (IC, FX, DC), main memory, and I/O is arbitrated by the SC. CPU sends I-cache reload, D-cache reload, and D-cache store-back requests to SCU over the bus, and SCU generates the appropriate memory control signals. SCU is the bus master for the memory and SIO buses. It controls the interface between D-cache and system memory and oversees DMA operations between main memory and the I/O unit.

All the chips were implemented using a 1 micron CMOS technology. One of the primary goals of the IBM second-generation RISC project was to design a high-performance and truly balanced machine that avoided bottlenecks in the CPU, caches, memory interface, and I/O subsystem. This was achieved by :

1. A superscalar implementation with multiple functional units that can execute concurrently.
2. Highly fine-tuned caches and memory subsystem.
3. A high bandwidth I/O subsystem.

3.10 THE ARM ARCHITECTURE FROM ACORN

The ARM (Acorn RISC Machine) architecture is produced by VLSI Technology Inc. under the reference VL86C010 [103]. The VL86C010 ARM is a full 32-bit general-purpose microprocessor designed using the RISC methodology. The processor is targeted for the microcomputer, graphics, industrial and controller markets, for use in stand-alone or embedded systems. Applications in which the processor is useful include laser printers, graphics engines and any other systems requiring fast real-time response to external interrupt sources and high processing throughput.

The VL80C010 features a 32-bit data bus, 27 registers of 32 bits each, a load-store architecture, a partially overlapping register set, 2.6 µs worst-case interrupt latency, conditional instruction execution, a 26-bit linear address space and an average instruction execution rate of from 4 to 5 MIPS.

Additionally, the processor supports two addressing modes : program counter (PC) and base register relative modes. The ability to do pre- and post-indexing allows stacks and queues to be easily implemented in software. All instructions are 32 bits long (aligned on word boundaries), with register-to-register operations executing in one cycle. The two data types supported are 8-bit bytes and 32-bit words.

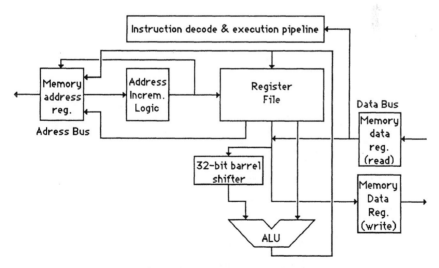

Fig.3.18 VL86C010 architecture.

Using a load-store architecture simplifies the execution unit of the processor, since only a few instructions deal directly with memory and the rest operate register-to-register. Load and store multiple register instructions provide enhanced performance, making context switches faster and exploiting sequential memory access modes.

The processor supports two types of interrupts that differ in priority and register usage. The lowest latency is provided by the fast interrupt request (FIRQ) which is used primarily for I/O to peripheral devices. The other interrupt type (IRQ) is used for interrupt routines that do not demand a low-latency service or where the overhead of a full context switch is small compared with the interrupt process execution time.

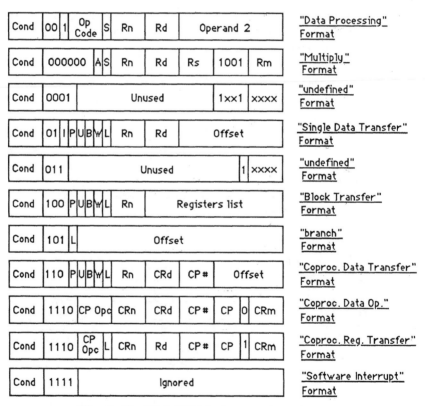

Fig.3.19 VL86C010 instruction formats.

The VL86C010 contains a large, partially overlapping set of twenty-seven 32-bit registers, although the programmer can access only 16 registers in any mode of operation. Fifteen of the registers are general-purpose ; with the remaining twelve dedicated to functions such as User Mode, FIRQ Mode, IRQ Mode, Supervisor mode and the Program Counter (PC)/Processor Status Register (PSR). Registers R0 to R13 are accessible from the user mode for any purpose. The fifteenth register, user-mode return-link register, is specific to the user mode. Its contents are mapped with those of other return-link registers as the mode is changed. The return-link register is used by the branch-and-link instruction in a procedure call sequence but may be used as a general-purpose register at other times. The least significant two bits of the processor status word (PSW) define the current mode of operation.

Seven registers are dedicated to the FIRQ mode and hide user-mode registers R8 to R14 when the fast interrupt request is being serviced. The registers R8 FIRQ to R13 FIRQ are local to the fast interrupt service routine and are used instead of the user-mode registers R10 to R13. Register R14 FIRQ holds the address used to restart the interrupted program instead of pushing it onto a stack at the expense of another memory cycle. Using a link-register helps provide very fast servicing of I/O related interrupts without disturbing the contents of the general-purpose register set although the FIRQ routine can access the R0 to R9 user-mode registers if desired. The FIRQ mode is used typically for very short interrupt service routines that might fetch and store characters in a disk or tape-controller application.

The next two registers are dedicated to the IRQ mode and hide user-mode registers R13 and R14 when the IRQ is being serviced. Once again R14 IRQ is the return-link register that holds the restart address and R13 IRQ is general-purpose and dedicated to the IRQ mode. This mode is used when the interrupt service routine will be lengthy and the overhead of saving and reloading the register set will not be a significant portion of the overall execution time.

Two registers are dedicated to the supervisor mode and overlay user-mode registers R13 and R14 when a supervisor mode switch is made using a software interrupt (SWI) instruction. Operation of these two registers is the same as previously discussed.

The last register (R15) contains the processor status word and program counter and is shared by all modes of operation. The upper six bits are processor status, the next 24 bits are the program counter (word address), and the last two indicate the mode.

The VL86C010 supports a partially overlapping register set so that when interrupts are taken, the contents of the register array do not have to be saved before new operations can begin. Improved response time is accomplished, in the case of the fast interrupt, by dedicating four general-purpose registers, in addition to a return-link register, that are only accessible in the FIRQ mode. These dedicated registers can contain all the pointers and byte-counts for simple I/O service routines thus incurring no overhead when context switching between processing and servicing interrupts at high rates. The other modes (IRQ and SUP) each have one general-purpose and one return-address (link) register dedicated to them. The general-purpose register is ideally suited for implementing a local stack for each mode. The need for dedicated registers in these modes is not as great since the time spent in an interrupt or supervisor routine is on the average much greater than the time spent in transition between the routines. The working registers can be saved and restored from stacks without significant overhead.

The VL86C010 supports five basic types of instructions, with several options available to the programmer. These instruction types are : data processing, data transfer, block data tranfer, branch, and software interrupt. All instructions contain a 4-bit conditional execution field that can cause an instruction to be skipped if the condition specified is not true. The execution time for a skipped instruction is one sequential cycle (100 ns for a 10 Mhz processor).

Data processing instructions operate only on the internal register file, and each has three operand references : a destination and two source fields. The destination (Rd) can be any of the registers including the processor status register, although some bits in R15 can only be changed in particular modes. The source operands can have two forms : both can be registers (Rm and Rn) or register (Rn) and an 8-bit immediate value. Both forms of operand specification provide for the optional shifting of one of the source values using the on-board barrel shifter. If both operands are registers, the Rm can be shifted. For the other case, it is the immediate value that can pass through the shifter. Another field in these instructions allows for the optional updating of the condition codes as a result of execution of the operation.

Data transfer instructions are used to move data between memory and the register file (load), or vice-versa (store). The effective address is calculated using the contents of the source register (Rn) plus an offset of either a 12-bit immediate value or the contents of another register (Rm). When the offset is a register it can optionally be shifted before the address calculation is made.

The offset may be added to, or subtracted from the index register Rn. Indexing can be either pre- or post- depending on the desired addressing mode. In the post-indexed mode the transfer is performed using the contents of the index register as the effective address and the index register is modified by the offset and rewritten. In the pre-indexed mode the effective address is the index register modified in the appropriate manner by the offset. The modified index register can be written back to Rn if the write-back bit is set or left unchanged if desired. When a register is used as the offset, it can be pre-scaled by the barrel shifter in a similar manner as with data processing instructions.

Data transfer instructions can manipulate bytes or words in memory. The VL86C010 supports both logical and physical address spaces at a lower level in hardware than other processors. Data transfer instructions contain a translate enable bit that allows non-user-mode programs to select the logical or physical address space as desired. The bit from the instruction is placed on the TRAN pin of the processor to signal an external memory management unit (MMU) whether to translate first or pass the address from the processor bus to the memory. This allows programs executing in the supervisor or interrupt modes to have easy access to user memory areas for page fault correction or to have bounds checking performed on dynamic data structures in the system space by the MMU. In the user mode, addresses are always translated by the MMU if it is implemented in the system.

The block data transfer instructions allow multiple registers to be moved in a single instruction. The branch instruction has two forms, branch and branch-with-link. The branch instruction causes execution to start at the current program counter plus a 24-bit offset contained in the instruction. The offset is left-shifted by two bits (forming a 26-bit address) before it is added to the program counter. Since all instructions are word-aligned, a branch can reach any location in the address space. The branch-with-link instruction copies the program counter and processor status register into R14 prior to branching to the new address. Returning from the branch-with-link simply involves reloading the program counter from R14.

The software interrupt instruction format is used primarily for supervisor service calls. Instructions operate at speeds dependent upon the options selected. The processor is able to take advantage of memories that have faster access times when accessed sequentially in the nibble or column mode.

The architecture uses a 3-stage pipeline. Due to its simplicity, the ARM architecture is a good target microprocessor for specific applications such as laser printers, embedded controllers, etc. The VLSI technology chip set includes also a memory controller (VL86C110), a video controller (VL86C310) and an I/O controller (VLC86C410). The integer unit is available in 10 and 12 Mhz versions. Another implementation, called VL86C020, designed using a CMOS 1.6 micron technology reaches 20 Mhz. A future implementation is planned for running at 32 Mhz using a 1 micron CMOS process.

3.11 THE IMS T800 TRANSPUTER ARCHITECTURE FROM INMOS

A transputer is a microprocessor with its own local memory and with links for connecting one transputer to another transputer [104].

The transputer architecture defines a family of programmable VLSI components. A typical member of the transputer product family is a single chip containing processor, memory and communication links which provide point-to-point connection between transputers. In addition, each transputer product contains special circuitry and interfaces adapting it to a particular use. For example, a peripheral control transputer, such as a graphics or disk controller, has interfaces tailored to the requirements of a specific device.

A transputer can be used in a single processor system or in networks to build high-performance concurrent systems. A network of transputers and peripheral controllers is easily constructed using point-to-point communication.

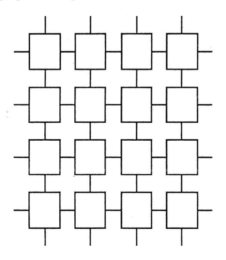

Fig.3.20 Transputer network.

The IMS T800 transputer is a 32-bit CMOS microcomputer with a 64-bit Floating-Point Unit and graphics support. It has 4 kbytes on-chip RAM for high-speed processing, a configurable memory interface and four standard INMOS communication links. The instruction set achieves efficient implementation of high-level languages and provides direct support for the OCCAM model of concurrency when using either a single transputer or a network. Procedure calls, process switching and typical interrupt latency are sub-microsecond.

The processor speed of a device can be pin-selected in stages from 17.5 Mhz up to the maximum allowed for the part. A device running at 30 Mhz achieves an instruction throughput of 30 MIPS peak and 15 MIPS sustained.

The IMS T800 provides high performance arithmetic and floating-point operations. The 64-bit Floating-Point Unit provides single and double length operation to the ANSI-IEEE 754 1985 standard for floating-point arithmetic. It is able to perform floating-point operations concurrently with the processor, sustaining a rate of 2.2 MFLOPS at a processor speed of 20 Mhz and 3.3 MFLOPS at 30 Mhz.

High performance graphics support is provided by microcoded block move instructions which operate at the speed of memory. The two-dimensional block move instructions provide for contiguous block moves as well as block copying of either non-zero or zero bytes only. Block move instructions can be used to provide graphics operations such as text manipulation, windowing, panning, scrolling and screen updating.

Cyclic redundancy checking (CRC) instructions are available for use on arbitrary length serial data streams, to provide error detection where data integrity is critical. Another feature of the IMS T800, useful for pattern recognition, is the facility to count bits set in a word.

The IMS T800 can directly access a linear address space of 4 Gbytes. The 32-bit wide memory interface uses multiplexed data and address lines and provides a data rate of up to 4 bytes every 100 nanoseconds (40 Mbytes/sec) for a 30 Mhz device. A configurable memory controller provides all timing, control and dynamic ram refresh signals for a wide variety of mixed memory systems.

System services include processor reset and bootstrap control, together with facilities for error analysis. Error signals may be daisy-chained in multi-transputer systems.

The standard INMOS communication links allow networks of transputer family products to be constructed by the direct point to point connections with no external logic. The IMS T800 links support the standard operating speed of 10 Mbits/sec, but also operate at 5 or 20 Mbits/sec. Each link can transfer data bi-directionally at up to 2.35 Mbytes/sec.

The transputer is designed to implement the OCCAM language [104], but also efficiently supports other languages such as C, Pascal and Fortran. Access to the transputer at machine level is seldom required, but is also possible if necessary.

The 32-bit processor contains instruction processing logic, instruction and work pointers, and an operand register. It directly accesses the high-speed 4 kbytes on-chip memory, which can store data or program code. Where larger amounts of memory or programs in ROM are required, the processor has access to 4 Gbytes of memory via the External Memory Interface (EMI).

The design of the transputer processor exploits the availability of fast on-chip memory by having only a small number of registers. Six registers are used in the execution of a sequential process. The small number of registers, together with the simplicity of the instruction set, enables the processor to have relatively simple (and fast) data-paths and control logic. The six registers are :

1. The workspace pointer which points to an area of store where local variables are kept.

2. The instruction pointer which points to the next instruction to be executed.

3. The operand register which is used in the formation of instruction operands.

4. The A, B and C registers which form an evaluation stack.

A, B and C are sources and destinations for most arithmetic and logical operations. Loading a value into the stack pushes B into C, and A into B, before loading A. Storing a value from A, pops B into A and C into B.

Expressions are evaluated on the evaluation stack, and instructions refer to the stack implicity. For example, the add instruction adds the top two values in the stack and places the result on the top of the stack. The use of a stack removes the need for instructions to specify the location of their operands. Statistics gathered from a large number of programs show that three registers provide an effective balance between code compactness and implementation complexity.

No hardware mechanism is provided to detect that more than three values have been loaded onto the stack. It is easy for the compiler to ensure that this never happens.

149

Any location in memory can be accessed relative to the workpointer register, enabling the workspace to be of any size.

The instruction set has been designed for simple and efficient compilation of high-level languages. All instructions have the same format, designed to give a compact representation of the operations occurring most frequently in programs.

Each instruction consists of a single byte divided into two 4-bit parts. The four most significant bits of the byte are a function code and the four least significant bits are a data value.

The representation provides for sixteen "direct" functions, each with a data value ranging from 0 to 15. The most common operations in a program are the loading of small literal values and the loading and storing of one of a small number of variables. The load constant instruction enables values between 0 and 15 to be loaded with a single byte instruction. The load local and store local instructions access locations in memory relative to the workspace pointer. The first 16 locations can be accessed using a single byte instruction.

The load non-local and store non-local instructions behave similarly, except that they access locations in memory relative to the A register. Compact sequences of these instructions allow efficient access to data structures, and provide for simple implementations of the static links or displays used in the implementation of high-level programming languages such as OCCAM, C, Fortran, Pascal or ADA.

Two more function codes allow the operand of any instruction to be extended in length : prefix and negative prefix. All instructions are executed by loading the four data bits into the least significant four bits of the operand register, which is then used as the instruction's operand. All instructions except the prefix instructions end by clearing the operand register, ready for the next instruction.

The prefix instruction loads its four data bits into the operand register and shifts the operand register up four places. The negative prefix instruction is similar, except that it complements the operand register before shifting it up. Consequently operands can be extended to any length up to the length of the operand register by a sequence of prefix instructions. In particular, operands in the range -256 to +255 can be represented using one prefix instruction.

The use of prefix instructions has certain beneficial consequences. Firstly, they are decoded and executed in the same way as every other instruction, which simplifies and speeds instruction decoding. Secondly, they simplify language compilation by providing a completely uniform way of allowing any instruction to take an operand of any size. Thirdly, they allow operands to be represented in a form independent of the processor wordlength.

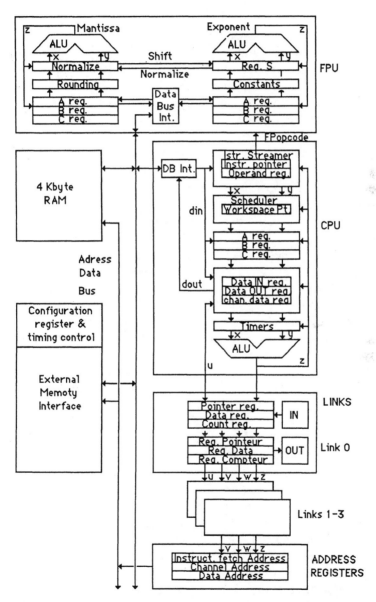

Fig.3.21 Transputer IMS T800 internal architecture.

The remaining function code, operate, causes its operand to be interpreted as an operation on the values held in the evaluation stack. This allows up to 16 such operations to be encoded in a single byte instruction. However, the prefix instructions can be used to extend the operand of an operate instruction just like any other. The instruction representation therefore provides for an indefinite number of operations.

Encoding of the indirect functions is chosen so that the most frequently occurring operations are represented without the use of a prefix instruction. These include arithmetic, logical and comparison operations such as add, exclusive or, and greater than. Less frequently occurring operations have encodings which require a single prefix operation.

Measurements show that about 70% of executed instructions are encoded in a single byte : that is, without the use of prefix instructions. Many of these instructions, such as load constant and add require just one processor cycle.

The instruction representation gives a more compact representation of high-level language programs than more conventional instruction sets. Since a program requires less store to represent it, less of the memory bandwidth is taken up with fetching instructions. Furthermore, as memory is word accessed the processor will receive four instructions for every fetch.

Short instructions also improve the effectiveness of instruction prefetch, which in turn improves processor performance. There is an extra word of prefetch buffer, so the processor rarely has to wait for an instruction fetch before proceeding. Since the buffer is short, there is little time penalty when a jump instruction causes the buffer contents to be discarded.

The instruction set includes process and concurrency support and a microcoded scheduler which enables any number of concurrent processes to be executed together, sharing the processor time.

Communication between processes is achieved by means of channels. Process communication is point-to-point, synchronized and unbuffered. As a result, a channel needs no process queue, no message queue and no message buffer.

Four identical INMOS bi-directional serial links provide synchronized communication between processors and with the outside world. Each link comprises an input channel and output channel. A link between two transputers is implemented by connecting a link interface on one transputer to a link interface on the other transputer. Every byte of data sent on a link is acknowledged on the input of the same link, thus each signal line carries both data and control information.

The quiescent state of a link output is low. Each data byte is transmitted as a high start bit followed by a high bit followed by eight data bits followed by a low stop bit. The least significant bit of data is transmitted first. After transmitting a data byte, the sender waits for the acknowledge, which consists of a high start bit followed by a zero bit. The acknowledge signifies both that a process was able to receive the acknowledge data byte only after the acknowledge for the final byte of the message has been received.

The IMS T800 links allow an acknowledge packet to be sent before the data packet has been fully received. The IMS T800 links support the standard INMOS communication speed of 10 Mbits/sec. In addition they can be used at 5 or 20 Mbits/sec.

The transputer has two 32-bit time clocks which "tick" periodically. The timers provide accurate process timing, allowing processes to deschedule themselves until a specific time.

The 64-bit FPU provides single- and double-length arithmetic to floating-point standard ANSI-IEEE 754-1985. It is able to perform floating-point operations concurrently with the central processor unit (CPU), sustaining in excess of 3.3 MFLOPS on a 30 Mhz device. All data communication between memory and the FPU occurs under control of the CPU.

The FPU consists of a microcoded computing engine with a three deep floating-point evaluation stack for manipulation of floating-point numbers. These stack registers are FA, FB and FC, each of which can hold either 32-bit or 64-bit data ; an associated flag, set when a floating-point value is loaded, indicates which. The stack behaves in a similar manner to the CPU stack.

The IMS T800 has 4 kbytes of fast internal static memory for high rates of data throughput. Each internal memory access takes one processor cycle. The transputer can also access 4 Gbytes of external memory space. Internal and External memory are part of the same linear address space. IMS T800 memory is byte addressed, with words aligned on four-byte boundaries. The least significant byte of a word is the lowest addessed byte.

Even if the transputer is not a pure RISC architecture, some of its original features take advantages of the RISC design methodology. As an example, the control is microcoded but the most frequent instructions are direct-instructions that execute in a single machine cycle.

3.12 OTHER RISC PROCESSORS

The RISC methodology has provided opportunities for new market entrants and resulted in major changes in industry structure. In addition to the processors described in the previous sections, many other companies have designed and introduced their own RISC architecture. In 1983, Ridge Computer Inc. released the RISC 32C, one of the first RISC systems to be actively promoted as such [105]. A few months later, Pyramid Technology Corporation followed with the announcement of its 90X [106]. In January 1986, IBM Corporation introduced the RT-PC, its first-generation 32-bit RISC architecture. A few weeks after the IBM RISC-based personal workstation, Hewlett Packard Corporation introduced the "Spectrum" architecture [107]. More recently, Hewlett Packard introduced its new generation "Precision" architecture [108]. Some other companies have rather designed dedicated architectures for specific application domains, like the Forth RISC chip from Novix [109] or the KIM20 symbolic processor from Sodima [110]. The latter will be described more precisely in the next chapter. However, before describing KIM20 in detail, the next sections give a complete set of comparison tables including the most important technical features, performance evaluations and application domains.

3.13 RISC ARCHITECTURE COMPARISON

3.13.1   CONFIGURATIONS

This section gives a synthesis of all architectures described in this book.

PROCESSOR	DEVELOPER	TECHNOLOGY
IBM801	IBM	MECL10K MSI board
RISC-I	U.C. Berkeley	VLSI NMOS 2μ
RISC-II	U.C. Berkeley	VLSI NMOS 2μ
SOAR	U.C. Berkeley	VLSI NMOS 4μ
SPUR	U.C. Berkeley	CMOS 2μ chip set
MIPS	Stanford University	VLSI NMOS 2μ
MIPS-X	Stanford University	VLIS CMOS 2μ
McD GaAs	Mc Donnell Douglas	GaAs VLSI E-JFET chip set
CDC GaAs	Control Data & Texas Inst.	GaAs HILL VLSI chip set
RCA GaAs	RCA	GaAs ED-MESFET
KIM200	SODIMA (F)	0,5μ CMOS
SPARC Sunrise	Fujitsu / SUN	CMOS 1,5μ gate array
SPARC 7C600	Cypress	CMOS 0,8μ custom
SPARC BIT	Bipolar Integrated Tech.	ECL
GaAs SPARC	Prisma	GaAs MSI board
KAP SPARC	Solbourne	CMOS VLSI chip
R2000	Mips Computer Syst.	CPU + FPU CMOS VLSIs
R3000	Mips Computer Syst.	CPU + FPU CMOS VLSIs
R4000	Mips Computer Syst.	CPU + FPU CMOS VLSIs
R6000	Mips Computer Syst.	CPU + FPU ECL VLSIs
AM29000	Advanced Micro Devices	1,2μ CMOS VLSI chip set
MC88000	Motorola	CPU/FPU + cache/MMU CMOS VLSIs
80960 K	Intel	1,5μ CMOS VLSI
80960 CA	Intel	1μ CMOS VLSI
i860	Intel	1μ CMOS VLSI
C100	Fairchild	CMOS VLSI microboard
C300	Fairchild/Intergraph	CMOS VLSI microboard
C400	Intergraph	1μ CMOS VLSI microboard
ROMP	IBM	1,8μ VLSIs
POWER	IBM	CMOS VLSIs
ARM VL86C010	VLSI Technology	2μ CMOS chip set
ARM VL86C020	VLSI Technology	1μ CMOS chip set
IMS T400	Inmos (GB)	CMOS VLSI
IMS T800	Inmos (GB)	CMOS VLSI
PRECISION	Hewlett Packard	1,5μ CMOS VLSI
WHESTONE I & II	Integrated Digital Prod.	ECL VLSIs

FAIM-I	Schlumberger (CA)	CMOS VLSI chip set
DRAGON	Xerox PARC	2μ CMOS VLSI chip set
RISC 32C	Ridge Computer	STTL & MOS VLSIs
90X	Pyramid Technology	STTL board
CRISP	AT & T	CMOS VLSI
NOVIX	NOVIX (US)	CMOS VLSI
KIM10	SODIMA (F)	Fast CMOS MSI board
KIM20	SODIMA (F)	1,5μ CMOS VLSI

3.13.2 ARCHITECTURAL FEATURES

This section gives a comparison of all major technical features of the RISC architectures described in the book.

PROCESSOR	CONTROL	GENERAL PURPOSE REGISTERS	WINDOWS	HARVARD	MULTIPLE UNIT
IBM 801	hardwired	32	no	yes	no
RISC-I	hardwired	(4+6+4)*6	yes	no	no
RISC-II	hardwired	(6+10+6)*8	yes	no	no
SOAR	hardwired	(8+8+8)*4	yes	no	no
SPUR	hardwired	(6+10+6)*8	yes	no	IU+FPU
MIPS	hardwired	16	no	no	no
MIPS-X	hardwired	32	no	no	coprocessors
MCDD GaAs	hardwired	16	no	no	IU+FPU
CDD GaAs	hardwired	16+16	no	no	IU+FPU
RCA GaAs	hardwired	16	no	no	1
KIM200	hardwired	32	no	no	coprocessors
SPARC Sunrise	hardwired	(8+8+8)*7	yes	no	coprocessors
SPARC 7C600	hardwired	(8+8+8)*8	yes	no	coprocessors
SPARC BIT	hardwired	?	yes	no	coprocessors
GaAs SPARC	hardwired	?	yes	no	?
SPARC KAP	hardwired	?	yes	yes	IU+FPU
R2000	hardwired	32+2	no	no	2
R3000	hardwired	32+2	no	no	2
R4000	hardwired	32+2	no	no	2
R6000	hardwired	32+2	no	no	2
AM 29000	hardwired	192	all modes	yes	2
MC 88000	hardwired	32+32	no	yes	2 to 8 units
80960 K	hardwired core + μprog.	32	register cache	no	CPU + FPU
80960 CA	hardwired	32	register cache	no	superscalar 3 units

i860	hardwired	32+32	no	yes	IU+FP adder+ FP multiplier
C100	hardwired + macros	32+8	no	yes	IU+FPU
C300	hardwired	32+8	no	yes	IU+FPU
C400	hardwired	32+8	no	yes	IU+FPU
ROMP	hardwired + μcode	16+10	no	no	IU+FPU
POWER	?	32+5	no	yes	IU+FPU + branch
ARM VL86C010	hardwired	27	no	no	no
ARM VL86C020	hardwired	27	no	no	no
IMS T400	μprogr.	6	no	no	no
IMS T800	μprogr.	6	no	no	IU+FPU
PRECISION	PLA+ μcode	32	no		
WHESTONE I & II	hardwired + μcode	4	no	?	?
FAIM-I	state machine	?	no	?	?
DRAGON	PLA	?	?	?	IU+FPU
RISC 32C	μprog.	16	?	?	IU + FPU
90X	μprog.	16*64	yes	?	?
CRISP	?	32	no	?	?
NOVIX	?				forth processor
KIM10	hardwired	(4+8+4)*4	yes	yes	no
KIM20	hardwired	(6+10+6)*8 +4	yes	yes	symbolic coprocessor

PROCESSOR	INSTRUC.	FORMATS	DELAYED BRANCH	LOAD/ STORE	PIPE STAGES
IBM 801	120	2	no	yes	2
RISC-I	31	2	yes	yes	2
RISC-II	39	2	yes	yes	3
SOAR	20	2	yes	yes	3
SPUR	38+25	?	yes	yes	4
MIPS	31	5	yes	yes	5
MIPS-X	40	4	yes	yes	5
MCDD GaAs	<64	1	yes	yes	4
CDD GaAs	29+37	?	yes	yes	6
RCA GaAs	<64	4	yes	yes	5
KIM200	16	2	yes	yes	4
SPARC Sunrise	55+13	6	yes	yes	4
SPARC 7C600	55+13	6	yes	yes	4
SPARC BIT	55+13	6	yes	yes	?

GaAs SPARC	55+13	6	yes	yes	?
SPARC KAP	55+13	6	yes	yes	?
R2000	74	3	yes	yes	5
R3000	74	3	yes	yes	5
R4000	74	3	yes	yes	
R6000	74	3	yes	yes	
AM 29000	112	1	yes	yes	4
MC 88000	51	?	yes	yes	4
80960 K	51+133	4	?	yes	3
80960 CA	51+133	4	?	yes	3
i860	76	?	yes	yes	
C100	101+67	15	?	yes	3
C300	101+67	15	?	yes	3
C400	?	?	yes	yes	?
ROMP	112	?	yes	yes	3
POWER	184	?	no	no	?
ARM VL86C010	44	11	yes	yes	3
ARM VL86C020	44	11	yes	yes	3
IMS T400	162	1	no	yes	?
IMS T800	162	1	no	yes	?
PRECISION	140		yes	yes	5
WHESTONE I & II	181	?	?	?	3
FAIM-I	64	?	yes	?	2
DRAGON	≈150	?	no	?	?
RISC 32C	170	?	no	yes	4
90X	90	?	yes	yes	3
CRISP	33	?	no	?	?
KIM10	32	1	yes	yes	3
KIM20	32	1	yes	yes	3

3.13.3 PERFORMANCE

This section gives various performance comparisons based on the information given by the developers.

PROCESSOR	TRANSISTOR (x 100)	CYCLE TIME (ns)	CPI	MIPS	MFLOPS
IBM 801	?	?	1,1	?	-
RISC-I	44,5	667	1,4	≈ 1	-
RISC-II	41	330	1,4	≈ 2	-
SOAR	35	360	1,4	≈ 2	-
SPUR	?	150	1,4	≈ 5	-

MIPS	25	250	1,4	8	-
MIPS-X	150	50	1,4	10	-
MCDD GaAs	41	10	?	100 peak	-
CDD GaAs	60	5	2,2	91	-
RCA GaAs	?	5	?	91	-
KIM200	50	5	1,4	100 peak	-
SPARC Sunrise	50	60	1,4	10	?
SPARC 7C600	?	25	1,6	20	?
SPARC BIT	?	?	?	?	?
GaAs SPARC	?	?	?	?	?
SPARC KAP	1000	25	?	40	20
R2000	100	60	1,4	12	?
R3000	115	40	1,25	16	4bp
R4000	1100	20	?	50	?
R6000	?	15	?	55	10,3bp
AM 29000	?	40	1,5	12	?
MC 88100	165	40	1,25	17	7bp
80960 K	350	50	2,7	7,5	?
80960 CA	575	30	?	25	?
i860	>1000	25	?	32	80sp
C100	?	30	6,7	4,9	?
C300	?	?	?	?	?
C400	160	20	0,9	50	21
ROMP	111	170	?	2	?
POWER	?	?	?		
ARM VL86C010	25	83	2	4	-
ARM VL86C020	?	50	?	?	?
IMS T400	?	50	1-48	10	-
IMS T800	200	33	1-48	15	3.3sp
PRECISION	115	33	?	?	?
WHESTONE I & II	?	50	?	5-13	?
FAIM-I	?	?	?	?	?
DRAGON	?	100	?	?	?
RISC 32C	?	125	?	1-4	?
90X	?	125	?	2-4	?
CRISP	172	62	?	10	?
KIM10	53	100	1,1	8	-
KIM20	53	62	1,2	10	-

3.13.4 APPLICATION FIELDS

For each RISC architecture, this section gives information about its application field.

PROCESSOR	COMMERCIAL PRODUCT	MICRO CONTROLLER	WORKSTATION	APPLICATION FIELD
IBM 801	no	+	-	GP
RISC-I	no	-	+	GP
RISC-II	no	-	+	GP
SOAR	no	-	+	AI
SPUR	no	-	+	AI
MIPS	no	-	+	GP
MIPS-X	no	-	+	GP
MCDD GaAs	no	-	+	GP
CDD GaAs	no	-	+	GP
RCA GaAs	no	-	+	GP
KIM200	yes	+	+	GP/FT
SPARC Sunrise	yes	+	+	GP
SPARC 7C600	yes	+	+	GP
SPARC BIT	yes	-	+	GP
GaAs SPARC	yes	-	+	GP
SPARC KAP	yes	-	+	GP
R2000	yes	+	+	GP
R3000	yes	+	+	GP
R4000	yes	-	+	GP
R6000	yes	-	+	GP
AM 29000	yes	+	-	GP
MC 88100	yes	+	+	GP
80960 K	yes	+	-	MC
80960 CA	yes	+	-	MC
i860	yes	-	+	Graphics
C100	yes	-	+	GP
C300	yes	-	+	GP
C400	yes	-	+	GP
ROMP	yes	-	+	GP
POWER	yes	-	+	GP
ARM VL86C010	yes	+	-	MC
ARM VL86C020	yes	+	-	MC
IMS T400	yes	+	+	DS
IMS T800	yes	+	+	DS
PRECISION	yes	-	+	GP
WHESTONE I & II	yes	-	+	GP

FAIM-I	n o	-	+	A I
DRAGON	n o	-	+	GP
RISC 32C	yes	-	+	GP
90X	yes	-	+	GP
CRISP	?	-	+	GP
KIM10	n o	+	-	A I
KIM20	yes	+	-	A I

GP = General Purpose   MC = Micro Controller
DS = Distributed Systems   AI = Artificial Intelligence
FT = Fault Tolerance

4

An example :
the KIM20 microprocessor

4.1 A RISC ARCHITECTURE FOR ARTIFICIAL INTELLIGENCE

4.1.1 THE AIM OF THE KIM PROJECT

As an example of a typical RISC architecture, this chapter describes more precisely the KIM20 microprocessor designed for efficient execution of symbolic processing.

Classical computing is efficient in applications for which numerical and algorithmic solutions are known. On the other hand, Artificial Intelligence is a part of Computer Science whose purpose is to solve problems traditionally considered to require a human-like behaviour. However, it is well known that conventional Von Neumann architectures ar not well suited for Symbolic Processing. By symbolic processing we mean the ability of a computer to manipulate symbols, which are used to represent knowledge in an abstract way, rather than simple numbers.

In this framework, various symbolic processing languages appeared in the last decade, such as Lisp, Prolog and Smalltalk. Studies of Artificial Intelligence programming show that most of these languages rely upon the same primitive tools, but these primitives are not very well suited for execution on a conventional computer. One way to gain speedup is to design hardware supports for them, focusing on the time-consuming operations.

According to that scheme, many Artificial Intelligence workstations have been designed : the Symbolics 3600 family [111], the Lambda machines [112], the Texas Instruments Explorers [113], and MAIA in France [114]. Most of these machines are inspired from the original Lisp machine, called CADR [115], which was developed at the MIT's A.I. Laboratory in 1978. They represent the first generation of symbolic processing computers, designed primarily for research, and mainly based on a mono-microcode processor.

Recent technological progress in circuit integration (VLSI Very Large Scale Integration), and the introduction of the RISC concept, now make possible the design of a new wave of symbolic processing systems. Examples of such projects are the SOAR chip (Smalltalk On A Risc), the SPUR workstation (Symbolic Processing Using RISC), the PEARLS project in France (Processeur Experimental Adapté à la Recherche sur les Langages Symboliques [116]). These new machines are all based on a multiprocessor "tagged-RISC" model.

In such a framework, the KIM20 architecture was designed in order to provide a custom symbolic microprocessor well-suited for a large range of Artificial Intelligence applications. Two key principles motivated the architecture of the machine :

1.   The specification of a virtual execution-oriented machine.
2.   A pure RISC approach.

The main idea was to design a reduced core of instructions that capture the fundamental primitives of symbolic processing, and to implement them directly into hardware. To meet this challenge, the KIM (Knowledge-base Integrated Machine) virtual machine was specified, consisting of an architectural model and a reduced and homogeneous set of instructions. Major part of this work was done during 1985 under the auspice of the HECATE project at the Perception System Laboratory of the ETCA (Etablissement Technique Central de l'Armement French Defense). During 1987, this virtual machine was tested in the execution of the KOS realtime executive [117], and validated on one hardware prototype using standard logic technology [118] (called KIM10). During 1988, the KIM machine was implemented on a single VLSI chip [119] (called KIM20).

4.1.2 SYMBOLIC PROCESSING REQUIREMENTS

In this section, we focus onto the four main obstacles to fast symbolic computation on conventional computers :

fast list processing,

procedure calls and returns,
dynamic type checking,
memory management.

The first fundamental requirement for an efficient execution of
Artificial Intelligence languages is the list and tree manipulation.
Even the simplest Common-Lisp primitives (i.e. car, cdr) require
approximately ten instructions with a 68000-like implementation.
M.F. Deering performed experimental measures to compare Lisp
systems on different processor instruction sets [120]. The next
table, as a representative sample, shows the timing results for a
simple Lisp function :

(defun foo (x) (+(car x)(cdr x)))

PROCESSOR	EXECUTION TIME
VAX	53.8 µs
68000	65.2 µs
68020	16.1 µs
CADR	19.0 µs
3600	6.4 µs

Fig.4.1 Timing results for a simple Lisp function.

Because of the recursive and modular nature of most Artificial
Intelligence languages, many more "call" and "return" operations
are executed than in other languages. For example, any application
written in Lisp spends more than 20% of the run-time on such
tasks, and it comes to nearly 50% for many Smalltalk
implementations. In addition to being frequent, these operations
are generally expensive, because of local variable-saving and
restoring, argument-passing, and recomputation of most call
destinations from the type of operands.

Efficient Artificial Intelligence program executions depend also
on dynamic type checking and generic operations. Most Artificial
Intelligence languages, like Lisp, use polymorphic functions, where
the operand types vary and are not known until run-time. A
polymorphic operator is defined to operate on arguments of more
than one type (i.e. an addition on binary words, small integers, long
integers, big numbers, floating-point values ...). Some languages
emphasize this problem by checking data-types at run-time, rather
than variable-types. Run-time data-type checking is one of the

most important features of symbolic programming, but as opposed to compilation-time type-checking, it is more CPU time-consuming.

The last important point which is emphasized in this paper is the need for fast dynamic creation and suppression of objects. As symbolic processing addresses complex applications, it requires an extensive amount of memory space with efficient reclamation algorithms garbage collection. In addition to the dynamic aspect, the low level of the locality property in Artificial Intelligence programs complicates the problem of storage management.

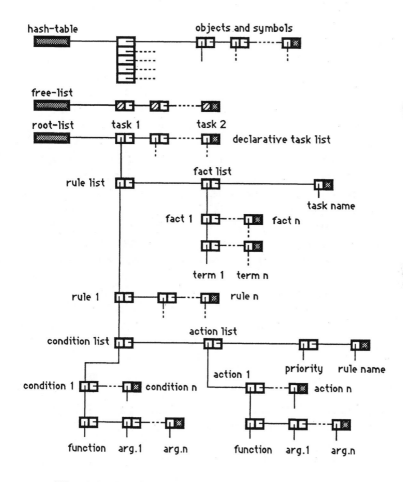

Fig.4.2 Example of a typical AI data structure.

4.1.3 EARLIER LISP MACHINES

All available Artificial Intelligence workstations, such as the Symbolics 3600 and the Explorers, are based on the original Von Neumann model with some architectural improvements related to the four critical points previously discussed. Roughly speaking, their common characteristics are :

1. Mono-microcoded processor.
2. Stack oriented.
3. Tagged architecture.
4. Paging virtual memory.

First, a microprogrammed processor allows designers to microcode time-consuming operations. Examples of such critical tasks are the garbage collector, and the evaluator itself. Using this technique, speedups are quite good, but in fact, due to the difficulty in coding and debuging microprograms, only a macro-code level is available for users, which looks like a more conventional assembly language. Beyond the increase in performance, microcoding provides a flexible interface between the hardware and the high-level language. The drawback is that multiple programming levels imply multiple execution levels that potentially reduce the efficiency. In most cases, the high-level language is compiled into macro-codes, which are converted as microcode sequences, and then decoded to produce hardware control words.

The second important requirement is to make function calls and returns as fast as possible. Such processors contain multiple stacks and buffers to solve this problem. For example, a given computation on a 3600 is always associated with a particular stack group, which has three components :

1. A control stack which contains the control and local environments, the caller list ; this stack is formatted into frames that correspond to function calls.

2. A binding stack which contains special variables and Lambda bindings.

3. A data stack for temporary objects such as arrays and lists.

These kinds of computer are not pure stack machines, but rather stack-oriented. This means that most of instructions use the stack in getting operands and storing the results.

The next improvement corresponds to the so-called "tagged architecture". Semantic information is attached to each memory word, by means of an additional bit-field called the "tag". Directly associating data-types with data-objects is the basic technique for implementing fast run-time data-type checking. Tag checking, in microprogrammed processors, is performed in parallel with arithmetic operations. It basically assumes that most operands are integers. For example, an ADD instruction causes the 3600's processor to perform the following operations :

1. Fetch the operands from the stack.

2. Check the data-type fields with a simple hardware automaton, and in parallel perform the operation on the ALU (Arithmetic and Logical Unit), assuming that operands are small integers.

3. If both operands are integers, the operation completes normally ; otherwise, the processor traps to a microcoded task which determines the types of operands, and performs the appropriate operation.

4. Check for overflow, upon which trap to microcode to return a "bignum" result.

5. Tag the result with the proper data-type.

6. Push the result onto the stack.

7. Dispatch to the microcode for the next instruction.

The last point is the need for dynamical management of a large memory space. All Artificial Intelligence workstations actually use paging virtual memory with an "ephemeral" reclamation algorithm [121]. Some of them rely only upon microprogramming and tagging, to gain efficiency (Explorers, etc.), other ones (Symbolics 3600, MAIA) provide hardware support to gain more efficiency.

4.1.4 THE KIM20 MICROPROCESSOR

As we mentioned in the previous section, most Artificial Intelligence machines are based on a stack-oriented microcoded architecture.

In contrast, KIM is a pure register machine which inherits work on "overlapped register windows" from the original RISC-II and SOAR project. This mechanism allows KIM to execute call and return operations in a single cycle, including context saving/restoring and argument/result passing. In addition to this window mechanism, the instruction set includes all basic operations for an efficient execution of list processing and dynamic type-checking required by symbolic computing. No microcode is used, hardwired control and direct implementation of operations in hardware are the key points of the design. KIM's instruction set is composed of 32 instructions, which manipulate three operands (two source and a destination).

They can be listed in four categories :

1.   Arithmetic and logical operations, with special support for dynamic type-checking.

2.   List processing operations, including CAR, CDR, RPLACA, RPLACD, CONS Lisp-like primitives and special hardware support for the reclamation algorithm (garbage collector).

3.   Control flow operations, including fast call and return operations which take advantage of the overlapped register windows.

4.   Special memory accesses like Last-In First-Out stack, etc.

KIM20 is based on a full Harvard architecture to achieve the execution of one instruction per machine cycle. All operations are encoded in a single instruction format. Like RISC-II, KIM20 is based on a regular 3-stage pipeline, where the first cycle fetches the instruction, the second cycle fetches operands and computes the appropriate operation, and the last one writes back the result into a register. Unlike previous RISC machines, only one instruction needs to include a no-operation in the instruction stream, to prevent breaks in the execution pipeline. This instruction, called cond, verifies a specified condition and a false result dynamically cancels the execution of the next instruction. This simple mechanism makes all instructions conditional in two cycles (i.e. cond-jump, cond-call, cond-xxx sequences). In the same meaning, call and jump instructions accept only an immediate address, to be able to compute the destination address before the end of the first pipeline stage.

Two main formats are available for data encoding : a classical 32-bit signed integer and a 32-bit tagged cell. The latter is composed of three fields. The first one encodes in two bits the remainder of the current list, using the CDR-code technique. The second field includes two special bits for the garbage collection algorithm and four bits for the object's type. These three fields form the 8-bit tag of each cell. The last 24 bits are used to encode an immediate value, a reference or a classical CAR pointer. Tagging data and the multiway branch are the basic mechanisms which allow fast execution of polymorphic functions needed by symbolic processing.

The preliminary version of the processor was designed on a Mentor Graphics system using Fast MSI CMOS parts. The resulting board was a triple height and full depth Eurocard (366.66 by 400 mm) including more than 400 standard chips. Then, we designed the first VLSI version using the NEC standard cell CMOS 1.2 micron technology with a Valid system and a Hilo-3 simulator. The implementation of the register windows requires a high speed dual-access memory of 128 16-bit words. Since these memories are in the main critical path of the microprocessor, the samples received were not totally functional due to technological problems. Thus, we decided to design a second version of the chip using the ES2 CMOS 1.5 micron technology and the Solo 2000 software environment. The use of a RAM compiler enables us to optimize the required memory and adjust its performance/consumption ratio. The resulting chip was functional with a performance improvement of 100% compared to NEC simulation results. The KIM20 microprocessor was then produced using a 176 pins PGA package. The complexity of the chip is approximately 17000 equivalent gates routed in a 1 cm square die. Notice that, the ES2 1.5 micron version was more efficient and smaller than the NEC 1.2 micron version. This shows that a good technology is important, but software development tools are also crucial.

4.2   THE PROGRAMMING MODEL

4.2.1 INTRODUCTION

This section gives a description of the KIM20 from the programmer point of view. It describes the programming model, the instruction format and the data format.

The processor architecture is based on two separate 32-bit buses. The first one is connected to the code memory, and the second one is connected to the data memory. A 24-bit bus addresses the code memory containing the instruction words, allowing a memory space up to 64 Mbytes. A 24-bit bus addresses the data memory containing the cells, allowing a memory space up to 64 Mbytes. This structure allows simultaneous instruction and data transfers. With a 10 Mhz internal clock, the maximum transfer rate is 80 Mbytes per second.

4.2.2 THE INSTRUCTION FORMAT

The KIM20 instructions are coded on a 32-bit word, in a unique format. The use of only one format makes it very easy to design the Instruction Decoding Unit.

The following figure gives the format of the instructions.

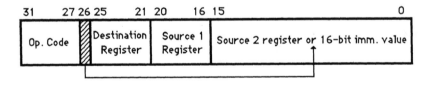

Instruction   Rd,S1,[#]S2

Fig.4.3 KIM20 single instruction format.

4.2.3   THE DATA FORMAT

The KIM20 manipulates two different types of objects coded on a 32-bit word. The first kind of object is called a "CELL" (tagged cell) and the second one is a 32-bit numerical value (signed integer).

A cell is composed of two fields, which allow a homogeneous and compact coding of lists and trees. The general format of a cell is given by the following figure.

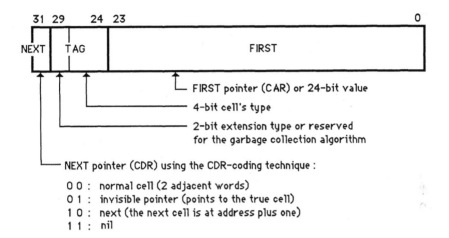

Fig.4.4 KIM20 cell format.

The "TAG" field (bits 24 to 31) is composed of 4 smaller fields, which can be written independently.

* The "CDR-code" field or "NEXT" field (bit 30 & 31)

   Theoretically, it represents the address of the next element in the list. The KIM20 processor takes advantage, of the CDR-coding technique to optimize the use of data memory. The "NEXT" field is only two bits wide, instead of the 24 bits usually required. Statistics measures have shown that 2 bits were enough in 61.3% of occurrences (53.7% to 75.8% depending on the application) but with a good linearizing algorithm during garbage collection, this success rate reaches 97%.

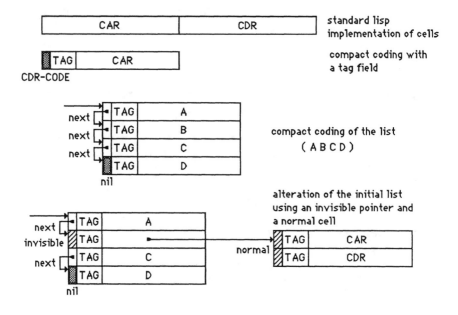

Fig.4.5 List encoding techniques.

The "NEXT" field built in "active-low-logic" uses the following values.

Value 3: CDR-NIL : The pointer to the next element in the list, is the NIL pointer. It indicates that the current cell is the last one of the list.

Value 2: CDR-NEXT : This value indicates that the following cell in the current list is located in the next memory word, in the adjoining cell.

Value 1: CDR-CELL : This value indicates that the current cell is coded on two adjacent 32-bit words. The location of the "NEXT" and "FIRST" fields belongs to the programmer.

Value 0: CDR-INVISIBLE : This value indicates that the address of the next cell is located in the "FIRST" field. This configuration is called the invisible pointer.

• The "MARK1" and "MARK2" bits (bit 29 and bit 28)

This bit does not have any special use. It can be undefined, used for the garbage collection algorithm, or as a type extention.

- The "TYPE" field (bits 27 to 24)

    This 4-bit field specifies the type of the element pointed to by the "FIRST" field of the cell. This field allows us to code 16 different object types.

- The "FIRST" field

    The "FIRST" field of a cell is composed of 24 bits (bit 23 to 0) and represents the address of the first element in the list.

A numerical value is a value coded on a 32 bit word without any "TAG" field. Its type is given by the cell that is pointing to it. Generally, data of the same type will be grouped in dedicated memory spaces, to optimize the memory management.

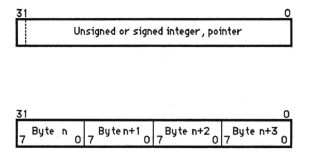

Fig.4.6 KIM20 numerical value and character formats.

4.2.4 REGISTER WINDOWS

The programming model of the KIM20 processor is composed of 138 registers organized as a circular buffer of overlapped register windows. At any time during processing, 32 registers can be accessed.

A group of 10 registers is dedicated to global data, and can always be accessed. Five of them are dedicated to special use which will be described in the following sections.

173

The 22 other registers belong to the current window associated with the executing procedure. The KIM20 processor includes 8 windows of this kind, partially overlapped, and organized as a circular buffer.

A window is composed of 22 registers of 32 bits. The first 6 registers (R0 to R5) and the last 6 (R16 to R21) are used for parameter and result passing. The 10 registers in between (R6 to R15) are reserved to deal with the current procedure local variables.

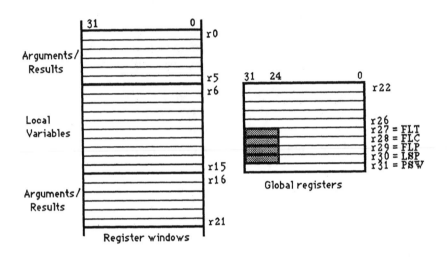

Fig.4.7 KIM20 register windows.

Two special fields of the Status-Word (SW) point out the current window (Window-Pointer : WP) and the first occupied window (Window-Overflow : WO).

During an instruction "CALL", the Window-Pointer (WP) is automatically incremented, thus passing the parameters, saving the local variables, and allocating a new working context. In such a case, if the Window-Pointer (WP) becomes equal to the Window-Overflow limit (WO), a window overflow exception occurs.

During an instruction "RETURN", the Window-Pointer (WP) is automatically decremented, returning the results, and restoring the previous context. Before decrementing, if the Window-Pointer (WP) is equal to the Window-Overflow limit (WO), a window underflow exception occurs.

During any overflow or underflow processing, saving or restoring of the different window registers has to be done by the exception handling software.

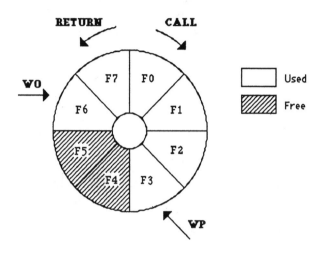

Fig.4.8 KIM20 window management.

4.2.5 GLOBAL REGISTERS

A group of 10 registers is dedicated to global data, and can always be accessed. Among these 10 registers, only 5 can be used for general purposes (R22 to R26).

The five others are dedicated to special tasks. They are the following :

• FLT Register (Free-List-Threshold)

The global register R27 is called FLT (Free-List-Treshold) and contains the minimum value at which the "STARVATION" exception will be generated.

During the execution of the instruction "NEW", if the value of FLT is greater or equal to the current value of FLC (Free-List-Counter), a STARVATION exception is generated. FLT is a 24-bit read/write register.

- FLC Register (Free-List-Counter)

  The global register R28 is called FLC (Free-List-Counter) and contains the current number of free cells, chained in the current Free-List. It is automatically updated during the execution of "NEW" and "FREE" instructions.

During execution of the instruction "NEW", if the value of FLT is greater or equal to the current value of FLC (Free-List-Counter), a STARVATION exception is generated. FLC is a 24-bit read/write register.

- FLP Register (Free-List-Pointer)

The global register R29 is called FLP (Free-List-Pointer) and contains the address of the first cell of the Free-List. It is automatically updated during the execution "NEW" and "FREE" instructions. FLP is a 24-bit read/write register.

- SP Register (Stack-Pointer)

  The global register R30 is called SP (Stack-Pointer) and contains the address of the top of a LIFO stack mapped in the data memory.

During the execution of instruction "PUSH" this register is automatically incremented before the memory access. If the lowest byte of this pointer becomes equal to the hexadecimal value "FF", a stack overflow is generated.
  During the execution of instruction "POP" this register is automatically decremented after the memory access. If the lowest byte of this pointer is equal to the hexadecimal value "FF", a stack underflow is generated. SP is a 24-bit read/write register.

4.2.6 THE STATUS WORD

The global register R29 is the Status-Word (SW) of the KIM20 processor.
  The Status-Word is divided into the following specific fields :

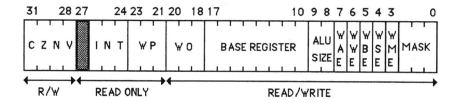

Fig.4.9 KIM20 status word.

- Underflow / Overflow bit (bit 27)

  This bit can only be read, but not written. It specifies, in cases of stack or window exceptions, whether there has been an overflow or an underflow. During a CDR-ESCAPE exception it tells whether the trap occurred during an instruction "NEXT" or "SETN".

- Exception bits (bits 26 to 24)

  This 3-bit field can only be read, but not written. It specifies, the level of the exception or interrupt being processed. Otherwise, it contains zero.

- The Window-Pointer (WP) (bits 23 to 21)

  This 3-bit field can only be read, but not written. It holds the current register window number. It is automatically updated by any "switching" instructions (CALL, RETURN, RETE).

- The Window-Overflow (WO) (bits 20 to 18)

  This 3-bit field can be written or read. It contains the number of the first window in use, which hasn't been yet saved in memory. During the "CALL" and "RETURN" instructions, it is compared to WP to prevent window overflow and underflow. It has to be updated by the software exception handling procedure. This mechanism implements a procedure saving and restoring part of the register window.

- The base register (bits 17 to 10)

  This 8-bit field can be written or read. Because the code memory addressing capabilities are divided into 256 pages of

64 Kwords of 32 bits, this field contains the number of the current page from where the instruction is fetched. There are two possibilities to perform a page change, the first one is to change this field with a write operation, the second one is performed by the "RETURN" instruction which automatically restores the page number saved during the corresponding "CALL" instruction.

- The ALU-SIZE (bits 8 &9)

  This 2-bit field can be written and read. It determines the virtual size of operands, used to compute the ALU code condition bits (bits 31 to 28 of the Status-Word).
  The meaning of the different values are : **0** (32-bit integer), **1** (24-bit integer), **2** (16-bit integer), **3** (8-bit integer). This field is cleared upon reset.

- The WAE bit (bit 7) "Write ALU Enable bit"

  This bit will be cleared every time it is read, and cannot be set. However to allow a write operation on the ALU-bit field (bits 31 to 28), you simultaneously have to attempt to set this bit.

- The WWE bit (bit 6) "Write WO Enable bit"

  This bit will be cleared every time it is read, and cannot be set. However to allow a write operation on the Window-Overflow field (bits 20 to 18), you simultaneously have to attempt to set this bit.

- The WBE bit (bit 5) "Write Base-register Enable bit"

  This bit will be cleared every time it is read, and cannot be set. However to allow a write operation on the Base-Register field (bits 17 to 10), you simultaneously have to attempt to set this bit.

- The WSE bit (bit 4) "Write ALU-Size Enable bit"

  This bit will be cleared every time it is read, and it cannot be set. However to allow a write operation on the ALU-SIZE field (bits 9 & 8), you simultaneously have to attempt to set this bit.

- The WME bit (bit 3) "Write Mask Enable bit"

  This bit will be cleared every time it is read, and cannot be set. However to allow a write operation on the MASK field (bits 2 to 0), you simultaneously have to attempt to set this bit.

- The MASK field (bit 2 to 0)

  This 2-bit field can be written and read. It specifies the level over which exceptions and interrupts are disabled and discarded (for more details refer to section 4.2.8).

- ALU-code condition bits (bits 31 to 28)

  This 4 bit field can be written or read and gives, after each instruction, the condition codes resulting from the latest Arithmetic & Logic instruction.

  The 31st bit is called the "carry", it is set when the result is equal to zero.
  The 30th bit is called the "zero", it is set when the result is equal to zero.
  The 29th bit is called the "negative", it is set when the sign bit of the result is equal to 1.
  The 28th bit is called the "overflow", it is set when the result cannot be represented on the same number of bits as the operands (signed overflow).
  The Arithmetic and Logic Unit (ALU) always computes 32-bit words, but the word length considered to compute the ALU-code condition bits can be one of the following : 8, 16, 24, 32 bits. This length is specified by the field ALU-size (bits 8 & 9) of the Status-Word.

4.2.7 THE INSTRUCTION SET

The instruction set of the processor KIM20 is composed of only 32 instructions, encoded using a single 32-bit format (section 4.2.2), The general syntax of an instruction is :

INSTRUCTION   Rd , S1 , (#) S2

"INSTRUCTION" represents the mnemonic of the instruction to be processed (bits 31 to 27 of the 32-bit instruction word).

"Rd" specifies a destination register among 32 registers (bits 25 to 21 of the instruction 32 bit word).

"S1" specifies a source register among 32 registers (bits 20 to 16 of the instruction 32 bit word).

"(#)" is an option which specifies the type of the operand S2. When not specified, this option is discarded (bit 26 = 0) and the operand S2 specifies a second source register. If this option is set (bit 26 = 1), the operand S2 corresponds to an immediate 16-bit value.

"S2" specifies, whether the option "#" is set or not, an immediate 16-bit value, or a second source register above the existing 32 registers (bits 15 to 0 of the instruction 32 bit word).

Unless otherwise specified the unused fields in the instruction word are left cleared. A register is modified by the execution of an instruction, only if it appears as the destination register.

The KIM20's instruction set can be listed in four classes :

1. Arithmetic and logical operations, including ADD, SUB, AND, OR, XOR, INSERT, EXTRACT, ROTATE, SHIFTRA, SHIFTRL, CASE, HASH, HYPER instructions.

2. Control flow operations, including CALL, RETURN, TRAP, RETE, BRANCH, COND instructions.

3. List processing operations, including FIRST, NEXT, SETF, SETN, WTAG, NEW, FREE instructions.

4. Special memory accesses, including SEND, LOAD, STORE, PUSH, POP instructions.

Instruction	Operands	Operation	Cycle
ADD	rd,s1,[#]s2	rd = s1+s2;	1
SUB	rd,s1,[#]s2	rd = s1-s2;	1
AND	rd,s1,[#]s2	rd = s1&s2;	1
OR	rd,s1,[#]s2	rd = s1 | s2;	1
XOR	rd,s1,[#]s2	rd = s1xors2;	1
ROTATE	rd,s1,[#]s2	rd = s1 shifted left by [#]s2 %32;	1
SHIFTRL	rd,s1	rd = s1 shifted right 1 bit; rd<31> = 0;	1
SHIFTRA	rd,s1	rd = s1 shifted right 1 bit; rd<31> = carry;	1
INSERT	rd,s1,[#]s2	rd = 0; rd<byte n°[#]s2<1-0>> = s1<7-0>;	1
EXTRACT	rd,s1,[#]s2	rd = 0; rd<7-0> = s1<byte n°[#]s2<1-0>>;	1
HASH	rd,[#]s2	rd = s2<31-24>+s2<23-16>+s2<15-8>+s2<7-0>;	1
HYPER	rd,s1,[#]s2	rd = 0; rd<4-0> = n°bit msb of (s1xor[#]s2);	1
CASE	rd,s1,[#]s2	rd = 0; rd<7-0> = s1 <tag> & [#]s2<7-0>;	1
CALL	rd,#s2	rd = pc+1; pc = #s2; wp = wp+1;	1
RETURN		wp = wp-1; pc = pc(wp-1);	1
TRAP	#s2	pc = 0;	1
RETE	s1,[#]s2	pc = s1+[#]s2; wp = wp-1;	2
JUMP	#s2	pc = #s2;	1
BRANCH	s1,[#]s2	pc = s1+[#]s2;	2
COND	s1,[#]s2	if (test1 op test2 false) cancel next instruction;	1
FIRST	rd,s1,[#]s2	if ([#]s2<0> = 0) rd = (s1); else rd <first> = (s1)<first>;	1
NEXT	rd,s1	rd<tag> = (s1)<tag>; if (rd<cdr-code> = 3) rd <first> = 0; if (=2) rd<first> = s1+1; else trap;	1
SETF	s1,[#]s2	(s1)<first> = [#]s2;	1
SETN	s1,[#]s2	if ([#]s2 = 0) (s1)<cdr-code> = 3; if ([#]s2 = s1+1) (s1)<cdr-code> = 2; else trap;	1
WTAG	s1,[#]s2	(s1)<tag> = [#]s2<15-8> sélecté par <7-0>;	1
NEW	rd,[#]s2	rd = flp; flp = (rd)<first>; (rd)<tag> = [#]s2<15-8> sélecté par <7-0>; if (flc <= flt) trap; flc=flc-1;	1
FREE	s1	(s1)<tag> = 0; (s1)<first> = flp; flp = s1 <first>; flc = flc + 1;	1
SEND	s1,[#]s2	(s1) = [#]s2;	1
PUSH	sp,[#]s2	sp = sp + 1; if (sp<7-0> = 0) trap; (sp) = [#]s2;	1
POP	rd,sp	rd = (sp); sp = sp -1; if (sp<7-0> = 0) trap;	1
LOAD	rd,s1	rd = (s1)<code>;	1
STORE	s1,[#]s2	(s1)<code> = [#]s2;	1

Fig.4.10 KIM20 instruction set summary.

4.2.8   EXCEPTIONS AND INTERRUPTS

4.2.8.1   INTRODUCTION

Interrupts and traps cause the KIM20 to suspend execution of an instruction sequence and to begin the execution of a new one. The processor may, or may not, later resume execution of the original instruction sequence.

The distinction between interrupts and traps is largely one of causation and enabling. Interrupts allow external devices to control the processor execution and are always asynchronous to program execution. Traps (or exceptions) are intended to be used for exceptional events which occur during instruction execution, and are generally synchronous to program execution (for example : the internal window overflow/underflow). When an exception or an interrupt is raised, the processor determines a 3-bit vector number associated with the exception or the interrupt. The vector number gives the number of a vector table entry. The physical address of the corresponding vector table is generated by the exception handling sequence located at address 0 (zero).

The eight possible levels of interrupts or traps are ordered. Level 0 has the highest priority while level 7 has the lowest.

The following table gives the interrupt and trap level assignments :

Level 0	no interruption or reset (NOINT/RESET)
Level 1	window overflow/underflow (WINDOV)
Level 2	stack overflow/underflow (STACKOV)
Level 3	miss of cells (STARVATION)
Level 4	CDR coding technique exception (CDR_ESCAPE)
Level 5	software trap (TRAP)
Level 6	external interrupt A (INTERRUPTA)
Level 7	external interrupt B (INTERRUPTB)

4.2.8.2 THE RESET

The level 0 of vectorized exceptions is the processor reset. A mask at this level disables all interrupts or traps but the hardware reset. A hardware reset on the processor KIM20 initializes the processor, but only the global registers R30 (SP) and R31 (SW) are automatically cleared. The initializing software will have to "clean" the other 8 global registers and all the window registers before the application starts.

4.2.8.3 WINDOW OVERFLOW/UNDERFLOW

This exception is generated during "CALL" or "RETURN" instructions, when the two fields of the Status Word, WP (Window-Pointer) and WO (Window-Overflow) become equal. The comparison is performed before decrementing during a "RETURN" instruction and after incrementing during a "CALL" instruction.

If this exception is generated during a "CALL" instruction, it is called a Window-Overflow and bit 27 of the Status Word is set.

If this exception is generated during a "RETURN" instruction, it is called a Window-Underflow and the bit 27 of the Status Word remains clear.

This exception indicates that the 8 register-windows are used (overflow) or empty (underflow), and that the exception handling software should save one (or more) windows, or restore one (or more) previously saved windows.

4.2.8.4 STACK OVERFLOW/UNDERFLOW

This exception is generated during "POP" or "PUSH" instructions, when the lowest byte of the Stack Pointer becomes equal to the value 0xFF. In both cases the comparison is performed after renewing the Stack Pointer.

If this exception is generated during a "PUSH" instruction, it is called a Stack Overflow and bit 27 of the Status Word is set.

If this exception is generated during a "POP" instruction, it is called a Stack Underflow and bit 27 of the Status Word remains clear.

The stack overflow/underflow exceptions provide a simple mechanism to control multiple LIFO stacks mapped in data memory. However, the different LIFO stack segments must not exceed 256 32-bit words and have to start at an address with the lowest byte zero.

4.2.8.5 STARVATION EXCEPTION

This exception is generated during an instruction "NEW", when the Free-List Counter (FLC = R28) is less than or equal to the Free-List Threshold (FLT = R27).

The comparison between the two registers is performed before updating register FLC by the "NEW" instruction.

This exception warns that the number of cells remaining in the Free-List has reached a critical level, stored in register FLT, and that garbage collection should be performed to recover the unused cells.

Because the three registers, FLP, FLC and FLT can be written and read, several Free-Lists can be handled simultaneously.

4.2.8.6   CDR-CODING EXCEPTION

The CDR-coding technique allows a compact representation of lists and trees. When it is impossible to code the address of the next cell relative to the address of the current one, a CDR-coding exception is generated.

This exception can be caused, while attempting to read the "NEXT" field during a "NEXT" instruction, or while attempting to write it during a "SETN" instruction.

This exception is generated during a "NEXT" instruction if the "CDR" field of the read cell is not equal to the values 2 (CDR-NEXT) or 3 (CDR-NIL).   The bit 27 of the Status Word remains clear.

This exception is also generated during a "SETN" instruction if the address of the pointed cell is not equal to NIL (zero) or to the address of the current cell +1. In such a case, the CDR field of the current cell is cleared, and bit 27 of the Status Word is set.

The CDR-coding exception handling and especially the appropriate chaining of cells belongs to the exception handling software, using for instance the invisible pointer technique.

4.2.8.7 THE TRAP INSTRUCTION

The execution of the TRAP instruction generates a "software" exception. This mechanism can be used to communicate with the operating system in a homogeneous exception way or to expand the instruction set of the processor.

4.2.8.8   EXTERNAL INTERRUPTS

The interrupt level 6 and 7 corresponding to external hardware interrupts of the KIM20 processor. These interrupts can be used to connect a real-time clock or any other peripheral device.

4.2.8.9   EXCEPTION ENABLING CONDITIONS

From a software point of view, exceptions can be temporarily disabled by using the "MASK" field in the Status Word. From a hardware point of view, they are also disabled during "critical sections", when their action would cause serious damage.

The "MASK" field in the Status Word filters the flow of exceptions. An exception is handled only if its level is not greater than the "MASK" level.

A "MASK" settled at the level 0 disables all exceptions but the hardware reset, while at level 7 it enables all of them.

From the hardware point of view, there are three cases which disable all exceptions.

The first case is during the execution of the instructions "COND", "BRANCH" and "RETE". These three instructions are affecting the execution of the instruction directly following them, they are also disabling exceptions to be taken into account just behind them, otherwise instruction sequencing information may be lost.

The second case which requires to disable exceptions is during the second and third cycle of a write operation on the Status Word (SW = R31). This restriction is caused by the use of the "Base-register". The processor shall not be interrupted during a page-switch, otherwise, when returning from the exception handling procedure, the appropriate code page number will be lost.

The critical section will be detailed later in the next section. It corresponds to the time necessary for the software system to identify the exception level and memorize the return address.

The exception handling method ensures that only the two external interrupts may fall into these three invalid cases, because they are asynchronous to the instruction execution.

None of the exceptions are memorized, which means that they are definitely lost if they occur while they are masked. Thus, external interrupts must be held long enough to be taken into account.

4.2.8.10   THE COURSE OF THE EXCEPTION HANDLING PROCEDURE

The internal processor exceptions are always generated during the second cycle of the instruction that caused them. On the other hand, they are always detected and taken into account during the first cycle of the following instruction (fetch).

To assume a perfect homogeneity of treatments, we choose to flush the pipeline between the generation of an interrupt and the beginning of its handling sequence. To do so, the generation of an interrupt automatically cancels the following instruction. When the interrupt is taken into account, during the first cycle of the second following instruction it also cancels it. Then the Program Counter (PC) is cleared, and the exception handling section begins by fetching the instruction located at address zero. From this time and until they are explicitly authorized, all exceptions are disabled.

The generation of an exception always leads to cancel temporarily the two following instructions. It is only after these cancelled instructions that the exception handling procedure effectively begins, at address zero of memory page zero. This operation doesn't lead to a change among the register windows. The exception handling program can use any of the 32 registers.

The first "CALL" instruction processed during the handling procedure, saves the returning address of the exception procedure, but not the return address of the usual "CALL" function (PC+1). This address is in any case the address of the first previously cancelled instruction.

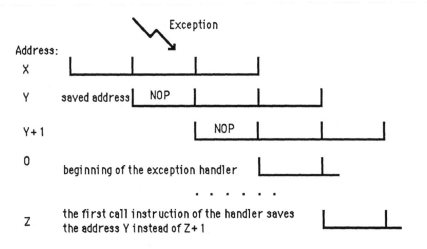

Fig.4.11 KIM20 exception handling.

At the end of the exception handling procedure, a "RETURN" or a "RETE" instruction restarts the interrupted task, and restores its working environment (the appropriate window).

Thus a "CALL" instruction is necessary in all the exception handling procedures. This instruction also enables the interrupts to be again taken into account according to the "MASK" field of the Status Word (SW(2:0)).

4.3   KIM20 HARDWARE ARCHITECTURE

4.3.1 THE DATA-PATH

The key principle of the KIM architecture is to reduce the semantic gap between Artificial Intelligence applications and the hardware machine. We have said in a previous section that a reduced and homogeneous set of operations is able to meet this challenge for both symbolic and numerical processing. Then, an important point is to map these operations directly on hardware using a simple and regular streamlined architecture. In this paragraph, we will give an overview of the KIM20 data-path. The next figure presents a simplified diagram of the KIM20 data-path.

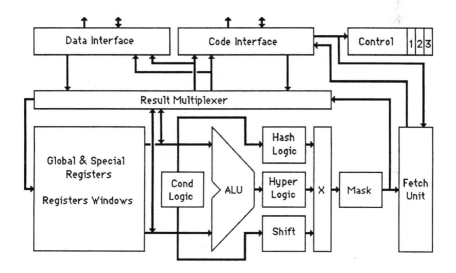

Fig.4.12 KIM20 data-path.

The KIM20 architecture is mainly based on a regular data-path inherited from the original RISC-II. The path followed by most instruction executions can be simply summed up by the following basic steps : after the instruction fetch and decode, two sources are read from the register file and routed to the Arithmetic and Logical Unit (ALU). Upon the completion of the operation, the result is then written back into the register file. Of course, this general description does not take into account all required operators in the data-paths, but two crucial design constraints are clearly brought to light. First, a very compact dual-port register file characterized by fast access-times is essential. The second important point is the time needed to perform a 32-bit signed addition on the Arithmetic and Logical Unit. These two parts (i.e. register file and ALU) of the circuit are critical paths, which will determine the final cycle-time. Lessons learned in previous implementations of the KIM architecture show that it is important to focus the hardware design on the pipeline scheme and to allocate hardware resources only to frequent operations. In this way, we must discard any mechanism which potentially breaks the pipeline execution scheme and increases delays and latencies.

4.3.2 ADDING A NEW INSTRUCTION

As shown in the previous section, the KIM20 data-path is based on a classical model including parallel and serial operators.

As an example, we can describe the HYPER instruction as an attempt to add a new operator into a simple RISC data-path.

Consider, as an example, simulating the behaviour of N electronic modules, as each of them is connected with the rest by input and output signals. The task can be started simply, but it requires hours, even days of sequential CPU time. Simulation of such large systems can run faster, with a performance improvement of several orders of magnitude, if we are able to compute the simulation on all N modules in parallel, updating their states by message-passing. Our approach to the problem is to create N objects, one for each electronic module. During a simulation phase, each object sends messages containing output information and receives similar messages from the other objects. This example emphasizes the capability of the object-oriented approach to model systems. To represent such structures, the object-oriented approach is probably best suited than a procedure-centred one. In this electronic simulation example, instead of passing data to procedures sequentially, objects are asked to perform operations on themselves in parallel. Thus, the object-oriented approach seems an elegant tool to implement software with inherent concurrency : we can use objects to model parallelism and the message-passing scheme for communication.

A computer architecture well-suited for implementation of this computational model may be conceived as a MIMD (Multi Instruction-stream Multi Data-stream) with each node based on a medium grain sized processing element. Typically, new technologies such as VLSI, permits us to fit one node on a single board. Among the parallel architectures for connecting processing elements in a distributed-memory scheme, a hypercube solves most of the drawbacks of simple topologies. One of the drawbacks is the problem of message-passing through the network without wasting a lot of computing power. For this particular problem, a boolean n-cube provides a good solution without requiring an unwieldy number of physical connections [122].

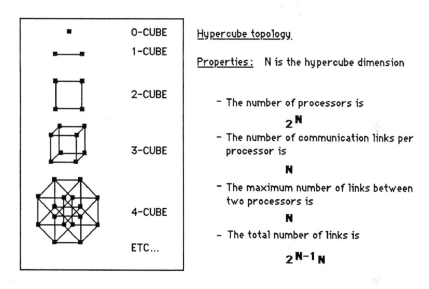

Fig.4.13 Hypercube architecture.

Nodes communicate directly with their N neighbours for a N-cube configuration. We assume that the nodes have identifiers 0 through 2^N-1. The hypercube can be interpreted as a generalization of a cube to an N-dimensional euclidian-space. Thus, each dimension corresponds directly to one bit in the node identifier. Therefore, an efficient routing algorithm can be simply implemented using a XOR operation between the source and destination node identifiers.

The HYPER instruction performs in one cycle the message routing algorithm when using KIM20 in a multiprocessor hypercube computer. Therefore, the design of the hardware operator, can take advantage of the basic KIM20 ALU executing an XOR instruction. In order to give as a result the number of the destination link (where the message must be sent), we must add a small encoder in the data-path. The latter is quite simple and we must only verify that the time required for the execution of the XOR operation added to the time required for encoding the result can fit in one machine cycle, like every other instruction.

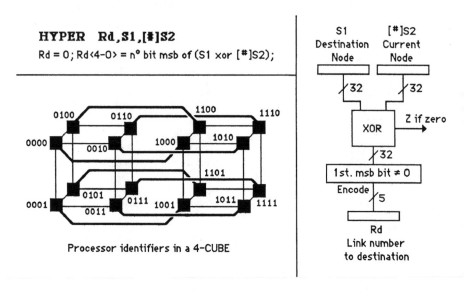

HYPER Rd,S1,[#]S2

Rd = 0; Rd<4-0> = n° bit msb of (S1 xor [#]S2);

Processor identifiers in a 4-CUBE

S1 — Destination Node

[#]S2 — Current Node

XOR — Z if zero

1st. msb bit ≠ 0

Encode

Rd — Link number to destination

Fig.4.14 KIM20 s hyper instruction.

4.3.3 THE PIPELINE AND DECODE UNIT

KIM20 is designed using a three-stage synchronous pipeline. The first cycle fetches the instruction from the program memory, the second cycle reads source operands from registers and computes the operation on the ALU, and the third cycle writes back the result in the destination register.

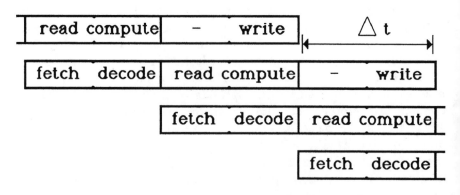

Fig.4.15 KIM20 pipeline architecture.

The fetch and decode unit of the KIM20 microprocessor is very close to the RISC-II one. In the next figure, you can notice all the pipeline registers that allow us to store source, destination operands, and operation codes for the pipeline instructions.

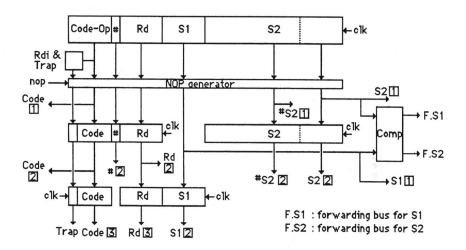

Fig.4.16 KIM20's decode unit.

4.3.4 INSTRUCTION EXECUTION

4.3.4.1 COMPUTE INSTRUCTIONS

This section describes the execution of arithmetic and logical instructions. All KIM20 instructions execute in three cycles following the pipeline model.

The first one is dedicated to the instruction fetch. This is done by applying the address of the instruction to be fetched on the program memory address bus, and then loading the corresponding instruction in the instruction register of the decode unit. At the same time, an incrementer computes the address of the next instruction to be fetched. Then, operand addresses are extracted from the instruction word before the beginning of the second cycle.

ALU instruction cycle #1

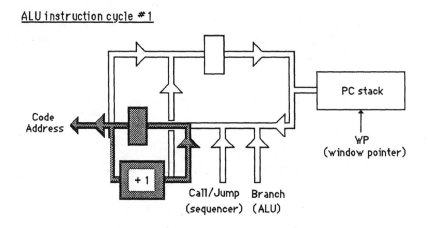

Fig.4.17 First cycle of ALU instructions

During the second cycle, three cases can occur :

1. Operand registers read, compute result in ALU (fig. 4.18.a).

2. Operand register read and constant read, compute result in ALU (fig. 4.18.b).

3. Operand register read and operand caught from one feedback bus, compute result in ALU (fig. 4.18.c).

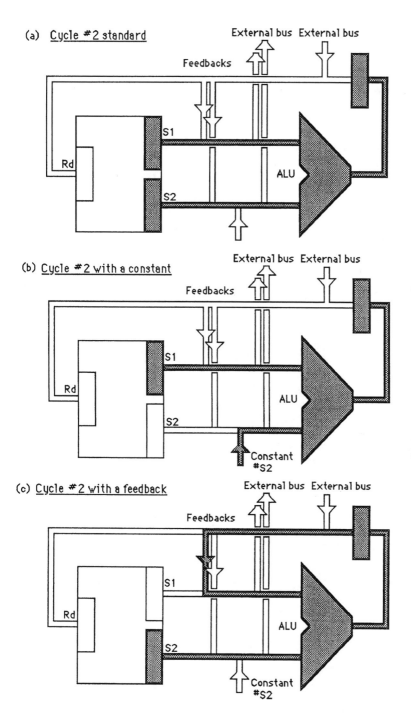

Fig.4.18 Second cycle of ALU instructions.

The third and last cycle writes back the result into the destination register.

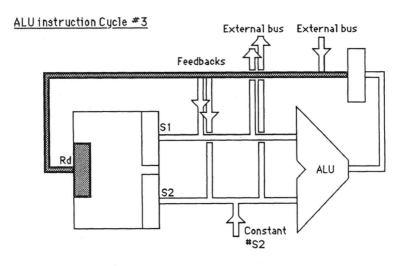

Fig.4.19 Third cycle of ALU instructions.

4.3.4.2   MEMORY ACCESS INSTRUCTIONS

The first cycle of all KIM20 memory access instruction is the same as for compute instructions (see previous section).

The second cycle reads operands from the register file and performs the external access.

For write instructions, the third cycle is not used, since no result needs to be writen in the register file. For read instructions, the third cycle writes back the data read from the memory into the destination register.

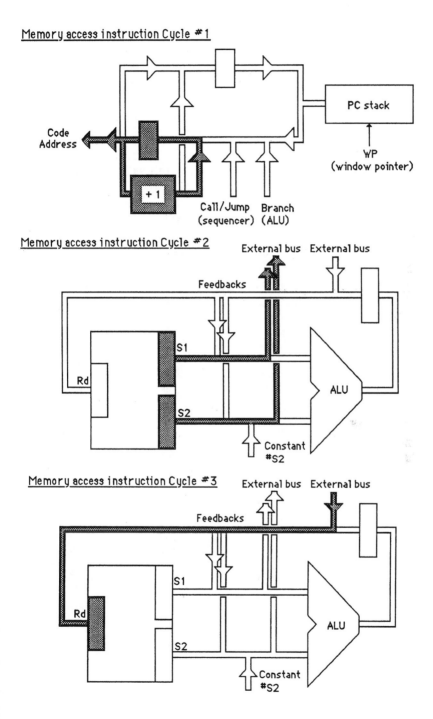

Fig.4.20 The three cycles of memory access instructions.

4.3.4.3 CONTROL FLOW INSTRUCTIONS

Most of the KIM20 control instructions use only the first cycle of the pipeline. The latter read the current instruction word from the program memory using the code bus, and store it into the instruction register. Then, the decode unit computes the command word and extracts operands, and finally computes the destination branch address.

The next figure gives the paths followed by the "JUMP", "BRANCH", "CALL" and "RETURN" instructions.

The second and third cycles are only used by the "CALL" instructions. A procedure call operation stores the return address in an internal stack coupled with the register windows during the second cycle. This value will be efficiently fetched by the return instruction.

The third cycle stores also the return address into a destination register for window overflow/underflow management or other software purposes.

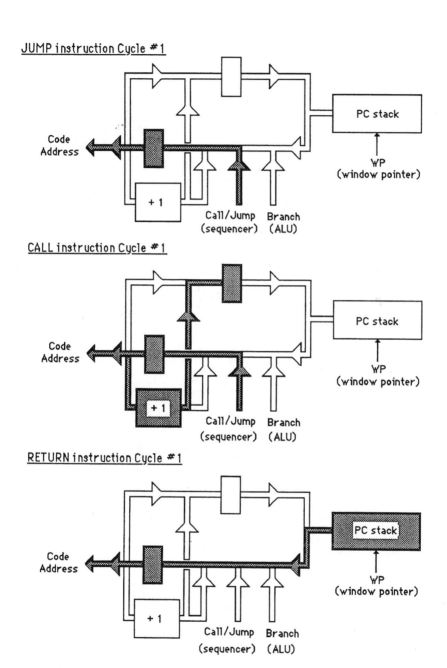

Fig.4.21 First cycle of control flow instructions.

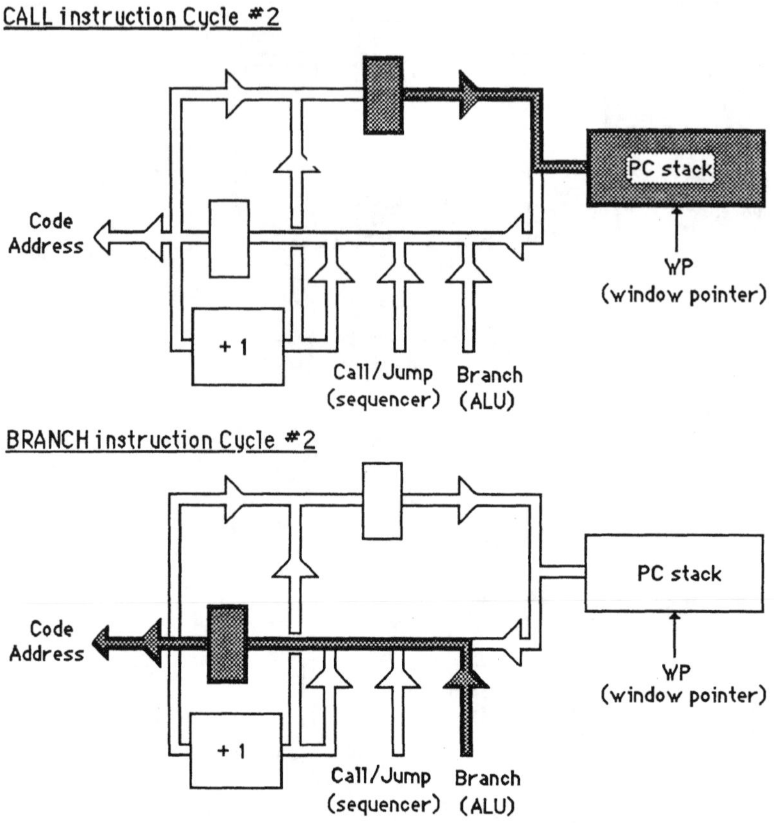

CALL instruction Cycle #2

Code
Address

PC stack

WP
(window pointer)

Call/Jump   Branch
(sequencer) (ALU)

BRANCH instruction Cycle #2

Code
Address

PC stack

WP
(window pointer)

Call/Jump   Branch
(sequencer) (ALU)

Fig.4.22 Second cycle of control flow instructions.

4.4. SOFTWARE AND PERFORMANCE ASPECTS

4.4.1 PROGRAMMING EXAMPLES

This section gives two examples of assembler programs that show the simplicity and efficiency of the resulting code. This efficiency and simplicity is largely due to the high-semantic level of symbolic processing instructions and the use of a RISC design approach.

The first example is a small Lisp (list processing) function that creates a binary tree. Both the Lisp code and resulting assembler code are given.

```
;; creates a 2**n binary tree
;;
;;     (defun 2NC (n)
;;        (if (> n 0) (cons (2NC (1- n))
;;                          (2NC (1- n)))))
;;

2NC:        equ       *                 ; 2NC entry
            sub       r4,r15,r0         ; test if > 0
            cond      psw,#NEGATIVE     ;
            jump      2NC_END           ; else return NIL
            new       r4,#NEW_CONS      ; allocate a cons
            sub       r8,r0,#1          ; n = n - 1
            call      lpc,#2NC          ; recursive call of 2NC
            setf      r4,r8             ; set CAR value
            sub       r8,r0,#1          ; n = n - 1
            call      lpc,#2NC          ; recursive call of 2NC
            setn      r4,r8             ; set CDR value
            add       r0,r4,#0          ; r0 points to the new cell
            return                      ; end
2NC_END:    add       r0,r15,#0         ; return NIL
            return                      ;
```

Fig.4.23 The 2NC list processing program.

The second example is a part of the implementation of a Lisp-evaluator on KIM20. Recall that the aim of a Lisp-evaluator is to return the value of a Lisp-object given its type. There are three categories of objects :

1. Self-evaluated objects : like numbers, strings, etc... for which the values are the object itself.

2. Functions : for which the value must be computed by calling the associated code with its arguments.

3. Symbols, for which the value must be searched from the variable-binding environment.

For more details on Lisp, refer to [123].

```
; beginning of a small lisp (scheme) evaluator
; r0 points to the object to be evaluated, the result is in r0

F_EVAL    first    r4,r0                  ; object type
          cond     r4,#OBJECT             ; is it a true object?
          jump     #F_UNDEFINED           ; else undefined
          case     r4,r4,#TYPE            ; type processing
          branch   r4,#TAB_OBJ            ; multiway branch

TAB_OBJ   return                          ; ()
          jump     #ER_UNBOUND            ; unbound
          jump     #EV_CONS               ; cons
          return                          ; character
          return                          ; string
          return                          ; vector
          jump     #EV_SYMBOL             ; symbol
          return                          ; fixnum
          return                          ; bignum
          return                          ; rational
          return                          ; real
          return                          ; complex
          jump     #ER_EVAL               ; stream
          jump     #ER_EVAL               ; process
          jump     #ER_EVAL               ; reserved
          jump     #ER_EVAL               ; reserved

; then follow the procedures for evaluation of each object type ...

; primitive examples ...              :
P_CAR     first    r0,r1        ; (car list)
          return

P_CDR     next     r0,r1        ; (cdr list)
          return

P_CONS    new      r0,#CONS     ; (cons car cdr)
          setf     r0,r1
          setn     r0,r2
          return
```

Fig.4.24 A small Lisp evaluator.

4.4.2   PERFORMANCE EVALUATION

Some performance measurments have been made using two benchmark programs. The first one is based on the famous Gabriel Benchmark [124] for Artificial Intelligence systems. The result is given in VAX MIPS, that is an acceleration ratio based on the time required by a VAX 785 to execute the Benchmark.

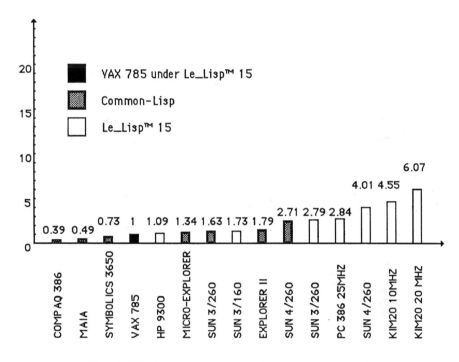

Fig.4.25 Performance evaluation using Lisp.

The second Benchmark was done using the KOS software prototype (release 2) [125]. The latter is an inference engine dedicated to real-time applications of Artificial Intelligence. Measurements show 10 sustained MIPS AT 16 MHZ (16 MIPS peak) and up to 5000 fired rules per second, to be compared to 350 with a MC68020 25 Mhz and near 1000 with a SPARC16 Mhz.

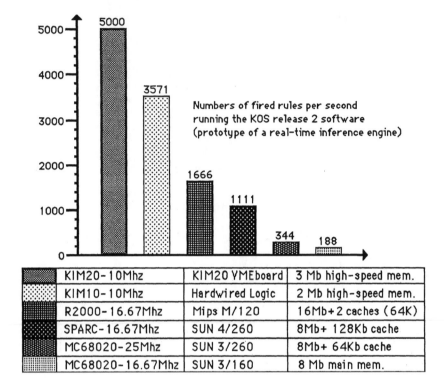

Fig.4.26 Performance evaluation using KOS.

Conclusion

Several years have elapsed since the early Reduced Instruction Set Computer architecture research was conducted at IBM, Stanford and Berkeley. In this book, we have surveyed modern Reduced Instruction Set Architectures.

The first chapter has described the history of the RISC research done by pioneers in universities and companies.

The second chapter has laid out the technical foundations of the RISC design methodology.

The third chapter has briefly surveyed the main commercial RISC products.

The last chapter has given a more detailed description of the KIM20 as an example of a RISC design dedicated to a specific application domain.

Finally, although this book does not provide much depth on each architecture, the reader interested in having more technical information about a particular product should refer to the references at the end of the book and directly contact the corresponding company.

However, a survey of this type helps illustrate the impact and application areas into which RISC has moved. In addition, the book is clearly useful for educational purposes and provides a good tool for selecting the right architecture for a given application.

The success of the RISC architecture is largely due to its history. RISC's originators derived the fundamental concepts of the design philosophy by carefully analyzing millions of lines of existing computer code. The analysis indicated that most of the software in use did not make optimal use of the CISC (Complex Instruction Set Computer) processor hardware. The RISC concepts developed from that research caused a major course correction that will continue to influence all computer architectures and systems for years to come.

Appendix

KIM20 INSTRUCTION SET

ADD   Integer   signed addition

Syntax   ADD Rd, S1, [#]S2

Operation   Rd = S1 + [#]S2

Description   Adds the content of source register S1, with the content of source register [#]S2, into the destination register Rd.

Condition codes   (depending on the ALU-SIZE field in the Status-Word)

     C   Set if a carry generated, otherwise cleared.
     Z   Set if the result is zero, otherwise cleared.
     N   Set if the result is negative, otherwise cleared.
     V   Set if an arithmetic overflow is detected, otherwise cleared.

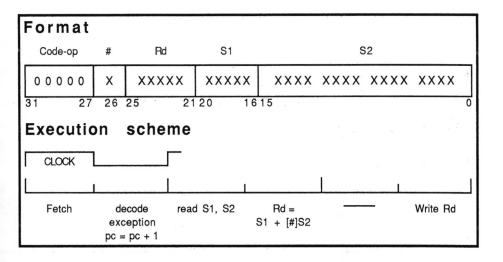

Format

Code-op	#	Rd	S1	S2
0 0 0 0 0	X	XXXXX	XXXXX	XXXX XXXX XXXX XXXX

31   27   26 25   21 20   16 15   0

Execution scheme

CLOCK

| Fetch | decode exception pc = pc + 1 | read S1, S2 | Rd = S1 + [#]S2 | —— | Write Rd |

SUB Integer signed subtraction

Syntax   SUB Rd, S1, [#]S2

Operation   Rd = S1 - [#]S2

Description   Subtracts the content of source register [#]S2 from the content of source register S1, into the destination register Rd.

Condition codes (depending on the ALU-SIZE field in the Status-Word)

C   Set if a carry generated, otherwise cleared.
Z   Set if the result is zero, otherwise cleared.
N   Set if the result is negative, otherwise cleared.
V   Set if an arithmetic overflow is detected, otherwise cleared.

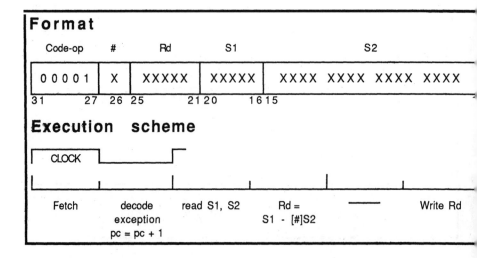

Format

Code-op	#	Rd	S1	S2
0 0 0 0 1	X	X X X X X	X X X X X	X X X X X X X X X X X X X X X X

31   27 26 25   21 20   16 15

Execution scheme

CLOCK

| Fetch | decode exception pc = pc + 1 | read S1, S2 | Rd = S1 - [#]S2 | ——— | Write Rd |

AND   Logical AND

Syntax   AND Rd, S1, [#]S2

Operation   Rd = S1 and [#]S2

Description   Computes a logical AND between the content of source register S1, and the content of source register [#]S2, into the destination register Rd.

Condition codes (depending on the ALU-SIZE field in the Status-Word)

C   Always cleared.
Z   Set if the result is zero, otherwise cleared.
N   Set if the result is negative, otherwise cleared.
V   Always cleared.

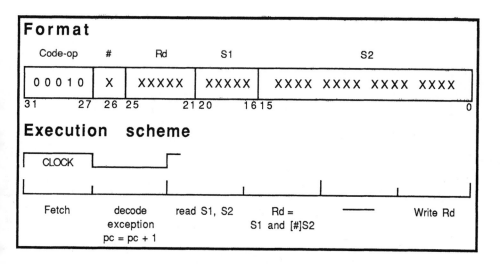

OR   Logical OR

Syntax   OR Rd, S1, [#]S2

Operation   Rd = S1 or [#]S2

Description   Computes a logical OR between the content of
                  source register S1, and the content of source
                  register [#]S2, into the destination register Rd.

Condition codes   (depending on the ALU-SIZE field in the Status-Word)

C   Always cleared.
Z   Set if the result is zero, otherwise cleared.
N   Set if the result is negative, otherwise
    cleared.
V   Always cleared.

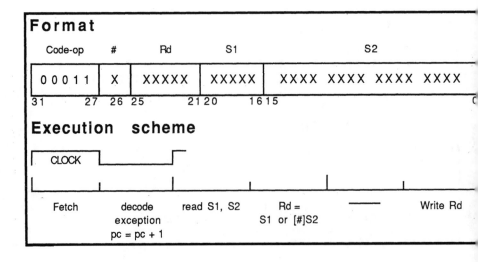

208

XOR   Logical exclusive OR

Syntax   XOR Rd, S1, [#]S2

Operation   Rd = S1 xor [#]S2

Description   Computes a logical exclusive OR between the content of source register S1, and the content of source register [#]S2, into the destination register Rd.

Condition codes   (depending on the ALU-SIZE field in the Status-Word)

C   Always cleared.
Z   Set if the result is zero, otherwise cleared.
N   Set if the result is negative, otherwise cleared.
V   Always cleared.

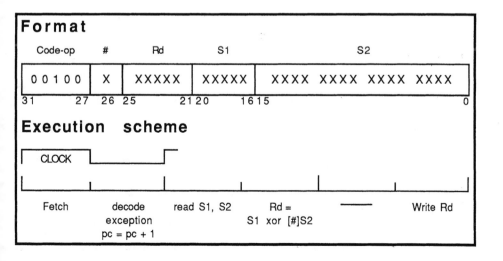

Format

Code-op	#	Rd	S1	S2
0 0 1 0 0	X	X X X X X	X X X X X	X X X X X X X X X X X X X X X X

31   27 26 25   21 20   16 15   0

Execution scheme

CLOCK

Fetch   decode   read S1, S2   Rd =   ————   Write Rd
             exception   S1 xor [#]S2
             pc = pc + 1

ROTATE   Left rotate

Syntax   ROTATE Rd, S1, [#]S2

Operation   Rd = S1 rotated [#]S2 times

Description   Computes a left rotation on the content of source register S1, into the destination register Rd. The rotate count is specified by the source register [#]S2.

Condition codes   (depending on the ALU-SIZE field in the Status-Word)

C   Always cleared.
Z   Set if the result is zero, otherwise cleared.
N   Set if the result is negative, otherwise cleared.
V   Always cleared.

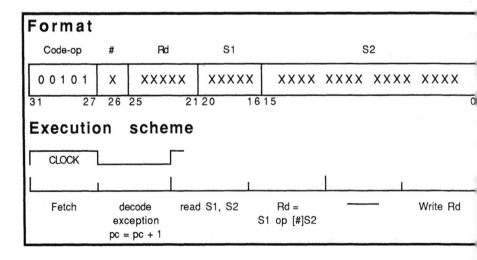

Format

Code-op	#	Rd	S1	S2
0 0 1 0 1	X	XXXXX	XXXXX	XXXX XXXX XXXX XXXX

31   27 26 25   21 20   16 15   0

Execution   scheme

CLOCK

| Fetch | decode
exception
pc = pc + 1 | read S1, S2 | Rd =
S1 op [#]S2 | —— | Write Rd |

SHIFTRL   Right logical shift

Syntax   SHIFTRL Rd, S1

Operation   Rd = S1 right shifted, Rd <31> = 0

Description   Computes a one-bit right shift on the source register S1 into the destination register Rd. The carry is set to the value of bit 0 of the source register S1, and the uppermost bit of the destination register is cleared.

Condition codes   (depending on the ALU-SIZE field in the Status-Word)

C   Equal to bit 0 of S1.
Z   Set if the result is zero, otherwise cleared.
N   Set if the result is negative, otherwise cleared.
V   Always cleared.

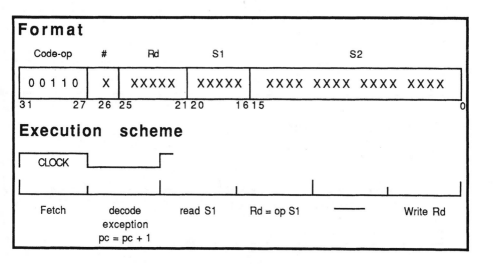

Format

Code-op	#	Rd	S1	S2
0 0 1 1 0	X	X X X X X	X X X X X	X X X X X X X X X X X X X X X X

31   27   26   25   21   20   16   15   0

Execution scheme

CLOCK

Fetch   decode exception pc = pc + 1   read S1   Rd = op S1   ——   Write Rd

SHIFTRA   Right arithmetical shift

Syntax   SHIFTRA Rd, S1

Operation   Rd = S1 right shifted, Rd <31> = carry

Description   Computes a one-bit right shift on the source register S1 into the destination register Rd. The uppermost bit of the destination register is set to the value of the carry, and the carry is set to the value of bit 0 of the source register S1.

Condition codes   (depending on the ALU-SIZE field in the Status-Word)

C   Equal to bit 0 of S1.
Z   Set if the result is zero, otherwise cleared.
N   Set if the result is negative, otherwise cleared.
V   Always cleared.

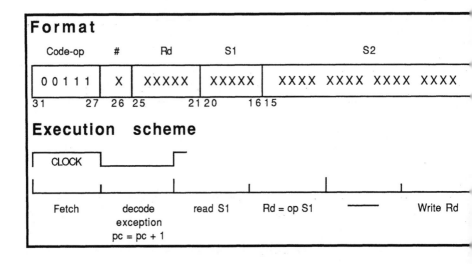

Format

Code-op	#	Rd	S1	S2
0 0 1 1 1	X	XXXXX	XXXXX	XXXX XXXX XXXX XXXX

31   27   26 25   21 20   16 15

Execution scheme

CLOCK

Fetch   decode exception pc = pc + 1   read S1   Rd = op S1   ———   Write Rd

INSERT   Byte insertion

Syntax   INSERT Rd, S1, [#]S2

Operation   Rd = 0 ;
                  Rd<byte nb.<[#]S2<1:0>>> = S1<7:0>

Description   Extracts the lowest byte from source register S1
                  and inserts it into the byte of the destination
                  register Rd indicated by the two lowest bits of
                  the operand [#]S2. The other bytes of the
                  destination register are cleared.

Condition codes   (depending on the ALU-SIZE field in the Status-Word)

   C   Always cleared.
   Z   Set if the result is zero, otherwise cleared.
   N   Set if the result is negative, otherwise
       cleared.
   V   Always cleared.

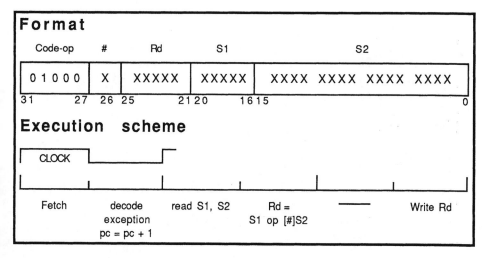

Format

Code-op	#	Rd	S1	S2
0 1 0 0 0	X	XXXXX	XXXXX	XXXX XXXX XXXX XXXX

31   27 26 25   21 20   16 15   0

Execution scheme

CLOCK

Fetch	decode	read S1, S2	Rd =	———	Write Rd
	exception		S1 op [#]S2		
	pc = pc + 1				

EXTRACT   Byte extraction

Syntax   EXTRACT Rd, S1, [#]S2

Operation   Rd = 0 ;
Rd<0:7> = S1<byte nb.<[#]S2<1:0>>>

Description   Extracts from source register S1, the byte indicated by the two lowest bits of the operand [#]S2 (highest byte is 3, lowest byte is 0) and inserts it into the lowest byte of the destination register Rd. The other bytes of the destination register are cleared.

Condition codes   (depending on the ALU-SIZE field in the Status-Word)

     C   Always cleared.
     Z   Set if the result is zero, otherwise cleared.
     N   Set if the result is negative, otherwise cleared.
     V   Always cleared.

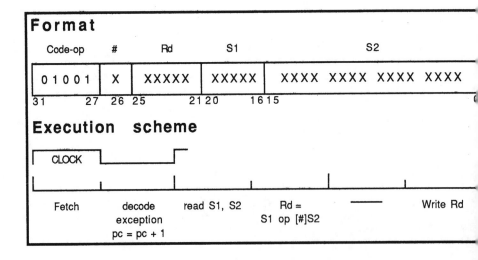

Format

Code-op	#	Rd	S1	S2
0 1 0 0 1	X	XXXXX	XXXXX	XXXX XXXX XXXX XXXX

31   27   26 25   21 20   16 15

Execution scheme

CLOCK

Fetch   decode   read S1, S2   Rd =   ——   Write Rd
          exception   S1 op [#]S2
          pc = pc + 1

HASH   Hash code processing

Syntax   Hash Rd, [#]S2

Operation   Rd<9:0> =
S2<31:24>+S2<23:16>+S2<15:8>+S2<7:0>
Rd<31:10> = 0

Description   Adds the 4 bytes of source register S2 into the destination register Rd. The result contains 10 significant bits.

Condition codes   (depending on the ALU-SIZE field in the Status-Word)

     C   Always cleared.
     Z   Set if the result is zero, otherwise cleared.
     N   Always cleared.
     V   Always cleared.

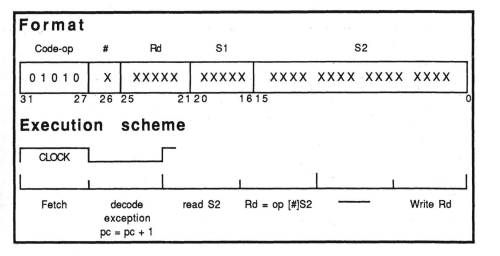

HYPER   Message routing

Syntax   HYPER Rd, S1, [#]S2

Operation   Rd = 0 ; Rd<4:0> = nb. of the most
                  significant bit of (S1 xor [#]S2)

Description   Computes an exclusive OR, between the source
                  register S1 and the source register [#]S2, and
                  writes into the destination register Rd the
                  number of the most significant bit of the
                  intermediate result.

Condition codes (depending on the ALU-SIZE field in the Status-Word)

     C   Always cleared.
     Z   Set if the result is zero, otherwise cleared.
     N   Always cleared.
     V   Always cleared.

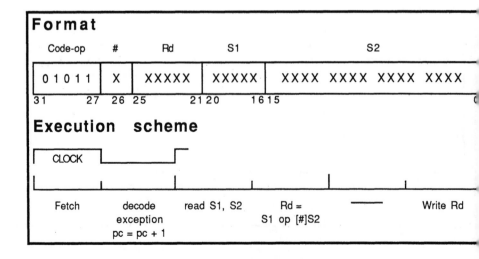

CASE   Case processing

Syntax   CASE Rd, S1, [#]S2

Operation   Rd = 0 ;
                  Rd<7:0> = S1<31:24> and S2<7:0>

Description   Computes a logical AND between the highest byte
                  of source register S1, and the lowest byte of
                  source register [#]S2 and writes the result into
                  the lower byte of destination register Rd. The
                  three higher bytes of destination register Rd are
                  set to null.

Condition codes   (depending on the ALU-SIZE field in the Status-Word)

C   Always cleared.
Z   Set if the result is zero, otherwise cleared.
N   Always cleared.
V   Always cleared.

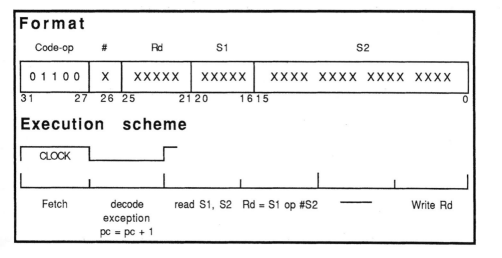

Format

Code-op	#	Rd	S1	S2

0 1 1 0 0	X	X X X X X	X X X X X	X X X X X X X X X X X X X X X X

31   27 26 25   21 20   16 15   0

Execution scheme

CLOCK

| Fetch | decode
exception
pc = pc + 1 | read S1, S2 | Rd = S1 op #S2 | ——— | Write Rd |

217

CALL   Call function

Syntax   CALL Rd, #S2

Operation   PC_save = PC + 1 (1) or PC_excep (2) ;
                 PC = #S2 ; WP = WP + 1 ; Test overflow ;

                 Rd = PC_save

Description Computes a window change (WP = WP + 1) and a
                 branch to the immediate address #S2. After WP
                 increment, if WP becomes equal to WO, a window
                 overflow exception is generated. The function
                 return address is saved into destination register
                 Rd. This return address is PC + 1 (1) unless this
                 call is the first being executed by an exception
                 handling procedure. In that case the return
                 address is the address of the interrupted
                 instruction (2).

Condition codes
       C   Unmodified.
       Z   Unmodified.
       N   Unmodified.
       V   Unmodified.

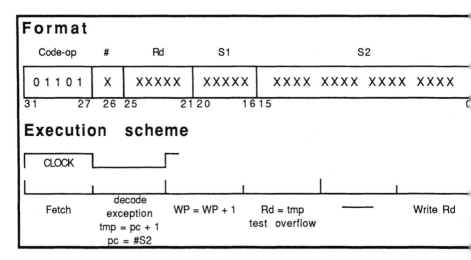

Format

Code-op	#	Rd	S1	S2
0 1 1 0 1	X	XXXXX	XXXXX	XXXX XXXX XXXX XXXX

31   27 26 25   21 20   16 15   0

Execution scheme

CLOCK

| Fetch | decode
exception
tmp = pc + 1
pc = #S2 | WP = WP + 1 | Rd = tmp
test overflow | — | Write Rd |

RETURN

Return from a function

Syntax   RETURN

Operation   WP = WP - 1 ;
PC<15:0> = PC_saved<15:0>
Base register = PC _saved<23:16>

Description   Computes a window change (WP = WP - 1) and a branch operation to the address saved during the corresponding call. The branch operation changes the content of the PC and base registers. If before decrementation WP is equal to WO, a window underflow exception is generated.

Condition codes

C   Unmodified.
Z   Unmodified.
N   Unmodified.
V   Unmodified.

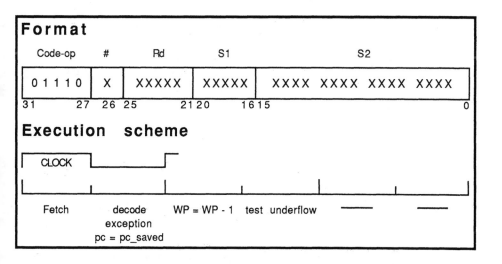

BRANCH Indexed branching

Syntax BRANCH S1, [#]S2

Operation PC = S1 + [#]S2

Description Computes a branch operation to the address resulting from the addition of the source register S1 and the source register [#]S2. This instruction needs two cycles to complete. A BRANCH instruction cancels automatically the execution of the following instruction. Exceptions are disabled during the second cycle of the BRANCH instruction.

Condition codes

C   Unmodified.
Z   Unmodified.
N   Unmodified.
V   Unmodified.

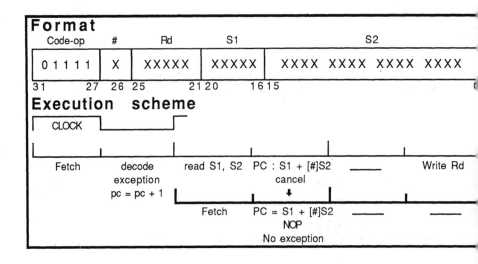

JUMP Immediate jump

Syntax   JUMP #S2

Operation   PC = #S2

Description Computes a branch operation to the immediate 16-bit operand #S2 address.

Condition codes

C   Unmodified.
Z   Unmodified.
N   Unmodified.
V   Unmodified.

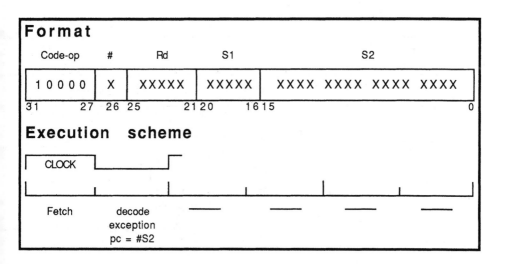

```
Format
   Code-op     #      Rd         S1                      S2

   1 0 0 0 0 | X | X X X X X | X X X X X | X X X X  X X X X  X X X X  X X X X
  31      27 26 25       21 20       16 15                                  0
Execution  scheme

   CLOCK


   Fetch      decode         ———        ———        ———        ———
              exception
              pc = #S2
```

COND   Condition test

Syntax   COND S1, [#]S2

Operation   Cancel the following instruction if
                    test (S1, S2) is false.

Description   Computes upon the most significant byte of
                    source register S1 the test specified by the
                    operand [#]S2. If false, the execution of the
                    following instruction is cancelled. The different
                    tests are specified on the next page.

Condition codes

C   Unmodified.
Z   Unmodified.
N   Unmodified.
V   Unmodified.

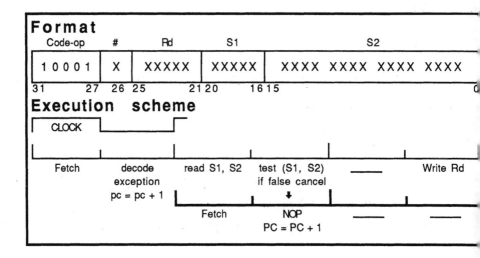

COND   Condition test

Description of the test determined by [#]S2 :

bits 0-7   : test2,
bits 8-11   : test1,
bits 12-14   : composed test with test1 and test2,
bit 15   : final test of the cond instruction.

Test 2 :
Test if : [#]S2<7:4> and [#]S2<3:0> = S1<27:24> and [#]S2<3:0> is true

Test 1 :   i = [#]S2<11:8>

i	formula	comments
0	<28>	overflow, mark2
1	<29>	negative, minus, mark1
2	<30>	zero, equal
3	<31>	carry, cdr-escape, higher or same*
4	<29> or <28>	less than
5	(<29> xor <28>) + 30	less or equal
6	<29> + <30>	negative or zero
7	!<30> and !<31>	invisible cell
8	!<30> and !<31>	cdr-cell
9	!<30> and !<31>	cdr-next
10	<30> and <31>	cdr-nil
11 to 15	0	(false)

Macro test : i = [#]S2<14:12>

0	test1
1	test2
2	!test1 and !test2
3	!test1 and test2
4	test1 and !test2
5	test1 and test2
6 or 7	0 (false)

Final test of the instruction : ([#]S2<15>)
If this bit is set, the result of the macro-test is inverted. If the final
test is true, then the following instruction is cancelled.

TRAP Software exception

Syntax TRAP #S2

Operation Generates a level 5 exception.

Description This instruction generates a level 5 exception which is processed as any other exception. Operand #S2 has no specific meaning.

Condition codes

C Unmodified.
Z Unmodified.
N Unmodified.
V Unmodified.

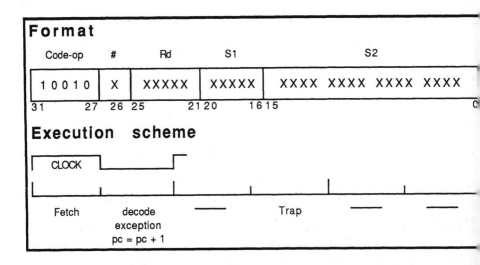

Format

Code-op	#	Rd	S1	S2
1 0 0 1 0	X	XXXXX	XXXXX	XXXX XXXX XXXX XXXX

31   27 26 25   21 20   16 15   0

Execution scheme

CLOCK

Fetch | decode exception pc = pc + 1 | —— | Trap | —— | ——

RETE   Return from exception

Syntax   RETE S1, [#]S2

Operation   PC = S1 + [#]S2 ; WP = WP - 1
Base register = PC_save <23:16>

Description   Computes a window change (WP = WP - 1) and a branch operation to the address which results from the addition of the source register S1 and the source register [#]S2. This instruction needs two cycles to complete. A RETE instruction cancels automatically the execution of the following instruction. Exceptions are disabled during the second cycle of the RETE instruction.

Condition codes

C   Unmodified.
Z   Unmodified.
N   Unmodified.
V   Unmodified.

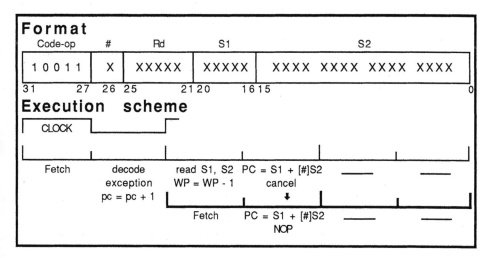

Format

Code-op	#	Rd	S1	S2
1 0 0 1 1	X	X X X X X	X X X X X	X X X X X X X X X X X X X X X X

31   27 26 25   21 20   16 15   0

Execution scheme

CLOCK

| Fetch | decode exception pc = pc + 1 | read S1, S2 WP = WP - 1 | PC = S1 + [#]S2 cancel | ——— | ——— |

| | | Fetch | PC = S1 + [#]S2 NOP | ——— | ——— |

FIRST   Read the "FIRST" field

Syntax   FIRST Rd, S1, [#]S2

Operation   Rd<23:0> = DATA(S1)<23:0>
If [#]S2<0>= 0 then
    Rd<31:24> = DATA(S1)<31:24>
If [#]S2<0> = 1 then
    Rd<31:24> = 0

Description   Performs a read of the cell located at the address given by the register S1 into the destination register Rd. If the lowest bit of the operand [#]S2 is set, the most significant byte of the destination register Rd is cleared.

Condition codes

    C   Unmodified.
    Z   Unmodified.
    N   Unmodified.
    V   Unmodified.

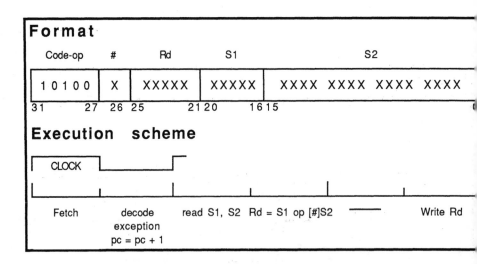

Format

Code-op	#	Rd	S1	S2
1 0 1 0 0	X	XXXXX	XXXXX	XXXX XXXX XXXX XXXX

31   27 26 25   21 20   16 15

Execution scheme

CLOCK

| Fetch | decode exception pc = pc + 1 | read S1, S2 | Rd = S1 op [#]S2 | — | Write Rd |

NEXT Read the "NEXT" field

Syntax   NEXT Rd, S1

Operation $Rd<31:24> = DATA(S1)<31:24>$
If $Rd<31:30> = 3$ then $Rd<23:0> = 0$
If $Rd<31:30> = 2$
Then $Rd<23:0> = S1<23:0> + 1$
Else $Rd<23:0> = 0$ and CDR-exception

Description   Performs a read of the "NEXT" field of the cell located at the address given by the register S1, and writes its extended value with the tag into the destination register Rd. The code 3 corresponds to the value 0 (nil) the code 2 to $(S1<23:0> + 1)$ (next cell) and the other codes to 0, with the generation of a CDR exception.

Condition codes

C   Unmodified.
Z   Unmodified.
N   Unmodified.
V   Unmodified.

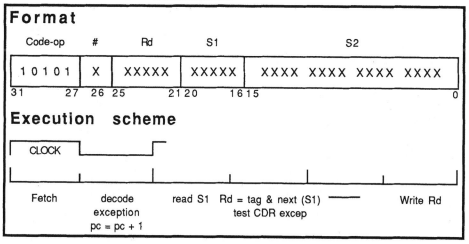

Format

Code-op	#	Rd	S1	S2
1 0 1 0 1	X	XXXXX	XXXXX	XXXX XXXX XXXX XXXX

31   27 26 25   21 20   16 15   0

Execution scheme

CLOCK

Fetch | decode exception pc = pc + 1 | read S1 | Rd = tag & next (S1) test CDR excep | Write Rd

SETF   Write the "FIRST" field

Syntax   SETF S1, [#]S2

Operation   DATA(S1)<23:0> = [#]S2<23:0>

Description   Writes the "FIRST" field of the cell pointed to by the source register S1, with the content of the source operand [#]S2.

Condition codes

    C   Unmodified.
    Z   Unmodified.
    N   Unmodified.
    V   Unmodified.

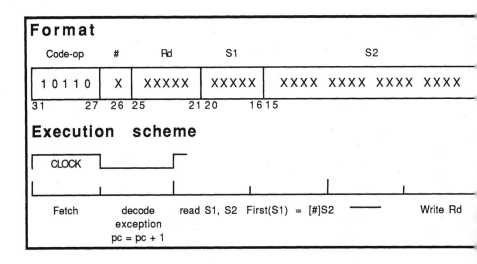

SETN Write the "NEXT" field

Syntax   SETN S1, [#]S2

Operation   If [#]S2 = 0 then DATA(S1)<31:30> = 3
If [#]S2 = S1 + 1
          then DATA(S1)<31:30> =2
Else DATA(S1)<31:30> = 0
     and CDR exception

Description   Write the "NEXT" field of the cell pointed to by the source register S1. The CDR code is computed with regard to the operands S1 and [#]S2.

Condition codes

C   Unmodified.
Z   Unmodified.
N   Unmodified.
V   Unmodified.

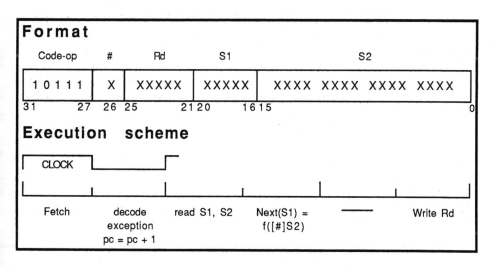

WTAG   Write the "TAG" field

Syntax   WTAG S1, [#]S2

Operation

If [#]S2<6> = 1	DATA(S1)<31:30> = [#]S2<15:14>
Else	DATA(S1)<31:30> = 0
If [#]S2<5> = 1	DATA(S1)<29> = [#]S2<13>
Else	DATA(S1)<29> = 0
If [#]S2<4> = 1	DATA(S1)<28> = [#]S2<12>
Else	DATA(S1)<28> = 0
If [#]S2<3> = 1	DATA(S1)<27:24> = [#]=S2<11:8>
Else	DATA(S1)<27:24> = 0

Description   Writes the "TAG" field of the cell pointed to by the source register S1. The value to write is contained in the 2nd byte of source operand [#]S2, while the first byte is a mask that authorizes the modification of the different fields of the tag (bit 3➔ type field ; bit 4➔ mark1 field ; bit 5➔ mark2 field; bit 6➔ cdr-code field).

Condition codes

C	Unmodified.
Z	Unmodified.
N	Unmodified.
V	Unmodified.

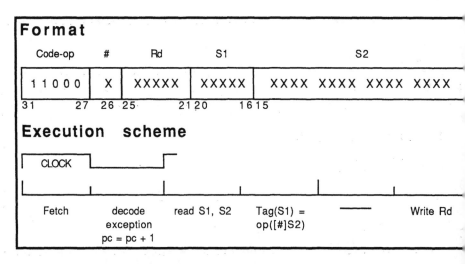

Format

Code-op	#	Rd	S1	S2
1 1 0 0 0	X	XXXXX	XXXXX	XXXX XXXX XXXX XXXX

31   27 26 25   21 20   16 15

Execution scheme

CLOCK

| Fetch | decode
exception
pc = pc + 1 | read S1, S2 | Tag(S1) =
op([#]S2) | ——— | Write Rd |

NEW   Cell allocation

Syntax   NEW Rd, [#]S2

Operation   Rd = FLP ; FLP = DATA(FLP)<23:0>
                  DATA(FLP)<31:24> = [#]S2 <15:8> masked
                  by [#]S2<7:0>
                  If FLC<= FLT then exception ; FLC = FLC - 1

Description   Allocation of a new cell, from the current free-
                  cell list called "Free-List". The tag field of the
                  allocated cell is initialized with the content of the
                  source operand [#]S2, like in the "WTAG"
                  instruction. The address of the allocated cell is
                  saved in the destination register Rd. The address
                  of the first cell of the Free-List is automatically
                  updated in FLP.

Condition codes

                  C   Unmodified.
                  Z   Unmodified.
                  N   Unmodified.
                  V   Unmodified.

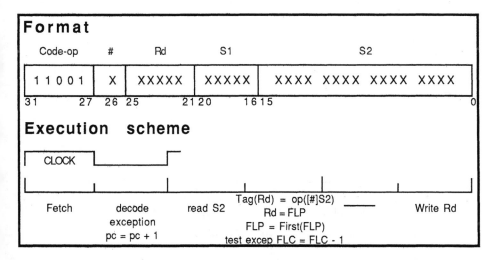

Format

Code-op	#	Rd	S1	S2
1 1 0 0 1	X	XXXXX	XXXXX	XXXX XXXX XXXX XXXX

31   27 26 25   21 20   16 15   0

Execution scheme

CLOCK

| Fetch | decode
exception
pc = pc + 1 | read S2 | Tag(Rd) = op([#]S2)
Rd = FLP
FLP = First(FLP)
test excep FLC = FLC - 1 | —— | Write Rd |

FREE   Cell garbaging

Syntax   FREE S1

Operation   DATA(S1)<31:24> = 0
                  DATA(S1)<23:0> = FLP
                  FLP = S1<23:0> ; FLC = FLC + 1

Description   Merges a free cell pointed to by the source
                  register S1 at the top of the current "Free-List".
                  The tag is automatically cleared, the CDR-code is
                  cleared, which assumes that the free cells are
                  chained with their "FIRST" field.

Condition codes

C   Unmodified.
Z   Unmodified.
N   Unmodified.
V   Unmodified.

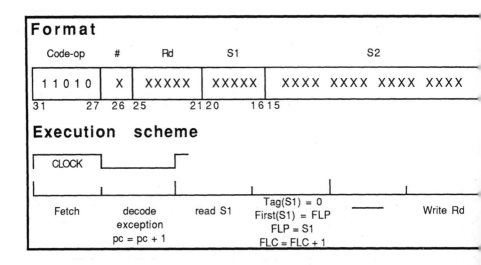

Format				
Code-op	#	Rd	S1	S2
1 1 0 1 0	X	XXXXX	XXXXX	XXXX XXXX XXXX XXXX

31   27 26 25   21 20   16 15

Execution scheme

CLOCK

| Fetch | decode
exception
pc = pc + 1 | read S1 | Tag(S1) = 0
First(S1) = FLP
FLP = S1
FLC = FLC + 1 | ——— | Write Rd |

SEND   Write the data memory

Syntax   SEND S1, [#]S2

Operation   DATA(S1)<31:0> = [#]S2<31:0>

Description   Writes a 32-bit word into the data memory. The source register S1 contains the memory address, while the source operand [#]S2 contains the 32-bit word to write at this address.

Condition codes

     C   Unmodified.
     Z   Unmodified.
     N   Unmodified.
     V   Unmodified.

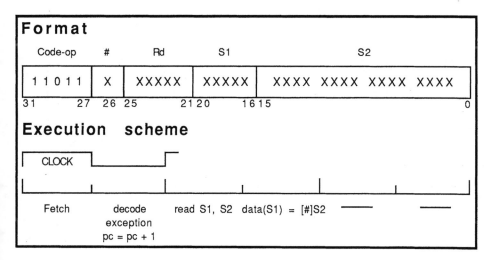

Format

Code-op	#	Rd	S1	S2
1 1 0 1 1	X	X X X X X	X X X X X	X X X X X X X X X X X X X X X X

31   27   26 25   21 20   16 15   0

Execution scheme

CLOCK

Fetch   decode   read S1, S2   data(S1) = [#]S2 ———   ———
                exception
                pc = pc + 1

233

PUSH

Push a data onto a LIFO stack

Syntax   PUSH SP, [#]S2

Operation   SP = SP + 1 ; If SP<7:0> = FF then exception
DATA(SP)<31:0> = [#]S2<31:0>

Description   Pushes a 32-bit word in a LIFO stack mapped in the data memory. The register SP contains the address of the top of the LIFO stack, while the source [#]S2 contains the 32-bit word to push. If the lowest byte of SP becomes equal to FF (hexadecimal) a stack underflow exception is generated.

Condition codes

C   Unmodified.
Z   Unmodified.
N   Unmodified.
V   Unmodified.

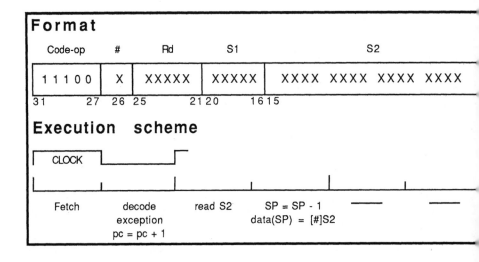

Format				
Code-op	#	Rd	S1	S2
1 1 1 0 0	X	X X X X X	X X X X X	X X X X X X X X X X X X X X X X

31   27 26 25   21 20   16 15

Execution scheme

CLOCK

Fetch | decode exception pc = pc + 1 | read S2 | SP = SP - 1 data(SP) = [#]S2

POP   Pop from a LIFO stack

Syntax   POP Rd

Operation   Rd<31:0> = DATA(SP)<31:0>
SP = SP - 1 ; If SP<7:0> = FF then exception

Description   Pops out a value from the current LIFO stack pointed to by the register SP. The result is stored in the destination register Rd. If the lowest byte of SP becomes equal to FF (hexadecimal), a stack underflow exception is generated.

Condition codes

      C   Unmodified.
      Z   Unmodified.
      N   Unmodified.
      V   Unmodified.

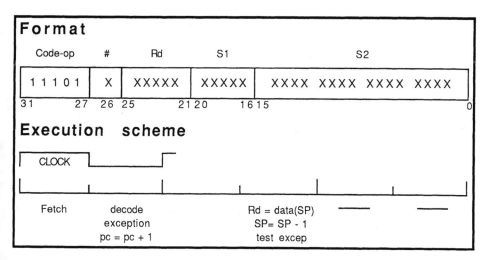

Format

Code-op	#	Rd	S1	S2
1 1 1 0 1	X	XXXXX	XXXXX	XXXX XXXX XXXX XXXX

31   27 26 25   21 20   16 15   0

Execution scheme

CLOCK

Fetch	decode	Rd = data(SP)
	exception	SP= SP - 1
	pc = pc + 1	test excep

LOAD Read code memory

Syntax   LOAD Rd, S1

Operation   Rd<31:0> = CODE(S1)<31:0>

Description   Performs a read of a 32-bit word of code memory at the address contained in the source register S1. The word read is stored into the destination register Rd.

Condition codes

C	Unmodified.
Z	Unmodified.
N	Unmodified.
V	Unmodified.

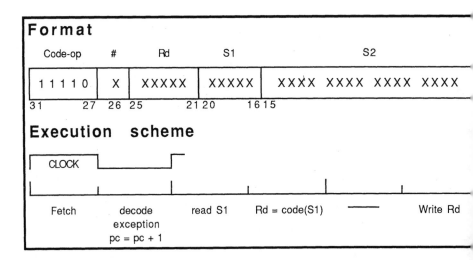

Format

Code-op	#	Rd	S1	S2
1 1 1 1 0	X	XXXXX	XXXXX	XXXX XXXX XXXX XXXX

31   27 26 25   21 20   16 15

Execution scheme

CLOCK

| Fetch | decode exception pc = pc + 1 | read S1 | Rd = code(S1) | —— | Write Rd |

STORE   Write code memory

Syntax   STORE S1, [#]S2

Operation   CODE(S1)<31:0> = [#]S2<31:0>

Description   Writes a 32-bit word into code memory at the address contained in the source register S1. The source operand [#]S2 contains the 32-bit word to write at this address.

Condition codes

        C   Unmodified.
        Z   Unmodified.
        N   Unmodified.
        V   Unmodified.

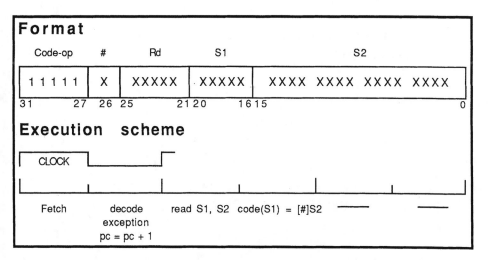

Format

Code-op	#	Rd	S1	S2
1 1 1 1 1	X	XXXXX	XXXXX	XXXX XXXX XXXX XXXX

31   27 26 25   21 20   16 15   0

Execution scheme

CLOCK

Fetch   decode   read S1, S2 code(S1) = [#]S2
               exception
               pc = pc + 1

References

[1]   MC68030 Enhanced 32-bit Microprocessor User's Manual
       Motorola Inc., 1987

[2]   Computer Architecture : A Quantitative Approach
       J.L. Hennessy, D.A. Patterson
       Morgan Kaufmann Publishers, 1989

[3]   A Unique Microprocessor Instruction Set
       Dennis A. Fairclough
       IEEE Micro, May 1982

[4]   A RISC Tutorial
       SUN Microsystems Inc., 1987

[5]   The CRAY-I Computer System
       Communication ACM, Vol. 21, no 1, 1978

[6]   The 801 Minicomputer
       G. Radin
       ACM symposium on architectural support for programming
       languages and operating systems, Palo Alto (USA), March
       1982

[7]   Reduced Instruction Set Computer for VLSI
       Manolis G.H. Katevenis
       The MIT Press, 1983

[8]   A VLSI RISC
       D.A. Patterson, C.H. Séquin
       IEEE Computer, September 1982

[9]   The C Programming Language
       B.W. Kernighan, D.M. Ritchie
       Prentice Hall Editions, 1978

[10]   A VLSI Pascal Machine
       F. Baskett
       Public lecture, U.C. Berkeley (USA), 1978

[11] How to Use 1000 Registers
R.L. Sites
Caltech Conference on VLSI, January 1979

[12] Architecture of a VLSI Instruction Cache for a RISC
D.A. Patterson, P. Garrison, M. Hill, D. Lioupis, C. Nyberg, T. Sippel, K. Van Dyke
Communication of ACM, 1983

[13] A Big RISC
R.A. Blomseth (capt. USAF)
Technical report of Computer Science Division
Department of Electrical Engineering and Computer Science
University of California, Berkeley (USA), July 1983

[14] The Symbolics 3600
Technical summary
Symbolic Inc., 1983

[15] Architecture of SOAR : Smalltalk On a Risc
D. Ungar, R. Blau, P. Foley, D. Samples, D. Patterson
11th ACM International Symposium on Computer Architecture, 1984

[16] What Price Smalltalk ?
D. Ungar, D.A. Patterson
IEEE Computer, January 1987

[17] SOAR Architecture
D. Samples, M. Klein, P. Foley
U.C. California, Berkeley Technical Report, 1985

[18] Smalltalk on a RISC CMOS Implementation
D. Samples, M. Klein, P. Foley
U.C. California, Berkeley Technical Report, June 1985

[19] RISC-taking in Symbolic Processors
A. Altman
Texas Instruments Engineering Journal, January 1986

[20] Design Decisions in SPUR
M. Hill ... D.A. Patterson
IEEE Computer, November 1986

[21]   Common-Lisp : The Language
        G.L. Steele
        Digital Press, 1984

[22]   IEEE Standard 754 1985 for Binary Floating-Point
        Arithmetic
        Order number CN 953, 1985

[23]   SPUR : A VLSI Multiprocessor Workstation
        M. Hill ... D.A. Patterson
        Technical Report of Computer Science Division
        Department of Electrical Engineering and Computer Science
        University of California, Berkeley, December 1985

[24]   The MIPS Machine
        J. Hennessy, N. Jouppi, F. Baskett, A. Strong, T. Gross, C.
        Rewen, J. Gill
        Proceeding COMPCON (Stanford University), February 1982

[25]   A Short Guide to MIPS Assembly Instructions
        T. Gross, J. Hill
        Computer Systems Laboratory Technical Note no 83.236
        Stanford University, November 1983

[26]   Summary of MIPS Instructions
        J. Gill, T. Gross, J. Hennessy, N. Jouppi, S. Przybylski, C. Rowen
        Computer Systems Laboratory Technical Note no 83.237
        Stanford University, November 1983

[27]   HLL Architecture from a RISC Perspective
        P. Steenkiste, T. Gross
        High-level Language Computer Architecture edited by V.M.
        Milutinovic, Computer Science Press, 1989

[28]   The MIPS-X Microprocessor
        M. Horowitz, P. Chow
        Computer Systems Laboratory, Stanford University, 1985

[29]   MIPS-X Instruction Set and Programmer's Manual
        P. Chow
        Computer Systems Laboratory Technical Report no 86.289
        Stanford University, May 1986

[30] MIPS-X : A 20-MIPS Peak 32-bit Microprocessor with On-Chip Cache
M. Horowitz ... J.M. Acken
IEEE Journal of Solid-State circuits, Vol. sc-22 no 5, October 1987

[31] Architectural Tradeoffs in the Design of MIPS-X
P. Chow, M. Horowitz
Communication of the ACM, 1987

[32] The MIPS-X RISC Microprocessor
P. Chow
Kluwer Academic Publishers, 1989

[33] An Evaluation of Directory Schemes for Cache Coherence
A. Agrawal, R. Simoni, J. Hennessy, M. Horowitz
Stanford University, IEEE Conference, June 1988

[34] PIPE : A High Performance VLSI Architecture
J.E. Smith, A.R. Pleszkun, R.H. Katz, J.R. Goodman
IEEE International Workshop on Computer System Organization, New Orleans (USA), March 1983

[35] Reduced-Instruction Set Multi-Microcomputer System
L. Foti, D. English, R.P. Hopkins, D.J. Kinniment, P.C. Treleaven, W.L. Wang
Proceedings of the NCC, July 1984

[36] The Architecture of a Simple, Effective, Control Processor
G.J. Lipovski
Microprocessing and Microprogramming, Euromicro 76
North-Holland, 1976

[37] Design Considerations of a Single Instruction Microcomputer : A case study
Microprocessing and Microprogramming, Vol. 11 no 3, March 1983

[38] The WISC Concept
P. Koopman (US Navy)
Byte, April 1987

39] How much of a RISC ?
P. Robinson
Byte, April 1987

[40] Reduced Instruction Set Architecture for a GaAs
Microprocessor System
E.R. Fox, K.J. Kiefer, R.F. Vangen, S.P. Whalen (Control Data)
IEEE Computer, October 1986

[41] A 32-bit RISC Implementation in Enhancement-Mode JFET
GaAs
T.L. Rasset, R.A. Niederland, J.H. Lane, W. A. Geideman (Mc
Donnell Douglas)
IEEE Computer, October 1986

[42] A GaAs 32-bit RISC Microprocessor
D.L. Havington, G.L. Troeger, W.C. Gee, J.A. Bolen, C.H.
Vogelsang, T.P. Nicalek, C.M. Lowe, Y.K. Roh, K.Q. Nguyen, J.F.
Fay, J. Reeder (Mc Donnell Douglas)
IEEE GaAs IC symposium, 1988

[43] Gallium Arsenide Computer Design
V.M. Milutinovic, D.A. Fura
IEEE Tutorial, 1988

[44] A DCFL E/D-MEFSET GaAs Experimental RISC Machine
W. Helbig, V. Milutinovic
IEEE Transactions on Computers, Vol. 32 no 2, February
1989

[45] KIM200 : A Tagged-RISC Architecture for Gallium Arsenide
Implementation
J.C. Heudin, C. Métivier (Sodima S.A. / Stanford University)
8th SPIE Conference Applications of Artificial Intelligence
Orlando (Florida, USA), April 1990

[46] Une mémoire cache multiniveau pour un processeur RISC en
Arseniure de Gallium
F. Poirier (Sodima S.A.)
DEA report, University of Paris XI at Orsay (France),
September 1989

[47]   Future Directions for RISC processors
       J. Hennessy
       Stanford University, Computer Systems Laboratory Draft
       Report, 1990

[48]   Very Large Instruction Word Architectures and the ELI-512
       J.A. Fisher (Yale University)
       ACM Conference, 1983

[49]   Trace Scheduling : A Technique for Global Microcode
       Compaction
       J.A. Fisher (Yale University)
       IEEE Transactions on Computers, July 1981

[50]   The RISC/CISC Melting Pot : Classic Design Methods Converge
       in the MC68030 Microprocessor
       T.L. Johnson (Motorola Inc.)
       Byte, April 1987

[51]   The Symbolics Ivory Processor : a VLSI CPU for the Genera
       Symbolic Processing Environment
       G. Efland et al.
       Symbolics Inc., January 1988

[52]   Core Set Assembly Language Instructions for MIPS-based
       Microprocessors - Version 3.2
       R. Firth, T. Gross
       Carnegie-Mellon University, Software Engineering Institute
       Technical Report, October 1987

[53]   Final Evaluation of MIPS M/500
       D.V. Klein, R. Firth
       Carnegie-Mellon University, Software Engineering Institute
       Technical Report, November 1987

[54]   Parallel Operation in the Control Data 6600
       J.E. Thorton
       Fall Joint Computer Conference, 1964

[55]   The IBM 360 Model 91 : Machine Philosophy and Instruction
       Handling
       D.W. Anderson, F.J. Sparacio, R.M. Tomasulo
       IBM Journal of Research and Development, January 1967

[56]   A Study of Branch Prediction Strategies
       J.E. Smith
       8th Symposium on Computer Architecture
       Minneapolis (USA), May 1981

[57]   Detection and Parallel Execution of Independent Instructions
       IEEE Transactions on Computers, October 1970

[58]   Windows of Overlapping Register Frames
       D. Halbert, P. Kessler
       Final class report of the Computer Science Department
       U.C. Berkeley, June 1980

[59]   Cache Memories
       A.J. Smith (U.C. Berkeley)
       Computing Surveys, Vol. 14 no 3, September 1982

[60]   On modeling Program Behavior
       P.J. Denning
       Spring Joint Computer Conference, Vol. 40
       AFIPS Press, Arlington, 1972

[61]   On-chip Instruction Caches for High Performance Processors
       A. Agrawal, P. Clow, M. Horowitz, J. Acken, A. Salz, J.
       Hennessy
       Computer Systems Laboratory Technical Report, Stanford
       University, 1985

[62]   RISCs Challenge Mini, Micro Suppliers
       A. Allison
       Mini-Micro Systems, November 1986

[63]   Chip Architecture : A Revolution Brewing
       F. Guterl
       IEEE Spectrum, July 1983

[64]   SUNRISE : A High-Performance 32-bit Microprocessor
       N. Namjero, A. Agrawal (SUN Microsystems)
       IEEE COMPCON, San Francisco (USA), March 1988

[65]   CMOS Gate Array Implementation of SPARC
       L. Quack, R. Cuch (Fujitsu Microelectronics)
       IEEE COMPCON, San Francisco (USA), March 1989

[66] CMOS Custom Implementation of the SPARC Architecture
N. Namjero et al. (SUN Microsystems, Cypress)
IEEE COMPCON, San Francisco (USA), March 1989

[67] RISC 7C600, RISC Family Users Guide
Cypress Semiconductor Corp.
June 1988

[68] Design Consideration for a Bipolar Implementation of SPARC
A. Agrawal, et al.
IEEE COMPCON, San Francisco (USA), March 1989

[69] The Scalable Processor ARChitecture (SPARC)
R. Garner, D.A. Patterson, et. al.
IEEE COMPCON, San Francisco (USA), March 1989

[70] A RISC Tutorial
SUN Microsystems Corp., 1987

[71] Implementing SPARC : A High-Performance 32-bit RISC
Microprocessor
N. Namjero, A. Agrawal (SUN Microsystems)
SUN Technology, 1988

[72] SUNOS on SPARC
S. Kleinian, D. Williams (SUN Microsystems)
IEEE COMPCON, San Francisco (USA), March 1989

[73] Optimizing Compilers for the SPARC Architecture : An
Overview
S. Muchnik et al. (SUN Microsystems)
IEEE COMPCON, San Francisco (USA), March 1989

[74] MIPS RISC Architecture
G. Kane
Prentice Hall, 1988

[75] MIPS RISCompilers
Mips Computer System, 1989

[76] R3000 & R3010 RISComponents
Mips Computer Systems, March 1988

[77] R3000/R3010 Users Manual
      Integrated Device Technology, Santa Clara (USA), 1989

[78] The MIPS RC6280 RISComputer
      Mips Computer Systems, November 1989

[79] RISC Processors : The New Wave in Computer Systems
      R. Weiss
      Computer Design, May 1987

[80] 32-bit Microprocessor Opens System Bottlenecks
      B. Case (Advanced Micro Devices)
      Computer Design, April 1987

[81] Am29000 Streamlined Instruction Processor Users Manual
      Advanced Micro Device, 1988

[82] 29K Family : The Next Standard 32-bit Microprocessor
      Advanced Micro Devices, 1988

[83] The Battle Royal in Chips
      R. Brandt, D.A. Depke, J.W. Verity
      Business Week, November 1989

[84] Supercomputing on Chip
      C. Dobbs, P. Reed, Tommy Ng (Motorola/SCS)
      VLSI Systems Design, May 1988

[85] MC88100-RISC Microprocessor
      User's Manual second edition
      Motorola, Prentice Hall Publisher, 1990

[86] MC88200 Cache/Memory Management Unit
      User's Manual - Second Edition
      Motorola, Prentice Hall Publisher, 1990

[87] Intel's Ambitious Game Plan in Embedded Chips
      B.C. Cole
      Electronics, April 1988

[88]   Intel 80960 Attacks Drawbacks of Prior RISC
       J.H. Wharton
       Microprocessor Architecture Reprints from Micro Design
       Resources Inc., 1988

[89]   A Programmer's View of the 80960 Architecture
       S. Mc Geady
       34th IEEE Computer Society International Conference,
       COMPCON, Spring 1989

[90]   Intel Symposium / Slide Reprint
       Paris (France), October 1989

[91]   The i960CA Superscalar Implementation of the 80960
       Architecture
       S. Mc Geady
       35th IEEE Computer Society International Conference,
       COMPCON, Spring 1990

[92]   80960CA 32-bit High-Performance Embedded Processor
       Intel Data Sheet, September 1989

[93]   Intel's i860 Sets New Performance Standard
       B. Case
       Microprocessor Report, Vol. 3 no 3
       Micro Design Resources Inc., March 1989

[94]   The Architecture of the Intel 860
       B. Smith
       MIPS, June 1989

[95]   i860 Single Chip Supercomputer User's Manual
       Intel Inc., 1990

[96]   The Fairchild Clipper
       A Microprocessor that Attempts to Balance the Best of CISC
       and RISC
       M. Ackerman, G. Baum
       Byte, April 1987

[97]   The C400 Chipset Architecture
       H. Sachs, H. Mc Ghan
       Intergraph Advanced Processor Division, 1991

[98] The 801 Minicomputer
G. Radin
SIGARCH Computer Architecture News, Vol. 10 no 2, March
1982

[99] IBM RT PC Architecture and Design Decisions
G.G. Henry
IBM RT Personal Computer Technology, 1986

[100] The IBM RT PC ROMP Processor and Memory Management
Unit
D.P. Hester, R.O. Simpson
IBM Systems Journal, Vol. 26 no 4, 1987

[101] An IBM Second-Generation RISC-Processor Architecture
R.D. Groves, R. Oehler
35th IEEE Computer Society International Conference
COMPCON, Spring 1990

[102] IBM Second-Generation RISC Machine Organization
H.B. Bakoglu et al. (IBM Advanced Workstation Division)
35th IEEE Computer Society International Conference
COMPCON, Spring 1990

[103] VL86C010 RISC Family Data Manual
VLSI Technology Inc., 1987

[104] The Transputer Data Book
Inmos Data Book Series, November 1988

[105] Ridge 32 Architecture : a RISC Variation
Proceedings of ICCD 83, October 1983

[106] The Pyramid 90x Architecture
Pyramid Technology Corp. Mountain View CA, 1983

[107] New RISC Machines Appear as Hybrids with both RISC and
CISC Features
Computer Design, April 1986

[108] Beyond RISC : High Precision Architecture
J.S. Birnbaum, W.S. Worley
Hewlett-Packard Journal, Vol. 36 no 8, August 1985

[109] NOVIX : A Radical Approach to Microprocessor Design
W. Watson, C. Stephens
Computer Solutions of Byfleet, Electronics & Wireless World,
1988

[110] KIM : Une nouvelle génération de processeurs RISC pour les
applications de l'informatique
J.C. Heudin (SODIMA)
French DGA/DRET conference on numerical and analogical
circuits, France, April 1989

[111] The Symbolics I Machine Architecture : A Symbolic
Processor Architecture for VLSI Implementation
Symbolics Inc. Cambridge Research Center, 1987

[112] Lambda Machines Technical Summary
Lisp Machine Inc. May 1985

[113] Lisp Hardware Architecture : The Explorer II and Beyond
P.H. Dussuq (Texas Instruments)
1st International Workshop on Lisp Evolution and
Standardization, Paris (France), February 1988

[114] A Real-Time Oriented Machine for Artificial Intelligence
Applications
J.P. Sansonnet, P. Clere, E. Papon, S. Bourgault, B. Grandjean
(CGE)
1st IEEE International Workshop on Computer Workstations,
San Jose CA (USA), November 1985

[115] Lisp Machine Progress Report
Geenblatt et al.
M.I.T. A.I. memo no 44, Cambridge, August 1977

[116] Reducing Memory Accesses on PEARLS : A Symbolic
Processor
D. Demigny, L. Kessal, C. Koester, J.C. Heudin, T. Maurin, F.
Devos
Microsystem BRNO, September 1987

[117] Les Implications Temps Réel dans l'Architecture des Machines Symboliques. Exemple : les commutations de tâches dans KIM
J.C. Heudin, et al.
6th Conference on Pattern Matching and Artificial Intelligence, AFCET/INRIA, Paris (France), November 1987

[118] A Compact Symbolic Processor for Artificial Intelligence Applications
J.C. Heudin, C. Métivier, P. Kajfasz, B. Zavidovique, F. Devos
2nd IEEE Conference on Computers and Applications, Peijin (China), Jun 1987

[119] KIM20 : A Symbolic RISC Microprocessor for Embedded Advanced Control
J.C. Heudin (SODIMA)
Euro ASIC 1990, IEEE Computer Society, June 1990

[120] Architectures for AI : Hardware and Software for Efficient Processing
M.F. Deering (Schlumberger Palo Alto)
Byte, April 1985

[121] Overview of Garbage Collection in Symbolic Computing
T.H. Mc Entee (Texas Instruments)
Texas Instruments Engineering Journal, January/February 1986

[122] Hypercube and Distributed Computers
F. André, J.P. Verjus, Editors,
North-Holland, 1989

[123] LISP
P.H. Winston, B.K.P. Horn
Addison Wesley, 1984

[124] Performance and Evaluation of Lisp System
R.P. Gabriel
The M.I.T. Press, 1985

[125] Toward Embedded Controllers for Real-Time Applications of Artificial Intelligence
J.C. Heudin, J.P Courrier, C. Métivier (SODIMA)
2nd ACM International Conference on Industrial & Engineering Applications of Artificial Intelligence & Expert Systems
University of Tennessee, Space Institute, Tullahoma, June 1989

Index

R3010 : 97, 99, 102

R4000 : 103, 155, 156, 158, 159, 160

R6000 : 103, 155, 156, 158, 159, 160

R6010 : 103

RCA : 44, 45, 155, 156, 157, 159, 160

Reading University : 40

RIDGE Computer : 21, 88 154

RIMMS : 40

RISC-1 : 21, 22, 23, 24, 25, 26, 27, 28, 29, 71, 73, 87, 155, 156, 157, 158, 160, 168

RISC-2 : 21, 27, 28, 29, 30, 31, 35, 69, 71, 87, 90, 94, 95, 155, 156, 157, 158, 160, 191

RISC32C : 154, 156

Santa Clara : 103

Schlumberger : 156

Séquin : 27, 28

Seymour Cray : 19

Sherburne : 27

Siemens : 103

Silicon Compiler Systems : 112

Sippel : 27

Site : 25

Smith : 80